ENDORSEMENTS FOR APOCALYPSE 2012

In *Apocalypse 2012: The Ticking of the End Time Clock*, author John Claeys takes readers on a journey into the near future where they encounter the ultimate battle of good versus evil—of Satan's king of the world overcoming the prophets of God, of war breaking out in heaven, and of the armies of the earth banding together to launch an assault upon God's King as He comes to the earth to claim His kingdom. This is a story that is packed with adventure, conflict, dramatic rescue, and an incredible climax. It describes worldwide cataclysms, demonic manifestations, and people rising from the dead. The best part is that it is entirely true!

As you can see, this is not a dull treatise about the future. Neither is it one based on some fanciful imagination of the author, but one that is a careful exposition of Biblical passages describing a real, seven-year period leading to the return of Jesus Christ to the earth.

If you are looking for clear and accurate revelation of the future that is a page-turner, you can do no better than *Apocalypse 2012*.

—**Earl Radmacher, Ph.D., President Emeritus Western Seminary in Portland, Oregon, general editor of *The Nelson Study Bible: New King James Version*, and author of ten books including *The Nature of the Church, Salvation, The Disciplemaker, The NIV Reconsidered, You and Your Thoughts, What May we Expect From the Holy Spirit,* and *Celebrating the Word*.**

John Claeys' *Apocalypse 2012: The Ticking of the End Time Clock* helps fill a noticeable void today as new works on biblical prophecy are sadly lacking. I found the book to be a refreshing change to the typical writings and commentaries. It contained material marked by simple and clear explanations of Scriptures, presented in a way that would both engage the avid Bible student as well as someone completely unfamiliar with the biblical text. Once you pick it up, you won't be able to put it down. The book will challenge you in a way that will make you excited to share it with friends and family.

—**J. Paul Nyquist, Ph.D., President Moody Bible Institute**

We are living in difficult times; for many, even frightening times. Where is God in the midst of all of this? What is God's purpose for these trying days? According to *Apocalypse 2012: The Ticking of the End Time Clock*, God is preparing the world for His coming kingdom. Combining Biblical accuracy and intriguing narrative, John Claeys draws us into the challenging world of Bible prophecy. There is a new world coming! What can we expect? Will you be ready? As never before in our days, we have needed a book like *Apocalypse 2012*. Read it for yourself and share it with your friends. It will change your life. And maybe, just maybe, it will change your friends' lives as well.

—**Barry R. Leventhal, Ph.D., Academic Dean and Professor, Southern Evangelical Seminary, Matthews, NC**

For many of us, the book of Revelation, rich in symbolism, can seem disturbing and complex. But in an easy to comprehend and simplified manner, author John Claeys establishes God's dramatic, electrifying word in our hearts and minds in *Apocalypse 2012: The Ticking of the End Time Clock*. In addition, Claeys has done a masterful job of pulling together passages from across Scripture about a coming seven-year period while remaining true to their context. He shows with clarity and astonishing revelation what is coming and how to prepare for it.

This is a timely book that needed to be written, and it has been written well. I recommend that you not only get this book, but that you get enough copies to give to family and friends. They will thank you for it.

—**Mark Gregston, Executive Director of Heartlight Ministries, author of *When Your Teen Is Struggling* and *What Happened to My Teen?***

Claeys' book, *Apocalypse 2012: The Ticking of the End Time Clock*, is well researched and engagingly written as to present a clearer understanding into the prophecies of the Bible concerning the Day of the Lord in biblical prophecy. He demonstrates that God is in control of the future and "He will make all things right" by His righteous judgment while at the same time showing that God works His plan out of an "immeasurable love for people." A must read.

—**Stephen R. Lewis, Ph.D., President Rocky Mountain Bible College, Rocky Mountain Seminary**

APOCALYPSE
2012:

TO: Billie

John Claeys

Jer. 29:11

APOCALYPSE
2012:

The Ticking of the End-Time Clock—
What Does the Bible Say?

BY JOHN CLAEYS

VMI Publishers
Sister, Oregon

APOCALYPSE 2012: The Ticking of the End-Time Clock—
What Does the Bible Say?
© 2010 by John Claeys. All rights reserved. Published 2010.

Published by VMI Publishers
Sisters, Oregon
www.vmipublishers.com

ISBN: 1-935265-16-4
ISBN 13: 978-1-935265-16-0
Library of Congress Control Number: 2010921415

Cover design by Joe Bailen and interior design by Juanita Dix

Table of Contents

Foreword

This book would not have happened without the provision and direction of God. His direction included the planting of a strong desire deep within my heart to share with all who are open to his Word what he has intricately communicated about his future plan. It also involved the encouragement from those who heard me teach this information to write and publish it.

I have the utmost gratitude for God's own Son, the Lord Jesus Christ, for his willingness to take my place by dying in payment for my sins—as well as for the sins of the entire world. I am also thankful that God opened my eyes to the truth—that I could not gain heaven or a relationship with him based on living a good life, being religious, or on any other effort or sacrifice one may attempt. He enabled me to see that his Son paid it all, and because he did, Jesus offers eternal life (a relationship with God that lasts forever) by simply believing him for it. When I believed Jesus—for his promise of eternal life—I not only entered into an eternal relationship with God, but he gave me so much more, including a life of purpose and meaning that I previously lacked, along with a strong interest in his Word—especially regarding his plan for the future.

In addition, I am indebted to God's provision of the people he has put in my life, many of whom contributed to this book in some way. I could never thank my wife, Connie, enough—for her encouragement, for her amazing patience while I worked on the manuscript nights and weekends, and for her support through the entire process. She continually demonstrates that "her worth is far above rubies" (Proverbs 31:10).

I am also very grateful for my wonderful sons, Scott and Jason, who have been wonderful gifts from the Lord. I couldn't love them any more than I do.

I also want to acknowledge my gratitude for my father. Dad, you have been an inspiration to me my entire life. Thank you for all you have done for me. I love you.

Zane Hodges deserves more than a mention here, as I would not have been able to write this book without his mentoring. Much of what I know from Scripture, and how to approach the Bible, came from his input, including how to understand God's teaching about the future. I feel honored to have known, and to have been mentored by, this special vessel of God, and I look forward to see his great kingdom reward.

Cindy Mallett spent untold hours proofreading my manuscript and offering many, many valuable suggestions. This may never have gotten to the publisher without her assistance. In addition, she put in even more time responding to the suggestions of my editor. Cindy, I cannot thank you enough! I know you will be greatly rewarded by our Lord for selflessly volunteering your service.

Dave Bolthouse gave me the idea for the title of this book and showed me why I should use it among other super ideas. Thank you, Dave, for lending your genius to me.

Deb Germain seriously took on the challenge of capturing me in the best way for this book via photograph. To do so, she assembled a team consisting of Connie Hill, my photographer, and Julie Simpson, my makeup artist (which this subject desperately needed for a good picture!). Then, Deb did her magic on computer. Thanks to each of you for lending your time, expertise, and passion to help me out. You were too much fun to work with!

I am also indebted to Ken Sladaritz for granting me the use of his brilliance in all things related to the computer and my Web site. Ken, your willingness to serve in any way you can in these areas has not only been a great help and encouragement to me, but I know God will use what you have done (and continue to do) to reach more people for Christ. I can't thank you enough for that.

I must also mention Bob Bryant, who has served as a mentor and friend. Bob, thank you for your interest in this project. In addition, thank you for providing such a great example of serving Christ, and for being such a careful exegete of God's Word.

In addition, I am thankful for the elders of Cypress Valley Bible Church with whom I have gratefully served. Thank you for your support and your examples of humble service for Christ.

Clearly, God hand-picked my editor, Susanne Lakin, for this project. She had the perfect background (Jewish and editor of a number of books on eschatology) to catch any mistake I may have made, provided the perfect touches to my manuscript, and was wonderful to work with. Thank you, Susanne, for making the editing process such a terrific experience. I hope we can work together again soon.

I owe so much to so many. For example, this book may never have been written were it not for the encouragement of a number of friends from Cypress Valley Bible Church to put it on paper and to submit it for publishing. There have been many people who have offered invaluable help through financial giving, persistent prayer, and continued encouragement. I have repeatedly thanked God for you and asked him to greatly reward you for your service to me—and for all who will be impacted by this book.

John Claeys
October 2009
Marshall, Texas

CHAPTER 1
2012

WORLDWIDE DROUGHTS, floods, hurricanes, tsunamis, earthquakes, and volcanic eruptions caused by solar storms, cracks forming in the earth's magnetic field, and mass extinctions brought on by nuclear winter, famine, human disease, wars, economic cataclysm, massive solar flares, polar reversals . . . These have all been predicted to occur in the year 2012. More specifically, based on the Maya calendar, more and more people believe that the world as we know it may change forever on December 21, 2012.

Patrick Geryl is one who has become convinced of this. In 2007, he quit his job as a laboratory worker for a French oil company to prepare for the apocalypse. He had saved up just enough money to last him until December 2012. After that, he thought, he wouldn't need it anyway.[1]

Geryl and others believe the world as we know it will end in 2012, pointing to the ancient Maya cyclical calendars. The longest of these last renewed itself approximately 5,125 years ago and is set to end again, supposedly with catastrophic consequences, in 2012.

But, Patrick Geryl certainly is not alone in this belief. As Christine Brouwer reports:

> Thousands of people worldwide seem to be preparing, in one way or another, for the end of days in 2012. Survival groups exist in Europe, Canada, and the United States. A simple Google search for "2012" and "the end of the world" brings up nearly 300,000 hits. And the video-sharing Web site YouTube hosts more than 65,000 clips informing and warning viewers about their fate in 2012.[2]

In fact, the growth of interest in 2012 has been so phenomenal that Hollywood hopes to cash in on it with the November (2009) worldwide release of a major motion picture entitled "2012," with such name actors as John Cusack, Amanda Peet, Woody Harrelson, and Danny Glover.

What Is the 2012 Phenomenon?

The 2012 phenomenon is based on the proposition that cataclysmic or transformative events will occur in 2012, reaching the apex of dramatic results on December 21 of that year. December 21, 2012 marks the ending of the current *baktun* cycle of the Mesoamerican Long Count calendar. The Long Count set its "time zero" at a point in the past marking the end of the previous world and the beginning of the current one, which corresponds to either August 11 or 13, 3114 BC in the Gregorian calendar (the calendar used by the West today), depending on the formula used.[3] As Vincent H. Malmström, Professor Emeritus of geography at Dartmouth College explains it, the long cycle "consists of 13 *baktuns*, each of which numbers 144,000 days, making for a grand total 1,872,000 days. This, in turn, equates to 5,139.44 solar years, and marks the number of days that have elapsed since the supposed beginning of the present world, as determined by some unknown priest in the year 236 B.C."[4] Supposedly, the Maya calendar ends on December 21, 2012, which has sparked many to believe that the world as we know it will end.

Though prognosticators such as Nostradamus (though no hard evidence has been surfaced about his prediction of 2012 as a significant year for the world) are sometimes mentioned in the discussion of 2012, there seems to be universal agreement that the 2012 phenomenon is primarily

2

based on the Maya calendar. However, Mayan expert David Webster argues against the Maya calendar signaling the end of the world as we know it. In a paper he presented at "The Emergence of the Modern World" conference, he argues that the Maya did not have in mind that the end of the current long cycle of their calendar would bring an end to the world as we know it. Instead:

> The Maya, of course, would simply have begun another cycle, just as they did before, and their world would have gone on. Here's my prediction: 2012 will come and go without the world falling apart (at least faster than it is at present), and people will forget about this particular intrusion of the ancient Maya into our lives.[5]

Moreover, according to Robert Stiler, writing in *Novo Religio*, states, "Hundreds of books and Internet sites speculate wildly about the 2012 date, but little of this conjecture has a factual basis in Mayan culture."[6] University of Florida anthropologist Susan Gillespie says the 2012 phenomenon comes "from media and from other people making use of the Maya past to fulfill agendas that are really their own."[7]

Why December 21, 2012?

It has been suggested that the Mayans fixed their calendar to end on winter solstice in order "to target when the cosmic alignment would maximize."[8] However, according to Dr. Malmström, "to suggest this date will have any meaning or importance to anyone but a historian of chronology is to embroider it with a significance it was never intended to have."[9] He points out that the calendar (which he shows was not constructed by the Mayans but by an Olmec priest)[10] was developed in 236 BC and could not have identified either the beginning of the world or any significance of its ending more than 2,300 years later.[11] Thus, it seems to be a random calendar with a random set (though one of pattern, but not of significance) of numbers attached to it.

> Dr. Karl S. Kruszelnicki provides a different take on this calendar by stating that when a calendar comes to the end of a cycle, it just rolls over into the next cycle. In our Western society, every year 31 December is followed, not by the End of the World, but by

1 January. So 13.0.0.0.0 in the Mayan calendar will be followed by 0.0.0.0.1—or good ol' 22 December 2012, with only a few shopping days left to Christmas.[12]

This reasoned approach demands the answer to this question: Simply because the calendar stops at a certain point (and all calendars eventually do), why is it necessary to jump to the conclusion that the end of the world as we know it is in view? This writer has yet to see a good answer to that question.

Does the Calendar Point to the End of the World?

Concerning whether December 21, 2012 is the end of the world or is a new beginning, one Web site dedicated to discussion of 2012 states: "As mentioned, some believe cataclysmic events will take place in December 2012 with the ultimate destruction occurring on December 21, 2012. Others believe that the world will not end, but instead humanity will enter a new age, marked by significant changes physically and mentally."[13] Spiritual healer Andrew Smith predicts a restoration of a "true balance between Divine Feminine and Masculine" in *The Revolution of 2012: Vol. 1*, The Preparation. In *2012*, Daniel Pinchbeck anticipates a "change in the nature of consciousness," assisted by indigenous insights and psychedelic drug use.[14]

Brooke Kenney explains the 2012 phenomenon in this way on her Web site: "The basis of this event lies in the Mayan calendar, in which time, as we understand it, comes to an end and a major shift occurs in human consciousness. Will this be the end of the world? Or, is it the beginning of a new world?"[15] She goes on to comment: "Some believe that the shift will reveal the 4th dimension (time) or maybe the 5th dimension (unity with the unseen Spirit World/Heaven). My spirit guide, Dew, has told of a time, near the end of time, when inanimate objects will come to life, including stones, and that our animals will speak to us, to prove God's dominion on earth."[16]

So, according to proponents of the 2012 phenomenon, maybe December 21, 2012 will signal the end of the world, and maybe it will not.[17] But if, in fact, it does signal the end of the world as we know it, what might produce this consummation? Let us look at some of the theories.

4

Geomagnetic Reversal of the Earth?

One theory suggested is a geomagnetic reversal of the earth. This means that whereas our magnets now point to the North Pole, they will, in that case, point south—to Antarctica. Supposedly, the last time this occurred with the earth was 780,000 years ago.[18] However, the evidence of this occurrence is scant and arguable at best—even if one accepts that the earth is that old. Yet, not only are advocates of the 2012 phenomenon predicting its occurrence once more, but they state with absolute certainty that it will occur in 2012.[19]

Some 2012 theories suggest that the earth's geomagnetic reversal is connected to the natural eleven-year solar cycle. However, according to Ian O'Neill—who possesses a doctorate in solar physics—there is absolutely no scientific evidence to support such a claim.[20] According to O'Neill, "Although there appears to be a current downward trend in magnetic field strength, the current magnetic field is still considered to be 'above average' when compared with the variations measured in recent history." According to researchers at Scripps Institution of Oceanography, San Diego, if the magnetic field continued to decrease at the current trend, the dipolar field would effectively be zero in five hundred years' time. However, the magnetic field is currently "healthy," and it is more likely that the field strength will rebound and increase in strength, continuing its pattern of natural fluctuations as it has over the past several thousand years.[21]

Polar Reversal?

Many 2012 theorists seem to confuse polar reversal, or polar shift, with geomagnetic reversal; however, the two are not the same. "The pole shift hypothesis is the hypothesis that the axis of rotation of a planet has not always been at its present-day locations or that the axis will not persist there; in other words, that its physical poles had been or will be shifted."[22]

Author Patrick Geryl writes:

> Life after a polar reversal is nothing but horror, pure unimaginable horror. All securities you presently have at hand, like—amongst others—food, transport, and medicines, will have disappeared in one big blow, dissolved into nothingness. As will our complete

civilization. It cannot be more horrifying than this; worse than the worst nightmare. More destructive than a nuclear war in which the entire global arsenal of nuclear weapons has been deployed in one blow. Are you grasping the facts?[23]

However, Ian O'Neill points out:
Polar shift is considered to be a less likely event that occurs a few times in the evolutionary timescale of the Solar System. There are a couple of examples of planets that have suffered a catastrophic polar shift, including Venus (which rotates in an opposite direction to all the other planets, therefore it was flipped upside down by some huge event, such as a planetary collision) and Uranus (which rotates on its side, having been knocked off-axis by an impact, or some gravitational effect caused by Jupiter and Saturn).[24]

In other words, there seems to be little evidence and even less likelihood that a polar reversal will occur in 2012.

Alignment of the Planets?

Another theory propounded by advocates of the 2012 phenomenon is that, right on cue with the Maya calendar, the sun will be in the center of our galaxy with all of the planets lining up behind it on December 21, 2012 which, they believe, will create increased instability in the inner core of the earth—and this instability could cause cataclysmic phenomena such as hurricanes, earthquakes, volcanic eruptions, massive tidal waves, and tsunamis. Also, "nuclear reactors will melt, buildings will crumble, and a cloud of volcanic dust will block out the sun for forty years. Only the prepared will survive," Geryl says, "and not even all of them."[25] Journalist Lawrence Joseph, author of *Apocalypse 2012: A Scientific Investigation into Civilization's End*, states that when this alignment occurs, "whatever energy typically streams to Earth from the center of the Milky Way will indeed be disrupted on 12/21/12 at 11:11 p.m. Universal Time."[26]

However, it has been pointed out that we could make that same statement about the sun, the planets, and our galaxy in the 1990s through

2020, yet there is no indication of greater instability of the earth's core.[27] This theory also seems to presuppose that the Mayans knew that the sun travels in an orbit through the galaxy just as the planets of the solar system travel in an orbit around the sun. However, as Professor Malmström points out, this would be to credit "a people who had no knowledge that the earth was even round, much less that it wobbled on its axis, with more than supernatural powers."[28]

In contradiction to the claim that the planets will be in alignment with the sun in 2012, Dr. Rosa Williams states that at no time in 2012 will the planets be in anywhere near this kind of alignment.[29] Dr. Donald Luttermoser, chair of the physics and astronomy department at East Tennessee State University, calculated the probability for an exact planetary alignment to occur to be once in eighty-six billion-trillion-trillion-trillion years! (That is eighty-six followed by forty-five zeros!) His conclusion is "The odds strongly favor that an exact planetary alignment will NEVER occur throughout the entire history of the solar system."[30]

Even if planetary alignment did occur, Philip Plait, author of *Bad Astronomy*, states that planetary alignments have relatively little to do with earthquakes or other cataclysmic possibilities. He states that "the total pull of all the planets combined is 0.017, not even 2% of the Moon's pull! . . . . The change in tidal force due to the Moon's elliptical orbit is hugely larger than the combined tides of all the planets."[31]

Regarding a planetary alignment, astronomers generally agree that "it would be impossible the Maya themselves would have known that," says Susan Milbrath, a Maya archaeoastronomer and a curator at the Florida Museum of Natural History. What's more, she says, "we have no record or knowledge that they would think the world would come to an end at that point."[32]

Planet X?

Some 2012 proponents are convinced that the Mayans knew about a rogue planet that will doom the Earth in 2012, and they associated it with the end of their calendar in December 2012. In Web sites, blogs, and radio talk shows, theorists insist that NASA is tracking Nibiru—but that this information is being kept from the public as part of a worldwide conspiracy. Some of these theorists postulate that "Planet X," or Nibiru as it is sometimes called, will pass by the earth, creating severe weather patterns.[33] Others believe the planet will collide with the earth.[34] From where did the idea of Planet X emanate?

Senior scientist David Morrison at NAI (NASA Astrobiology Institute) claims that Planet X originated with Zecharia Sitchin, a writer of fiction regarding the ancient Mesopotamian civilization of Sumer. According to Morrison, Sitchin claimed he found and translated Sumerian documents that identify that the planet Nibiru orbits the Sun every 3,600 years,[35] though Sitchin later denied any connection between his work and claims of a coming apocalypse.[36]

The Nibiru story was advanced by Nancy Lieder (a self-declared psychic who claims she channels aliens), who wrote on her Web site Zetatalk that the inhabitants of a fictional planet around the star Zeta Reticuli warned her that the earth was in danger from Planet X or Nibiru.[37] "This catastrophe was initially predicted for May 2003, but when nothing happened the doomsday date was moved forward to December 2012. Only recently have these two fables been linked to the end of the Mayan long-count at the winter solstice in 2012—hence the predicted doomsday date of December 21, 2012."[38]

As solar physicist Ian O'Neill states, "The Planet X theory is based on very dubious astronomical 'discoveries.' " Planet X came from a story run in newspapers in 1983; however, it turns out there is no evidence that Planet X is even a planet.[39] O'Neill cites Washington Post staff writer Thomas O'Toole as stating, "So mysterious is the object that astronomers do not know if it is a planet, a giant comet, a nearby 'protostar' that never got hot enough to become a star, a distant galaxy so young that it is still in the process of forming its first stars, or a galaxy so shrouded in dust that none of the light cast by its stars ever gets through."[40]

The newspaper account did not provide any indication that this mystery mass would collide with our planet, let alone a projected date of 2012 when it would cause cataclysmic effects on earth. But, a dubious story is all it took for 2012 theorists to latch onto it and adapt it to fit their construction of the end of the world as we know it on December 21, 2012.

Could December 21, 2012 Be the End of the World?

When one objectively examines the evidence of the 2012 phenomenon, sorting through the reports and innuendos, it seems one is left with *only* reports and innuendos. There is a complete void of scientific evidence for the theory that December 21, 2012 will be the end of the world as we know it.

Does that mean the end of the world cannot occur on that date? Interestingly, God has answered that question for us. In fact, he has provided us with very detailed information about the future, including a coming seven-year period that will be far different than anything this world has ever experienced.

God has shown us exactly how this coming era will begin and what it will look like, so that from his explicit presentation we know the world has not yet entered into it. Though it could begin very soon, we know that from God's time frame, the world will not end in 2012. However, while this author is certainly not setting a date for its inception, the evidence we have before us suggests it could commence by the end of 2012—or sooner!

Be Forewarned

God's revelation of this future era is a compelling and stunning account. This near-future period will bring such change to the earth that, at its inception—to borrow a phrase from some 2012 theorists—the world "as we know it will end." However, the world itself will *not* end, and "harmony and convergence" (to borrow another phrase from proponents of the 2012 phenomenon) will *not* arrive upon the earth before the consummation of that era.

The apocalyptic account you are about to read is also a gripping story of adventure and conflict, of the ultimate battle of good versus evil, of suffering and heroic rescue, building toward an incredible climax—but, it is entirely true. God has verified this information in many different ways over a three-thousand-year time frame of communicating it through his prophets, apostles, and even his own Son.

We have "listened" to the reports of the 2012 theorists, and we have examined the testimonies of the scientists. Perhaps it is now time to see what God has to say about our near future. Because God has much to say about it, the rest of this book is dedicated to *his* testimony.

CHAPTER 2
Caught Unaware

In 1947, scientists created the Doomsday Clock to symbolically show how close they believe the world is to a nuclear holocaust. In 1953, after the US tested a hydrogen bomb, the hands were set at two minutes before midnight. Since then, they have been pushed back and forth thirteen times. The clock's safest setting was in 1991, after the US and Russia signed an arms-reduction treaty. The time was then set at seventeen minutes before midnight. But, in May 1999, after India and Pakistan set off nuclear blasts, the hands were advanced to 11:51. Today, the clock is set at five minutes till midnight.[1]

These scientists believe we are close to the end of our era—and we may be. However, does the general population believe that? It seems the world is focused on preserving the planet for the next ten thousand years. So, if things as we know it were to end any time soon, the world would certainly be caught unaware.

Surprise!

Though God has been warning for eons that he will bring a seven-year era of judgment upon the earth, the Bible announces the world will be caught unaware by its arrival.[2] Notice how the apostle Paul, under the inspiration of the Holy Spirit, describes this surprise: "But concerning the times and the seasons, brethren, you have no need that I should write to you. For you yourselves know perfectly that the day of the Lord so comes as a thief in the night" (1 Thessalonians 5:1–2).

This prophetic declaration uses a key phrase, "the times and the seasons," to refer to a future period of time.[3] Paul, the founder of the church at Thessalonica, had taught those Christians well regarding the future, for he stated they had no need for him to write to them about those things. So, what was it that Paul's readers knew? Among other things, they knew that the day of the Lord comes as a thief in the night.

The Day of the Lord?

But, what is "the day of the Lord"? The answer to that question is found in the Old Testament. There we discover it describes a future era in which God will pour out his wrath of judgment upon the earth. An example of its use is found in Isaiah chapter 2, which describes the day of the Lord as being connected with "the terror of the Lord."[4] According to this description, the day of the Lord will be a terrifying time—especially for the proud and lofty. At that time, God will judge the arrogance of man, when he causes "the loftiness of men to be bowed down."

Pride does not bow easily. To bring down the extreme haughtiness of men, God will cause the world's inhabitants to experience "the terror of the Lord." His judgment will be so traumatic that people will crawl "into the holes of the rocks, and into the caves of the earth" in their attempts to escape the Lord's anger toward their rebelliousness.

Here is how the Old Testament prophet Amos described the future day of the Lord:

> Woe to you who desire the day of the Lord! For what good is the day of the Lord to you? It will be darkness, and not light. It will be as though a man fled from a lion, and a bear met him![5]

As described, it will be a time of darkness and woeful judgment upon those who mock God's judgment (those who desire the day of the Lord). According to the prophet Zephaniah, the day of the Lord will be a bitter, devastating, gloomy, and distressful experience.[6] It is a future era in which God's wrath will be poured out upon the rebellious, and they will not escape!

A Thief in the Night

As revealed in 1 Thessalonians 5, the day of the Lord will catch many unaware. But, upon whom will "the day of the Lord so come as a thief in the night"? The answer, revealed in that same passage, is that it will catch by surprise *unbelievers*—those who have not believed in Jesus Christ.[7] And since, as we will learn in the next chapter, all believers will have been removed from the earth at the inception of this seven-year period of tribulation upon the earth, this means the day of the Lord will catch the unbelieving world off guard.

The apostle Paul further explains this statement when he proclaims in 1 Thessalonians 5:3: "For when they say, 'Peace and safety [security]!' then sudden destruction comes upon them, as labor pains upon a pregnant woman. And they shall not escape."

Sudden Destruction

The phrase "sudden destruction comes" is parallel to the phrase "the day of the Lord so comes," from the previous verse. This indicates that the day of the Lord will begin with sudden destruction. Therefore, the seven-year day of the Lord will be initiated by something violent that catches people by surprise.

It seems that the sudden destruction will be linked with something Jesus described as being part of the *beginning* of the day of the Lord in Matthew 24:6–8:

> "And you will hear of wars and rumors [reports] of wars. For nation will rise against nation, and kingdom against kingdom. And there will be famines, pestilences, and earthquakes in various places. All these are the beginning of *sorrows*." [emphasis added]

In the language in which the New Testament was originally written (Greek), the word *sorrows* is the same word used for *labor pains* in 1 Thessalonians 5:3. Just as the term *labor pains* is used as a picture of the day of the Lord, so *sorrows* is an apt description of that future era. And, since Jesus proclaims that the cataclysmic events described by him in

Matthew 24:6–8 are "the beginning of sorrows," this means these calamities occur in the first part of the day of the Lord.

The Cause of Destruction

Since the sudden destruction of 1 Thessalonians 5 comes at the very beginning of the day of the Lord, and since Matthew 24:6–8 describes the very beginning of the day of the Lord, it seems that the sudden destruction that initiates the day of the Lord is linked with "nation rising against nation."

The question that arises at this point is: What causes the sudden destruction? Of course, it is merely an educated guess, but since the sudden destruction is linked with nation rising against nation, and since sudden destruction refers to an abrupt annihilation, it is likely it is caused by some kind of nuclear attack.

Peace and Security

As pointed out in 1 Thessalonians 5:3, sudden destruction occurs when the unbelieving world believes it has attained peace and safety, or, because the Greek word translated as *safety* also means *security*, when the world feels at that time that it resides in a time of security. This means that immediately prior to the beginning of the day of the Lord, the world will be proclaiming peace and security.

Currently, the world is experiencing an unprecedented amount of terrorism. In fact, well-publicized attacks in several different countries have shown that no country is safe from sudden destruction. However, in the (near?) future, the world will appear to have become a better place, experiencing a brief period of time when it believes it has finally achieved peace and security from violent attacks.[8]

But then, sudden destruction will hit, and "they shall not escape!" Unbelievers will not be able to escape the destructive and horrifying effects of the day of the Lord that will be poured out upon the earth. This means that these judgments of God will be universal in scope—the entire world will experience them.

As we have seen, the world's belief that it is residing in peace and security when sudden destruction hits, along with the announcement that they shall not escape, underlines Paul's assertion that "the day of the Lord so comes as a thief in the night." The day of the Lord catching the world by surprise is a key concept in Paul's explanation of the day of the Lord.

As in the Days of Noah

To illustrate that the day of the Lord will catch the world by surprise, the apostle Paul used a comparison, and so did Jesus. He made this comparison in Luke 17:26–27: " 'And as it was in the days of Noah, so it will be also in the days of the Son of Man: They ate, they drank, they married wives, they were given in marriage, until the day that Noah entered the ark, and the flood came and destroyed them all.' "

This scene from the time of Noah portrays the world being caught unaware. In this comparison, people are presented carrying on normal activities (eating, drinking, marrying) as if nothing unusual—and certainly not cataclysmic—is about to occur.

With this illustration, Jesus portrays a worldwide catastrophe similar to what will occur in the day of the Lord. In the same way people in Noah's day were surprised by a cataclysmic judgment, people alive when the day of the Lord arrives will also be caught by surprise—as a thief in the night—and they shall not escape!

As in the time of Noah, the world today seems unaware that worldwide cataclysmic events are coming. Mankind seems focused on day-to-day survival, and news and discussions seem focused on the challenges of the here and now, with little consideration for the future. In addition, if there is warning regarding the future, it seems focused on such slower developing challenges such as global warming, or on economic challenges— not on the kind of sudden destruction God warns about.

Asleep at the Wheel?

It is understandable that non-Christians do not realize that the day of the Lord is approaching, but what is disturbing is that most Christians do not seem to realize it is coming. Why is that? It seems that the vast majority of teaching from pastors and church leaders today is centered on the here and now—how to deal with day-to-day issues and how to have a better life now. Unfortunately, this focus comes at the exclusion of teaching about the future, as indicated by the focus of books and articles written and sermons preached. Thus, Christians as a whole do not seem to be educated about future events.

The Importance of Knowing

It is important to realize that God does not give us this information simply to satisfy our curiosity about the future. Just because believers in Christ will not experience the day of the Lord, this does not mean this biblical teaching has no application for us. Indeed, we can learn much about God from this instruction about the future, information that will help us to trust him more and to respond in greater obedience.

Properly understanding the teaching of the day of the Lord enables us to see that God has a specific plan regarding the unbelieving world. We see that he is in control of the future.

In addition, biblical teaching on the day of the Lord shows that God works his plan out of an immeasurable love for people. He demonstrates his love for the unbelieving world by using these judgments to seek to bring people into an eternal relationship with him by faith in Jesus Christ for eternal life.[9]

This information can help us respond to God better as we realize he is in control and by understanding he has a specific plan for our future, borne out of love for us. A fuller understanding of God's plan regarding the day of the Lord also helps us to trust him in unfair situations by realizing that he is just and he will make all things right one day. As a result of trusting him more, we can respond to him better through obedience to him.

It Is Coming!

There is coming a brief period in which unbelievers will proclaim that the world has attained peace and security; but this will be immediately followed with the initiation of the day of the Lord by sudden destruction. We have also seen that the day of the Lord will be a devastating period containing great destruction. Clearly, this will be anything but a fun time to be alive on the earth.

However, with the approach of the day of the Lord, there is good news for those of us who have believed in Christ for eternal life. In the next chapter, we will center on this good news, which includes the escape of believers.

The Day of the Lord (7 years)

	3½ years (1,260 days)	3½ years (1,260 days)
1 2	3	

1. A brief period in which the world will proclaim "peace and security!"
2. The beginning of the day of the Lord—the seven-year tribulation period.
3. The midpoint of the day of the Lord, which is divided into two halves of 3½ years each.

CHAPTER 3
Taken

The story is told of an old farmer who, many years ago, brought his family to the big city for the first time. Upon arrival, they saw sights they had never seen before—skyscrapers, massive stores with beautiful display windows, and traffic everywhere.

The farmer dropped his wife off at the department store and took his son with him to the bank—the tallest of all the buildings. As they walked into the lobby, they saw something else they had never before seen. Two steel doors opened, revealing a small room. Into this tiny room, a large aged woman entered, and the doors closed behind her. The dial over the door swept to the right and then back to the left. The doors opened once more, and a beautiful young lady walked out.

The amazed farmer turned to his son and said, "You wait right here! I'm goin' to get your mother and run her through that thing!"

Of course, what appeared to be a physical transformation in this anecdote was only an apparent one. However, in our last chapter, we learned that a *real* physical transformation will occur with all Christians at the rapture of the church, which is that future event in which Jesus will come from heaven into the air and suddenly take all Christians off the earth to be with him.

In chapter 1 we learned that a brief era is approaching in which the world will proclaim peace and security. However, this period of tranquility will be broken by sudden destruction at the initiation of the day of the Lord. In addition, not only will the day of the Lord begin with devastation, its entire seven-year era will be one of massive death and destruction.

The Great Escape

But, there is good news for those of us who have believed in Christ for eternal life: God has provided a great escape! This escape is described in the passage that immediately precedes some verses we observed about the day of the Lord in the last chapter. Our good news is found in 1 Thessalonians 4:13–18.

Paul's concern is expressed in verse 13: "But I do not want you to be ignorant, brethren, concerning those who have fallen asleep [died], lest you sorrow as others who have no hope." He does not want Christians to be ignorant regarding the situation of deceased believers in Christ. Instead, he wants believers to have hope, so they will not grieve in a hopeless fashion (as do others who have no hope).[1]

The great "hope" described in this passage is oftentimes called the "rapture of the church."[2] The word *rapture* is from the Latin word *rapturo*, meaning "to [suddenly] snatch away." And though the word *rapture* does not appear in the Bible, the concept certainly does, as we see in this passage.[3]

Escape Details

In describing the rapture of the church, this passage announces that one day in the future, Jesus will descend from heaven and suddenly take from the earth every living believer in Christ in order for them to be united with him in the air. In joining Jesus in the air, they will also be gathered with Christians who had died and had been in heaven with the Lord. Thus, from this passage we discover three major things that will occur at this great event.

First, Jesus will bring with him from heaven believers in Christ who had previously died. As the New Testament clearly presents, when a Christian dies, he immediately goes into the presence of the Lord.[4] From the time of their deaths, Christians are in heaven enjoying an experience that is beyond what we can currently comprehend. However, while their experience in heaven is an amazing one, they are not yet complete without the physical bodies they left behind at death. This brings us to the second major occurrence at this wondrous event.

When Jesus brings departed believers with him from heaven into the air, they will then receive their resurrected bodies. In a moment in time, they will be reunited with their bodies, which will be perfected from that point on. Their glorified bodies will be completely healed and will function perfectly. They will never again experience sickness, pain, lameness, deafness, blindness, aging, or death.

Thirdly, when Jesus comes in the air, Christians who are alive at that time will be caught up with him and with the departed believers. As we examine these verses, we notice an order: raptured Christians will receive their resurrected bodies *after* the deceased believers receive their resurrected bodies.

Changed in a Moment

At the moment living Christians are caught up into the air, they will receive their glorified bodies. The apostle Paul describes this phenomenon like this in 1 Corinthians 15:51–52:

> Behold, I tell you a mystery: We shall not all sleep [die], but we shall all be changed—in a moment, in the twinkling of an eye, at the last trumpet.[5] For the trumpet will sound, and the dead will be raised incorruptible, and we shall be changed.

These verses reiterate something we saw in 1 Thessalonians 4: not all Christians will die. Specifically, Christians who are alive when the rapture of the church occurs will not die. Instead, their corruptible bodies will be changed into incorruptible (glorified) bodies as they are suddenly taken into the air to be with Christ.

In addition, we see information on the rapture in these verses that we did not see in the 1 Thessalonians passage. Believers will "be changed (and caught up in the clouds) in the twinkling of an eye"—faster than one can blink! No one who is left behind will see this event happen because believers in Christ will be here one moment and gone the next!

When?

Therefore, we have seen that believers who are alive when Jesus comes from heaven to the clouds will suddenly be caught up to be with Christ. But, when does this great event occur? We cannot predict a specific date for it, but the Bible does tell us when it will occur in relation to the day of the Lord.

Our first clue to the timing of the rapture comes in 1 Thessalonians 1:9–10. These verses give us a basic, chronological outline to the book of 1 Thessalonians,[6] and based on this outline, the rapture of the church will occur *before* the day of the Lord. Verse 10 of chapter 1 agrees with that chronological ordering, for it announces that at the rapture of the church, Jesus will deliver believers in Christ from the coming wrath.

Two other expressions for "the wrath to come" (or, the coming wrath) are "the day of the Lord" and "the tribulation period." Thus, when Jesus comes in the air to take believers out of the world, he will deliver them from the coming wrath, which is the day of the Lord, which is also the tribulation period.

Deliverance

As the teaching that believers will be delivered from the day of the Lord from which unbelievers will *not* escape concludes, we are presented with this very comforting thought:

> For God did not appoint us to wrath, but to obtain salvation [deliverance] through our Lord Jesus Christ, who died for us, that whether we wake or sleep, we should live together with Him. Therefore comfort each other and edify one another, just as you also are doing. (1 Thessalonians 5:9–10)

The comfort we receive from these verses is this: Christians will be delivered from the day of the Lord by Jesus, because God determined we would not experience this future period of wrath. To help us better understand this promise of deliverance from the coming wrath, it is important to note that the Bible does not refer to wrath as hell. God's wrath, in the Bible, is God's temporal judgment upon sinful mankind. That means that the wrath from which Jesus will deliver Christians is not eternal hell, but a temporary period of time (seven difficult years) called the day of the Lord.

This deliverance is for *all* believers alive at that time, whether we wake or sleep. Since this phrase refers to a believer's spiritual health, it is saying to us that whether a believer is *awake* to the soon return of Christ and demonstrating that alertness by faithfully serving Christ, or is *asleep* and showing spiritual lethargy by not being faithful to Christ, Paul promises that all believers who are alive at the time Christ comes in the air will be taken up to be with him. In other words, all Christians, whether they are faithful or unfaithful, will be delivered from the coming wrath by the rapture.

Imminent and Coterminous

While teaching us that believers will be delivered from the day of the Lord by the rapture, Paul exhorts Christians in 1 Thessalonians 5:4 not to be caught off guard (as a thief in the night) by the appearing of the day of the Lord. In fact, both the rapture and the day of the Lord are described as events catching people off guard as a thief in the night.[7] This indicates that both events are presented as being imminent— meaning, that there is no other event predicted by the Bible as taking place before these two. These events can only be described in this way if both the rapture and the beginning of the day of the Lord occur at the same time.

Earlier, in Matthew 24:36–41, Jesus also indicated that the rapture and the initiation of the day of the Lord will occur at the same time. The reference to the rapture in these verses can be seen in the repeated phrase "the coming of the Son of Man," referring to Jesus' return to establish his rule upon the earth.[8] His return will commence with him coming from heaven into the air for the rapture of the church. This will be followed by a seven-year hiatus, during which time Jesus and Christians will have a layover in the air,[9] while those dwelling on the earth will experience the day of the Lord. At the end of this seven-year period, Jesus will continue his return to the earth by landing on the Mount of Olives. Therefore, his coming (return) is actually a seven-year trip in all.

Some Christians have become confused when comparing the coming of the Son of Man in verses 29–37. Verse 37 refers to the rapture of the church at the *beginning* of the tribulation period, while verses 29–31 refer to Jesus' coming to the earth at the *end* of the tribulation period. It is the same "coming,"[10] though it is accompanied by a seven-year delay.[11]

Notice that Jesus not only pictures the rapture in this passage, He also portrays the day of the Lord. While the rapture of the church is represented by the ark that delivered Noah and his family, the flood in Jesus' description stands for the day of the Lord. Just as the Genesis flood was a worldwide judgment by God, so the day of the Lord, following the rapture of the church, is presented as a period of God's cataclysmic judgment upon the world, affecting everyone.

On the Same Day

You will notice that Jesus announced that before the flood came, "people were eating, drinking, marrying, and giving in marriage." By providing a description of people participating in mundane activities, Jesus' point is that those in Noah's day were unaware that a worldwide cataclysm was about to occur; they continued as if nothing was about to happen, missing the opportunity to escape from God's judgment about to be poured out upon the earth.

But, if we look even closer, we will see indication that the rapture of the church (portrayed by the ark) and the initiation of the day of the Lord (pictured by the coming of the flood) will occur on the very same day. Jesus links the two events by announcing that "the coming of the Son of Man" will be like the coming of the flood in Noah's day. He also commented that people simply carried on with their life activities until the day that Noah entered the ark. In addition, Jesus stated that these same people "did not know until the flood came and took them all away." These statements show that nothing about these people's lives changed until Noah entered the ark *and* the flood came and took them all away. In order for *each* of these descriptions to be true regarding the rapture and the beginning of the day of the Lord, they would need to occur on the same day.[12]

What Noah's Day Shows Us

In addition, we can see that the description of the mundane activities of verses 37–39 demonstrate a comparison between the setting leading up to, and including, the deliverance of Noah and his household from the universal flood and the future setting of "peace and security" along with the rapture of the church. By linking Noah's day with the coming rapture of the church, Jesus presents a parallelism to show that the age prior to the rapture is similar to life prior to the flood of Noah's day. Preceding the flood, life continued with people focused on life's activities and with no awareness of the cataclysm about to occur. In the same way, the world continues prior to the day of the Lord with no thought of what is coming.

Taken

To enhance his teaching of the imminence of these events, Jesus presents this picture in verses 40 and 41: " 'Then two men will be in the field: one will be taken and the other left. Two women will be grinding at the mill: one will be taken and the other left.' "

The word *then* connects these verses to Jesus' coming, which is mentioned immediately prior. The word *taken*, which is used twice in these verses, is the Greek word *paralambano*, which is defined by the standard Greek lexicon as "to take into close association, take (to oneself) take with/along."[13] It is a different Greek word than the one (*airo*) translated as *taken* in the announcement "the flood came and took them all away" in verse 39.[14] In verse 39, Jesus speaks of judgment, while in verses 40 and 41 he pronounces that believers in him will be taken to be with him.

The message communicated by the two abbreviated scenes in verses 40 and 41 is this: While people are going about their normal life activities, Jesus will suddenly take believers to himself from among unbelievers, leaving behind the unbelievers in the world. This message is driven home by the repetition of the phrase, "one will be taken, the other left."

So, just as the ark delivered those (Noah and his family) who believed God's message, so Jesus will deliver those who believe his message of eternal life. Noah and his family were untouched by God's judgment poured out upon the earth in the same way those who will be delivered by the rapture will be untouched by the judgments God will pour out during the seven-year tribulation period.

Watch

The application of Jesus' proclamation of the rapture follows in two parts. Part one is presented in verses 42–44:

> "Watch therefore, for you do not know what hour your Lord is coming. But know this, that if the master of the house had known what hour the thief would come, he would have watched and not allowed his house to be broken into.[15] Therefore you also be ready, for the Son of Man is coming at an hour you do not expect."

Here is what Jesus is announcing to us in these verses: Be ready at all times for his coming. Here is why we should be ever ready: We do not know when he will come for us.

At the point Jesus made that announcement, not even *he* knew when the rapture and the day of the Lord would occur.[16] This shows that these events will be surprise occurrences, and, as such, they are imminent.

Getting Close?

However, though Jesus presented these as events that will occur suddenly, catching many off guard, this does not mean we cannot know we are getting close to them. As we see prophecy being fulfilled, we can know that these events are drawing near. For example, the continued influx of Jews into the land of Israel in fulfillment of Ezekiel 37 to prepare for the salvation of Israel, (which will occur during the tribulation period), indicates we are getting close to those predicted events.

Another observable fulfillment of Scripture demonstrating we are getting close to the day of the Lord is the gained control of Jerusalem by Israel in 1967. This fulfilled prediction of Jesus in Luke 21:24 signaled the fulfillment of "the times of the Gentiles" in which God began to turn his focus from the Gentiles to Israel for salvation. This new focus of the Lord also indicates that the salvation of Israel in the day of the Lord is drawing nigh.[17]

So, we *can* know these events are drawing near. And God wants us to be ever ready so we will finish well—because to finish well means the opportunity to rule with Christ in God's kingdom.

A Tale of Two Servants

As we return to Jesus' teaching in Matthew 24, we see him illustrating the importance of being ready for his coming with the following parable in verses 45–51. Here Jesus presents a representation of a Christian entrusted with a ministry of serving others.[18] In verse 41, this Christian (servant) is described as applying Jesus' exhortation of verses 42–44 (to watch, to be ready, for his coming) in this way: He faithfully obeys his master (carries out the charge to give them food in due season)[19] right up to his master's return. As a result, the master responds to his servant's readiness at his return by rewarding him with rule over his household.

As a result of the faithfulness of this servant, Jesus states: "Assuredly, I say to you that he will make him ruler over all his goods." This announcement represents the reward of rule in Christ's kingdom for the believer who finishes his life faithfully to Christ. Therefore, verses 45–47 illustrate the important truth other passages teach, which is that only those believers who *finish* their lives faithfully to Christ will rule with him. Therefore, the first half of this parable presents an illustration of a believer responding well to his exhortation of living in readiness to his coming—and being well rewarded for it.

A Different Response

However, the focus of the parable makes an important change in verses 48–51. There Jesus shows by illustration that the same believer who responded so well in verses 45–47 could actually respond very differently: "But if that evil servant says in his heart, 'My master is delaying his coming,' and begins to beat his fellow servants, and to eat and drink with the drunkards. . ." By using the word *that*, Jesus shows that this different response refers to the *same* servant mentioned in verses 45–47. In other words, Jesus is teaching by this presentation that a believer in Christ can respond to his imminent return by serving faithfully until he returns, or a Christian can, unfortunately, respond very differently.

Verse 49 portrays the *opposite* of living in readiness for the coming of Christ. We see that the servant "begins to beat his fellow servants, and to eat and drink with the drunkards." Instead of living in readiness for the coming of Christ, the believer described in this verse mistreats his fellow Christians and lives for self-gratification, while keeping company with those who live without restraint.[20] From this we can conclude that living

27

in readiness for Christ's return involves serving others, living soberly (in self-control), and keeping company with committed believers.[21]

What causes the differing behavior between these two pictures of Christians presented in this passage? What is it that creates the second picture—that of a Christian who finishes unfaithfully to his Master? The fatal mistake this believer makes in verses 48–51—which leads him to live such a wasteful life—is that he believes his Master will not soon return (verse 48).

Unfortunately, it seems many Christians think this way. Not many churches seem to teach on the imminent return of Jesus. Thus, many Christians appear to have the mindset of the scoffers described in 2 Peter 3:3–4, questioning the soon return of Christ.[22]

Regret for Ignoring God's Warning

Instead of being rewarded with rule in Christ's kingdom, the unfaithful believer depicted in verses 49–51 will experience great regret at the judgment seat of Christ.[23] When believers appear before Christ in the future, they will have a complete absence of sin. Since sin is what impedes our desire to please Christ, then when we appear before him one day, we will, at that time, want to please Christ with 100 percent of our being! Imagine, then, how a Christian will feel appearing before Christ and realizing he finished his life in self-gratification instead of living for Christ! At that point, any word of rebuke from Jesus[24] will be like cutting the sensitive believer in two!

The unfaithful believer will then have the unfortunate fate of being assigned a portion with the hypocrites. A hypocrite is one who misrepresents who he really is. For a Christian, this would mean not living as a child of God—in other words, not living as a faithful follower of the Lord Jesus Christ.[25]

To be assigned a portion with the hypocrites means this unfaithful Christian will possess the same reward in the kingdom as other hypocritical Christians—those who did not live as children of God. This may not sound so serious; after all, this individual will still be in the kingdom forever, and his experience will be far better than life here and now. However, this is a very serious consequence of unfaithfulness! It will result in an eternal experience that will be far less fulfilling than it could have been. A believer with this kind of experience will miss out on a kind of joy, intimacy with Christ, awesome honor from him, significant position, fulfilling service, etc. that God desires for us in his eternal kingdom.

The Importance of Seeing His Imminence

It is very important, then, for us to continue to believe what Jesus says about his coming for us—that it is imminent. He could return at any time—even before you finish reading this chapter! If we truly believe that important teaching, we will live as if he may return tomorrow—or even by the end of today.

Therefore, while the rapture will deliver believers out of the world to keep them from undergoing the day of the Lord, it will actually occur on the same day as the commencement of the day of the Lord. Because we know Jesus will not allow us to experience God's wrath that will be poured out on the world during the day of the Lord, this understanding can motivate us to live for Christ. In addition, because Jesus could come for us at any time, this imminence should motivate us to continue in faithfulness day by day so as not to be caught by him in unfaithfulness.

This last point can be illustrated by a time when my parents went to Belgium for two weeks to visit my younger sister, Donna, who was there at the time as an exchange student. My other sister, Rita, and I were home from college at spring break during the last week of their trip.

The mistake my parents made was to tell Rita and me exactly when they would return. We knew when their plane was scheduled to touch down at the airport, and because we knew how long it would take them from the airport to our front door, we had their arrival at our house calculated down to the minute.

That meant we could party heartily at the house with full confidence we would not get caught. We could trash the home and know how much time we had in order to clean up. Thus, we were able to behave the way we wanted and get our act together before our parents arrived. However, if our parents had not told us when they were returning, we would have been motivated to behave much differently.

In the same way, because the rapture occurs as a thief—prior to the day of the Lord—we have no signs that are noted to occur before the Lord comes in the air for us. Since Jesus' return is imminent, we have a greater motivation to remain faithful to him in order to finish well—so we might be found faithful when he comes for us.

Living with Expectation

Bud Wood used to run Shepherd's Home, a home for the educable retarded and those with Down's syndrome. He taught them the gospel of Christ, but he also stressed to the residents that Jesus may appear in the air at any moment for believers in Christ. As a result, the worst maintenance problem at the home during Bud Wood's tenure there was dirty windows. The reason is residents at the home would constantly go to the windows, and while pressing their faces against the glass, would excitedly look into the sky and ask, "Is Jesus coming?! Is he coming?!"

The Bible teaches that Christians are to live with this kind of expectation. After all, it will not be good to be caught by surprise by Jesus' coming in the air for us.

As we have seen, once the rapture occurs, the seven-year day of the Lord will begin. However, something else will cause the clock to begin ticking, heralding in the tribulation period. In the next chapter, we will examine that event.

CHAPTER 4
Seventy Sevens

In Dr. Donald Campbell's commentary *Daniel: Decoder of Dreams*, he tells of how Leopold Cohn, a European rabbi, came to the conclusion that the Messiah had already come. Based on his study of Daniel 9:24–26, he reasoned that the Messiah's coming was slated to occur prior to the destruction of Jerusalem in 70 AD.

Interestingly, this led him to speak about this to an older rabbi, who told him that he would find information about the Messiah if he went to New York. So, he sold his belongings to purchase passage to the big city. After he arrived, he wandered the streets seeking information on the Messiah. Then, one day he heard singing coming from a building, so, out of curiosity, he entered and sat among the congregation. There he heard a message about Jesus Christ, and responded by believing in him for eternal life.

He then dedicated himself to reaching Jews for Christ. Shortly thereafter, he established an outreach that was to become the American Board of Missions to the Jews.

This true story demonstrates that Daniel 9:24–27 can lead to an eternal impact. In addition, we will see in this chapter that this same brief passage presents a detailed version of God's prophetic plan over a period of four hundred and ninety years, culminating in the return of Christ to establish his kingdom on earth.

We previously saw that the Bible foretells a seven-year period called the day of the Lord in which God's wrath is poured out upon the earth. The day of the Lord is initiated by an important event that begins the clock ticking on this seven-year period; however, we cannot fully understand or appreciate that event—or the period following it—without seeing it in the context of God's purposes and time frame, which are located in Daniel 9:24–27.

The Significance of Seventy

Daniel, who wrote the book in which this verse appears, was a godly Jew living in Babylon at the time—along with many other Jews. These Jews were all originally from southern Israel, called Judah, the area in which Jerusalem is located. However, due to Judah's disobedience against God, God used Nebuchadnezzar and his army to discipline southern Israel by attacking that area and evacuating ten thousand young Jewish men to Babylon. In addition, almost seventy years before the scene in Daniel chapter 9 was to take place, Nebuchadnezzar, with his army, overran Jerusalem, looted the Jewish temple, and set up his own puppet government there.

This period of time (seventy years) takes on great significance for Daniel as he reads the scroll (book) of Jeremiah,[1] for he comes to realize that the captivity of Judah will last seventy years.[2] This understanding moves Daniel to begin praying fervently for his people, asking God to fulfill his word by delivering the Jews from captivity. In response, God sends the angel Gabriel to announce to Daniel that Israel would be delivered. However, the message the angel proclaims to Daniel is not about the *immediate* deliverance of Israel but about the *long-range* deliverance of Israel. It is as if God is saying to Daniel, "I will answer your prayer for the deliverance of Israel. But I will do so in a far greater way than you can imagine!"

The Overview of God's Plan for His People

It was through this revelation that the angel delivered an amazing proclamation, which begins in verse 24: " 'Seventy weeks [sevens] are determined for your people and for your holy city, to finish the transgression, to make an end of sins, to make reconciliation for iniquity, to bring in everlasting righteousness, to seal up vision and prophecy, and to anoint the Most Holy.' "

This verse presents an overview of God's incredible plan for his people, while the verses that follow (25–27) provide key elements of that plan and their God-ordained timing. The word *week* in this passage is a translation of a Hebrew word that literally means *seven*. Seven, in this context, refers to a unit of time, but the question is: *What* unit of time? Is it referring to days, weeks, or years?

Interpretive Clues

As we go through the context, it becomes evident that this prophecy is referring to units of years.[3] The phrase *seventy weeks* literally means *seventy sevens*. Seventy sevens refer to seventy *times* seven, which equals 490 years. Therefore, the prophecy of verses 24–27 describes a 490-year period of time.

Verse 24 provides us with some key interpretive clues to help us understand the prophecy. For example, there are two subjects mentioned, around which this prophecy is built.

The first subject mentioned is "your people." Thus, it is important to see the identity of "your people" in this verse. This identity can be readily seen by understanding that Daniel, to whom this prophecy is addressed by the angel, is a Jew. Since this prophetic announcement concerns Daniel's ("your") people, we can see, then, that it deals with the Jews, or Israel.

The second subject of this prophecy is the city mentioned, identified as "your holy city." That can only refer to Jerusalem, since Jerusalem was the capital city of Israel and its religious center. This means that Jerusalem is a key part of this prophecy. It also means that God designated a specific 490-year period (seventy weeks) to complete his plan for Israel, a plan that not only centers on the Jews in the land of Israel but also on Jerusalem and the temple.

A Plan with a Purpose

At first glance, there appear to be six purposes for this plan of God. However, it is more likely there is *one* major overall purpose, which is achieved by fulfilling five other purposes. We can recognize each of these purposes in verse 24 by noticing the signal word *to*.

To Finish Transgression

The first of these refers to God's overall plan for Israel and is presented in this way: "to finish the transgression." We can understand this phrase better by going back to verse 5 in chapter 9, which is a part of Daniel's prayer, to which the angel Gabriel was sent in response. There he made this confession: "We [the Israelites] have sinned and committed iniquity, we [the Israelites] have done wickedly and rebelled" (verse 5).

Though Daniel is presented as a very godly individual, he humbly identifies himself with the history of the Israelites. In that identification—and Daniel's prayer for his Jewish brethren—we learn that the Jews have had a history of apostasy (departing from) and rebellion against God. Thus, God was announcing through the angel that he would use this 490-year period to answer Daniel's prayer by finishing Israel's transgression. As verse 24 continues, we gain insight into how God will do that.

To Make an End of Sins

The second phrase presents the first of five subpurposes indicating how God will achieve the major purpose within this time frame. He will use this time period "to make an end of sins."

God will use the day of the Lord toward the goal of making an end of sins through the judgments he will pour out on a sinful world. Those judgments will bring about faith in Christ and national repentance by Israel,[5] as well as bring many Gentiles to faith in Christ.

The phrase *to make an end of sins* can also be translated *to seal up[6] sins*, as in not allowing sinfulness to have free rein upon the earth. This meaning fits well with the context surrounding verse 24.

Though the day of the Lord begins the process of making an end of sins, the event that will produce this sealing of sinfulness is the return of Christ to establish his kingdom. During the first thousand years of his kingdom rule on earth, Jesus will "rule with a rod of iron"[7] and cause justice and holiness to be manifested on the earth.[8] Following that millennial reign, the Lord will destroy the present world and create a new one[9] "in which righteousness dwells."[10] Thus, Jesus, at his return to the earth, will seal up sins, fulfilling this second purpose of Daniel 9:24.

To Reconcile

The second fulfillment toward the achievement of God's overall purpose for Israel is presented in this way: "to make reconciliation for iniquity." The New Testament shows us that making reconciliation for iniquity refers to the death Christ died to make payment for the sins of the world—to reconcile Israel (and all believers) to God.[11]

However, though Jesus did what was necessary to accomplish reconciliation, Israel, as a whole, will not actually receive reconciliation until Jews in the nation believe in Jesus as the Christ, the giver of eternal life. That will not occur until the day of the Lord nears an end. This means God will use the tribulation period to bring Israel into reconciliation with him. Thus, Israel will experience reconciliation for iniquity by the time of the return of Jesus to establish his kingdom upon the earth. Therefore, the third phrase of verse 24 focuses on the return of Christ in the same way the first two do.

To Bring Everlasting Righteousness

The third fulfillment toward the achievement of God's overall purpose for Israel is listed in this way: "to bring in everlasting righteousness." The future seven-year tribulation period will prepare for this everlasting righteousness, which will be displayed in the following way:

"Behold, the days are coming," says the Lord, "That I will raise to David a Branch of *righteousness*; a King shall reign and prosper, And execute judgment and *righteousness* in the earth. In His days Judah will be saved, And Israel will dwell safely; Now this is His name by which He will be called: THE LORD OUR *RIGHTEOUSNESS*" (Jeremiah 23:5–6, emphasis added).

These verses in Jeremiah describe what will occur following the return of Christ. Notice the emphasis on righteousness, for when he returns, he will initiate his reign of righteousness over all the earth. At that time, Jesus, the branch of righteousness and descendant of David, will rule. He will execute worldwide judgment and righteousness, and according to other Bible passages, once Jesus initiates righteousness upon the earth, it will continue eternally.[12]

Notice that this promise revolves around Israel, for at that time, Israel will be delivered from her enemies and will dwell safely upon the earth. For the first time since the introduction of sin into human history, righteousness will reign on the earth, and once universal righteousness comes to the earth, it will last forever! Thus, everlasting righteousness, mentioned in Daniel 9:24, will be present on our planet following the return of Christ to the earth.

To Finish Transgression

This brings us to the fourth fulfillment toward the achievement of God's overall purpose for Israel, that of finishing Israel's transgression. The fourth fulfillment is announced by the fifth infinitive phrase of verse 24: "to seal up vision and prophecy."

The Hebrew word translated to *seal up* means to enclose something because its functions are completed, while the word for *vision* carries the meaning of revelation. Putting these meanings together, we can see that this phrase refers to the fulfillment of God's prophetic revelation. This means that God will use the plan he outlines in verses 24–27 to fulfill his promises to Israel—promises that will be experienced in God's future kingdom upon the earth. Therefore, this statement "to seal up vision and prophecy" (along with the previous four infinitive statements in verse 24) will also be fulfilled at the return of Christ to establish God's kingdom upon earth.

To Anoint the Most Holy

The sixth and final phrase in verse 24 is announced in this way: "to anoint the Most Holy." This refers to the temple in Jerusalem. "The Most Holy" is a translation of two Hebrew words, *qodesh qadashim* (holy of holies), that are used together thirty-nine times in the Old Testament, always in reference to the tabernacle or temple in Jerusalem, or to the holy articles used in the tabernacle or temple. More specifically, this final infinitive statement refers to the temple erected according to God's direction, as indicated by the word *anoint*. Since each of the other five infinitives in verse 24 points to a fulfillment in conjunction with the return of Christ to establish his kingdom upon the earth, this sixth statement undoubtedly also refers to that time frame. That would mean that this anointing of the Most Holy refers to the temple that will be built for Christ's thousand-year rule.[13]

Pointing to Christ's Return

As mentioned, verse 24 gives an overview of God's timetable for accomplishing his overall purpose for Israel, achieved through the fulfillment of five other stated purposes. All of these purposes point to the future return of Jesus to the earth. This means that God appointed a 490-year period (seventy sevens) of time to prepare Israel for his future kingdom on earth.

The First 483 Years

Verses 25 and 26 present key events and their timing in the first 483 of the 490 years of this prophetic revelation in this way:

Know therefore and understand, that from the going forth of the command to restore and build Jerusalem until Messiah the Prince, there shall be seven weeks [sevens] and sixty-two weeks [sevens]; the street shall be built again, and the wall, even in troublesome times. And after the sixty-two weeks [sevens] Messiah shall be cut off, but not for Himself; and the people of the prince who is to come shall destroy the city and the sanctuary. The end of it shall be with a flood, and till the end of the war desolations are determined.

We have seen from verse 24 that God's purpose for Israel would be fulfilled in a 490-year time period, which equals seventy sevens. Verses 25–26 divide the first sixty-nine *sevens*, or 483 years, into two major periods of time.

The First 49 Years

The first of those periods of time is seven sevens, which equal forty-nine years. This first era began with "the going forth of the command to restore and build Jerusalem." This command represents the decree from King Artaxerxes to Nehemiah, which was a response to Nehemiah's request to rebuild the wall of Jerusalem.[14] The decree occurred on March 5 (Nissan 1 on the Jewish calendar), 444 BC.[15] Though the decree of Artaxerxes dealt with rebuilding the wall around Jerusalem, verse 25 shows that this forty-nine-year period also involved a complete restoration of the city.

The Next 434 Years

Another key event is mentioned in verse 26: "Messiah shall be cut off." *Messiah* is the English translation of the Hebrew word for *anointed*,[16] while *Christ* is the English translation from its Greek equivalent.[17] The phrase *cut off* is a translation of a Hebrew word that is used elsewhere in the Old Testament of *being put to death*,[18] indicating that the phrase "Messiah shall be cut off" refers to the crucifixion of Christ. Verse 26 announces that this event would occur *after* the 434-year period (sixty-two sevens) following the restoration of Jerusalem. In fact, Messiah was cut off one week after this 434-year measurement of time ended.

Notice that this 434-year period begins with the completion of the Jerusalem building project—forty-nine years after the rebuilding began—and ends with the introduction of Messiah the Prince. It is *after* the 434-year period that Messiah shall be cut off.

Messiah the Prince

Thus, Jerusalem was restored in forty-nine years. Four hundred and thirty-four years after the restoration was completed, Jesus was publicly recognized as "Messiah the Prince" at his triumphal entry. This can especially be seen in Matthew 21:8–11 and John 12:12–13.

In fulfillment of Daniel 9:25, both of these New Testament passages show the Jewish crowd acknowledging Jesus as Messiah (Jewish deliverer and king). He is called "king" in John 12, while in Matthew the multitude cries out that he is "God's deliverer" or "salvation," and he is introduced as such to the entire city of Jerusalem! This clearly fulfills Daniel 9:25 in amazing fashion.

Perfect Timing

It has been calculated that Jesus' triumphal entry into Jerusalem—when he was acknowledged as Messiah the Prince—occurred on March 30 (Nissan 10 on a Jewish calendar), AD 33.[19] Using a Jewish calendar, this date would be 483 years (49 years [seven sevens] + 434 years [sixty-two sevens]) to the very day![20] Because a Jewish calendar year is 360 days (rather than 365 days of a solar year), the time period from March 4, 444 BC ("from the going forth of the command to restore and build Jerusalem") to March 30, AD 33 ("until [the introduction of] Messiah [as] the Prince") is 173,880 days, which equals 483 prophetic years to the very day!

This perfect fulfillment of God's prophetic word clearly shows us that God is in complete control.[21] It also demonstrates that God's word is absolutely trustworthy! This should encourage us to trust him all the more, knowing he is in control of the future, and he will fulfill his word completely and perfectly—down to the minutest detail!

God's Answer to Prayer

At the beginning of this chapter, we saw that when Daniel realized Israel's captivity was nearing the end of the seventy-year period of time God had determined, he prayed according to God's will, asking God for Israel's deliverance. In response to his prayer, God sent the angel Gabriel to announce God's ultimate deliverance of Israel through his 490-year plan for the nation. This teaches us that when we pray according to God's will, he answers (1 John 5:14–15).

When Daniel prayed for God to deliver Israel by restoring the Jews to Judah, he most likely did not anticipate that God would answer with the ultimate deliverance of Israel at the return of Christ. This passage illustrates that God may answer in ways far greater than we imagine[22]—and in ways that go well beyond the scope of time we may envision!

We have seen, thus far, that God's plan for Israel involves a 490-year time frame (seventy sevens) to bring in everlasting righteousness (see the timeline below). This plan includes three major divisions: 1) a forty-nine-year period, beginning with the decree to rebuild the wall of Jerusalem by Artaxerxes in 444 BC, to restore Jerusalem; 2) a 434-year era from the completion of the restoration of Jerusalem until the public introduction of Jesus as Messiah the Prince; and 3) a future seven-year era.

In the next chapter, we will explore this last and very significant, division. We will learn how significant it will be for Israel, as well as for the entire world, when the clock begins ticking.

The First 483 Years of God's Prophetic Plan for Israel

Restore Jerusalem	Till Messiah the Prince (Triumphal Entry of Jesus)
444 BC	AD 33
49 years (seven sevens)	434 years (sixty-two sevens)

CHAPTER 5
The Clock
Begins Ticking

The *Guinness Book of Records* recognized the Olsen clock, installed in the Copenhagen Town Hall, as the most accurate and complicated clock in the world. It contains more than 14,000 units, took ten years to make, and the mechanism of the clock functions in 570,000 different ways! "The celestial pole motion of the clock will take 25,753 years to complete a full circle," and the clock is accurate to one-half of one second every three hundred years![1]

However, there is no more accurate measure of time than that presented in Daniel 9:24–27. Those four verses present a time period of 490 years, containing amazing events announced prophetically—with perfect accuracy!

In our last chapter, we were introduced to God's amazing 490-year plan for Israel, revealed by the angel Gabriel to a godly Jew named Daniel. We saw that a majority of that prophetic program has already been fulfilled, but there remains a very important period of time that will usher in the kingdom of God upon the earth.

490 Years

Before we examine that remaining prophetic period, it will help to review what we learned in the last chapter. The word *week* in Daniel 9:24–27 literally means *seven*. We also saw that the time period represented by this number is seven years.

Verse 24 provides an overview of this prophecy, which is for a period of seventy weeks. These seventy weeks represent a 490-year period God designed for Israel's salvation. This verse also refers to Jerusalem (presented as "your holy city"). This capital of Israel is mentioned because it is the city around which this prophecy revolves.

Looking to the Return of Christ

We also observed one major purpose to fulfill God's overarching plan for this *seventy-week* time frame and five "subpurposes." These statements all look to the return of Christ to the earth. To reach completion, God predetermined a particular 490-year period divided into three parts. Part one, which extended from the decree of King Artaxerxes in 444 BC until Jerusalem was completely restored, was deemed to last forty-nine years (seven sevens). Part two, which began once the restoration of Jerusalem was completed and ended at the triumphal entry of Jesus into Jerusalem (just days before he was crucified), is the longest period of time of the 490-year period, lasting 434 years (sixty-two sevens). A few days after part two of this 490-year prophetic plan for Israel was fulfilled, Messiah was cut off, referring to the crucifixion of Jesus.

Prediction of the Crucifixion of Jesus

The crucifixion of Jesus signaled the rejection of the Messiah by Israel and led to this significant event, presented in the last half of verse 26: " 'And the people of the prince who is to come shall destroy the city and the sanctuary. The end of it shall be with a flood, and till the end of the war desolations are determined.' " This refers to the monumental event of AD 70 in which the Roman legions destroyed Jerusalem and the temple. The prince identified in this verse refers to the Roman general, Titus, who led the large military force into Israel at that time. Therefore, the people of the prince are the people of the Roman Empire.

Destruction of Jerusalem

Verse 26 announces that this destruction of Jerusalem would be with a flood of troops[2] leading to great destruction, described as desolations. These desolations resulted in the slaughtering of approximately one million Jews in the Jewish wars with Rome in AD 66–70.

Only Seven Years Left to Fulfill

If we totaled the amount of years from this prophetic plan that has already been fulfilled, we would come up with 483 years. However, as a result of the crucifixion and rejection of the Messiah by Israel, God introduced an interruption in this prophetic program, which has now lasted close to 2,000 years. This means that the final seven years of this prophetic vision, leading to the return of Christ to establish his kingdom upon the earth, are yet to be fulfilled.

This final seven-year period is presented in verse 27:

> "Then he [they] shall confirm a covenant [treaty] with many for one week [seven]; but in the middle of the week [seven] he [they] shall bring an end to sacrifice and offering. And on the wing of abominations shall be one who makes desolate, even until the consummation, which is determined, is poured out on the desolate."

We know that this has not yet been fulfilled. The word *then* that begins verse 27 shows that this description occurs *after* the events of verse 26. But, how long after those events?

Rebuilding the Temple

Verse 27 announces that as a result of breaking the treaty (covenant), sacrifices and offerings end. This shows us that sacrifices and offerings are connected to the making of the treaty, but, in order for the Jews to make sacrifices and offerings, a temple is needed.[3] In order for Israel to rebuild the temple,[4] the nation would need to be in possession of Jerusalem—for Jerusalem has always been, and will always be, the city where the temple is located. Though Jerusalem was lost to Israel in AD 70, Israel reacquired the city of David in 1967 (nearly 1,900 years later!) as a result of being victorious in the Six-Day War.[5]

A Treaty between Israel and Ten Nations

English translations usually translate verse 27 in this way, "Then he shall confirm a covenant . . . he shall bring an end . . ." However, the more natural way to translate the verse is to replace *he* with *they*. "Then they shall confirm a covenant . . . they shall bring an end . . ." This translation makes more sense, because the subject is the people of verse 26, not the prince.[6] Therefore, the people will make a treaty, and the people will break that treaty.

As we learned earlier, the people are those living within the boundaries of the old Roman Empire. Though we are not told in verse 27 how many nations from the old Roman Empire will make this treaty with Israel, the clues elsewhere indicate there will be ten—five from the West and five from the East. The two legs and ten toes in the vision of Daniel 2 portray both the old Roman Empire and a future, revived one. The ten toes point to the future fulfillment of Revelation 17 with ten kings giving their power to a man who becomes the world ruler. This can also be seen in Daniel 7, where a vision pictures the same four world powers as in Daniel 2, with the fourth power—also portraying a future revived Roman Empire—having ten kings arising from it (7:24). The two legs of Daniel likely indicate the two known divisions of the Roman Empire into East and West. Thus, the treaty will be made between ten nations that exist within the boundaries of the old Roman Empire and Israel, which are referred to as "many" in verse 27.[7]

Based on what we have seen thus far, we could translate verse 27 in this way: " 'Then ten nations existing within the boundaries of the old Roman Empire shall confirm a treaty with Israel for seven years, but in the middle of this seven-year period those nations shall bring an end to sacrifice and offering.' " Thus, this treaty will be intended as a seven-year treaty, but it will be broken three and a half years after it begins.

The Man of Sin

While the first half of verse 27 refers to (ten) nations, the last half of the verse refers to an individual. He will be "one who makes desolate."

We can determine that this individual will be the Man of Sin described by the apostle Paul in 2 Thessalonians 2:3–4: "The man of sin . . . the son of perdition, who opposes and exalts himself above all that is called God or that is worshiped, so that he sits as God in the temple of God, showing himself that he is God." After all, this description in 2 Thessalonians 2 will take place when the treaty of Daniel 9:27 is broken. In addition, if we look closely, we will see another similarity between 2 Thessalonians 2:3–4 and Daniel 9:27.

According to Daniel 9:27, the breaking of the treaty, which will occur three and a half years into it, will bring an end to sacrifice and offering. As we noted earlier, "sacrifice and offering" implies that the Jews have access to the temple.

In putting the two passages together, we see that a man will enter into the temple to be worshipped as God at the time the treaty is broken. This act by the Man of Sin will be an abomination to the temple and will put an end to sacrifice and offering.

Abomination of the Temple

Thus, the description of Daniel 9:27 corresponds to the abomination of the temple by the Man of Sin. This means the Man of Sin presents himself to the world as God for three and a half years prior to the return of Christ. This also identifies him as the man described in Revelation as "the beast" who will rule the world for forty-two months (Revelation 13:5)—three and a half years—until Jesus returns to the earth (cf. Revelation 19:11–21).

The abomination this man will perform to the temple is hinted at in the last sentence in Daniel 9:27: " 'And on the wing of abominations shall be one who makes desolate, even until the consummation, which is determined, is poured out on the desolate.' " Jesus referred to this abomination when he made this announcement in Matthew 24:15: "Therefore when you see the 'abomination of desolation,' spoken of by Daniel the prophet, standing in the holy place . . . then let those who are in Judea flee to the mountains [hills].' " [8]

Though Jesus was speaking to his Jewish disciples in the first century at the time he gave this proclamation, he actually intended this warning for his Jewish followers living three and a half years before his return to the earth. As we see, Jesus described this man as "the abomination of desolation"; or, as presented in Daniel 9:27, he is the "one who makes desolate." In addition, he not only is "the abomination," but he also causes abominations. He will seek to bring desolation upon Jews who believe in Jesus Christ by bringing abominations upon them through severe persecution.

As Jesus mentions, this abomination will occur when this man stands in "the holy place," the holy of holies within the temple. He will abominate the temple by going where no man but the high priest is allowed to go.

Notice what Jesus commanded of those living at the time this abomination occurs: "Then let those who are in Judea flee to the mountains [hills]." This warning is to believing Jews living in southern Israel (Judea) at the time this man abominates the temple by entering it to be worshipped as God. When that abomination occurs, Jews who have believed in Jesus for eternal life are to flee to the mountains. The purpose of Jesus' command is to warn and protect Jewish believers from the attempts of the Man of Sin to eliminate them.

God in Control

The last half of Daniel 9:27 implies how bad things will get after this treaty with Israel is broken. But, in the midst of this seemingly bad news, there is also good news. Although the desolating activity will be poured out upon southern Israel, God is in control! This good news is declared by the phrase *which is determined.*

The book of Daniel stresses again and again that God is sovereign—he is in full control of all things. The consummation is not determined by the Man of Sin, nor is it determined by Satan; it is determined by God. God is in control—even of the abomination of the Man of Sin.

But, this is how God works. He is in control of even the most heinous acts, for he uses them for the greatest good. An example of this can be seen in the words of the apostles in Acts 4:27–28. There they acknowledged in prayer that God used men such as Herod, Pilate, and the Roman soldiers to accomplish exactly what he had planned from all eternity past when they handed Jesus over to be crucified. From that horrendous event, God brought about the greatest good—the opportunity for all people to be saved from their sins and receive eternal life.

God Intends It for Good

The phrase *which is determined* also indicates that because God is in control—and because he is perfectly good—he will work it for good for his people as they respond by trusting him through it. This is an illustration of Romans 8:28–29, which lies in the context of a discussion on Christians and suffering. These verses show us that God uses suffering for good for those who love God, so that they might be conformed to the image of his Son.

So, how will God use this horrible three-and-a-half-year period for good? Aside from the fact that he will use it to bring Jews (and Gentiles) to believe in Christ for eternal life,[9] he will use it to prepare his people through suffering, for an even greater experience in his kingdom.[10] That difficult period of suffering will conform believers into the image of God's Son so that they can share in the inheritance of his Son, the Lord Jesus Christ. This inheritance will include the joy and incredible fulfillment of ruling with Christ in the future kingdom of God.[11]

God will also use that very difficult time to prepare for the return of Christ to establish his kingdom. The suffering and persecution Israel will experience in the latter half of the seven-year tribulation period will cause the nation to repent,[12] and as a result, Jesus will return to establish his kingdom.[13]

Finally, the phrase *which is determined* also indicates the good news that the horrible great tribulation[14] has a definite end. God has determined that it will only last three and a half more years.

God's Plan

As we have seen in Daniel 9:24–27, God has a definite plan, with a very definite timetable that involves Israel at the center of it all. We have seen that the culmination of this plan involves a seven-year treaty with Israel made and guaranteed by ten nations that come out of the old Roman Empire. It will be the initiation of this treaty that will cause the clock to begin ticking on the seven-year day of the Lord.

All of this should encourage us that no matter how bleak things may look—in the world or in our own lives—God is in control, working all things for good according to his definite plan. In the next chapter, we will see that, in the bleakness of the future tribulation period, God will show his sovereign goodness by providing two amazing witnesses to Israel.

Daniel 9:24–26

Restore Jerusalem	Till Messiah the Prince (Triumphal Entry of Jesus)

444 BC   AD 33

   49 years *(seven sevens)*   434 years *(sixty-two sevens)*

Daniel 9:27: A Covenant for One "Week" (7 years)

3½ years (1,260 days)	3½ years (1,260 days)

1   2   Desolation upon Israel

1 = Covenant (treaty) goes into effect;
2 = Abomination of desolation, sacrifices end (treaty is broken)

CHAPTER 6
Prophets of
Power and Plagues

Two events that occurred a little more than a year apart illustrate the power of God. On March 5, 1979, the most powerful burst of energy was recorded by man. In its publication on January 28, 1980, the *Dallas Times Herald* described it in this way: "The burst of gamma radiation picked up by the satellites lasted for only one-tenth of a second. But, in that brief instant, it emitted as much energy as the sun does over a period of 3,000 years. If the sun had belched out the same amount of energy, the earth would have vaporized instantly."

The second demonstration of pure power occurred on May 18, 1980. It was then that Mt. St. Helens exploded with what is probably the most visible indication of the power of nature that the modern world has ever seen. In their January 1981 edition, *National Geographic* described the blast in this way: "At 8:32 that morning, the explosion ripped 1,300 feet off of the mountain with a force of ten million tons of TNT, or roughly equal to five hundred Hiroshimas. Sixty people were killed, most by a blast of three-hundred-degree heat traveling at two hundred miles per hour. Some people were killed as far as sixteen miles away.

"The blast also leveled one-hundred-fifty-foot Douglas firs, as far away as seventeen miles, and a total of 3.2 billion board feet of lumber were destroyed, enough to build 200,000 three-bedroom homes."

Though that kind of cosmic power is truly mind-blowing, neither one of those examples is really anything more than God moving his little finger. Glimpses of God's staggering power are presented in the Bible through prophets of God.

According to Philip Yancey, "The prophets are the Bible's most forceful revelation of God's personality."[1] Aside from the Lord Jesus Christ himself, the prophets are also the best human communicators of God's supernatural power.

But, of all the great prophets who have roamed the earth and served as God's agents of displaying his power, possibly the two greatest have yet to begin their ministry. God is saving these two for an amazing prophetic ministry to Israel during the first half of the day of the Lord.

What Have We Learned?

We have learned that the world will announce that peace and security have arrived. Then the Lord Jesus will descend from heaven into the air to take believers off the face of the earth to be with him. At the same time, a seven-year treaty between ten nations and Israel will go into effect (but will be broken after three and a half years). This will set off the day of the Lord, a seven-year tribulation period in which God will pour out his judgments upon the earth.

However, though Jesus will remove all believers from the earth, the Bible reveals there are many who will believe in Jesus Christ for eternal life following that event.[2] But, this raises a question: If all believers have been removed, who will reach people with the gospel during that final seven-year period before the return of Christ to the earth?

1,260 Days

The answer to that question comes in the form of two mysterious men of God presented in Revelation 11. They are introduced to us in verse 3: " 'And I will give power to my two witnesses, and they will prophesy one thousand two hundred and sixty days, clothed in sackcloth.' "[3]

These are the words of a mighty angel[4] who brings God's message to the apostle John.[5] This verse introduces two men calling others to repentance (clothed in sackcloth), whose prophetic ministry will endure for only 1,260 days.

Because the book of Revelation has a Jewish orientation,[6] it makes sense that its measurement of time is based on a Jewish calendar. Since a Jewish calendar consists of twelve months of thirty days each, then the prophets' ministry of 1,260 days represents three and a half years to the very day!

You may recall, according to Daniel 9:27, the final seven years before Jesus returns will be introduced by a treaty with Israel. Though that treaty will be intended for seven years, it will be broken after three and a half years—the exact period of time the two prophets of God will prophesy in Jerusalem.

Since the future tribulation period will consist of two periods of 1,260 days each, then the time frame in which the ministry of God's two prophets occurs represents one of those three-and-a-half-year periods. But, the question is: Which one?

Which Half?

Daniel 9:24 tells us that this final seven-year period before the return of Christ to the earth will bring in everlasting righteousness. The last three and a half years will end in righteousness introduced by Christ's return to establish his kingdom.

Keeping this in mind will be very helpful in determining when the two prophets of God will prophesy. For example, take note of Revelation 11:7–9:

> When they [the two prophets] finish their testimony, the beast that ascends out of the bottomless pit will make war against them, overcome them, and kill them. And their dead bodies will lie in the street of the great city which spiritually is called Sodom and Egypt, where also our Lord was crucified. Then those from the peoples, tribes, tongues, and nations will see their dead bodies three-and-a-half days,[7] and not allow their dead bodies to be put into graves. And those who dwell on the earth will rejoice over them, make

merry, and send gifts to one another, because these two prophets tormented those who dwell on the earth.

Based on this passage, how will the three-and-a-half-year ministry of the two prophets end? As we can see, this half of the seven-year period prophesied in Daniel 9 will conclude with the silencing of the ministry of God's prophets, for they will be put to death by a man empowered by Satan.[8] In addition, the bodies of these godly men will suffer the humiliation of not being buried in order to display the apparent triumph of evil over God and his prophets. Finally, the conclusion of this three-and-a-half-year prophetic period will be accompanied by a celebration of the demise of these godly prophets by the ungodly world. This is certainly not a picture of the triumph of righteousness.

This clearly shows that the period in which the two prophets minister certainly does *not* end with righteousness triumphing. Instead, the conclusion of this half of Daniel's seventieth week[9] shows the apparent triumph of evil.

The two prophets of God will carry out their ministry during the *first* half of Daniel's seventieth week. They will prophesy to Israel from Jerusalem during the same three and a half years the treaty with Israel will be in effect.

While verse 3 of Revelation 11 introduced us to the *power* of the two prophets, verses 4–6 describe that power more fully:

> These are the two olive trees and the two lampstands standing before the God of the earth. And if anyone wants to harm them, fire proceeds from their mouth and devours their enemies. And if anyone wants to harm them, he must be killed in this manner. These have power to shut heaven, so that no rain falls in the days of their prophecy; and they have power over waters to turn them to blood, and to strike the earth with all plagues, as often as they desire.

Shining for God

Verse 4 portrays these two prophets as faithful instruments of God. As lampstands, they will shine with the glory of God. Their description as olive trees pictures a continually shining light, providing the oil needed to perpetually light the lamps. Thus, they will ceaselessly reflect the command of Jesus in Matthew 5:16. By doing so, they will shine with the glory of the gospel (as described by the apostle Paul in 2 Corinthians 4:6).

In addition, the illustrations of Revelation 11:4 originate in Zechariah 4, showing that the ministry of these two prophets was predicted to Israel long ago.[10] This reminds us that God is not only in control of the future, but also of everything that will occur during the seven-year tribulation period.

The Untouchables

Notice what is announced about these two in verse 5: "And if anyone wants to harm them, fire proceeds from their mouth and devours their enemies." From this we learn several important pieces of information. First, these prophets of God will have enemies. Unfortunately, this fits the pattern regarding prophets of God. Jesus himself spoke of a long history of persecution against God's emissaries sent into the world.[11]

We also learn from verse 5 that those enemies will try to harm these men of God. Again, this is no different than the way the world treated past prophets and even Jesus Christ, whom the world put to death on a cross.

Third, verse 5 portrays the power of these prophets. As a result of the authority given to them by God, their enemies will not be able to harm them. In addition, they will possess such power that everyone who seeks to harm them will be killed.

Imitating Moses and Elijah

The power described in verse 6 reflects the ministries of Moses and Elijah, two of the greatest and most prominent Old Testament prophets.[12] Just as with Moses and Elijah, the kind of power we see displayed in verse 6 is the power of God's judgment. In the ministries of both Moses and Elijah, fire devoured their enemies. For example, in Numbers 16:35, when men rebelled against Moses, God used fire against them in this way. And when Ahaziah, the king of Israel, sent a captain and fifty men after Elijah to take him captive, God once again used fire in judgment.[13]

Impressive Power

Though the two future prophets will also have this judgmental power against their enemies, there is a significant difference pictured in Revelation 11:5. The difference is that the fire which devoured the enemies of Moses and Elijah came directly from God, whereas the fire that will destroy the enemies of the two prophets of Revelation 11 proceeds from their mouths. The power of the two prophets of Revelation 11 will be greater than the power God granted to Moses and Elijah. As powerful as the impact of Moses and Elijah was upon God's chosen people, the impact and ministry of the two latter-day prophets described in Revelation 11 will be even greater! In verse 6, the word *power* is used twice to introduce God's judgment through the prophets to two different groups of people.

The identity of the first people group is revealed through their "power to shut heaven" so that it doesn't rain for three and a half years.[14] This is a reference to Elijah's Old Testament ministry to Israel.[15] Thus, the identity of the first group to whom God's judgment will be introduced is the Jews.

We can discern the identity of the second people group by understanding that the phrases *power to turn waters to blood* and *to strike the earth with plagues* serve as reminders of God's powerful judgments through Moses upon Egypt. Egypt, as the most powerful nation upon the earth in Moses' day, is representative of the Gentile nations.

Thus, the ministry of these prophets includes the power of God's judgments upon both Jews and Gentiles. But, their prophetic ministry will not simply consist of judgment; it will also result in a very fruitful response from Israel and the nations. We will see in the next chapter that thousands upon thousands of Jews in Israel will believe in Christ for eternal life as a direct result of the two prophets. And then, through those thousands of Jews, the two prophets will indirectly reach the nations of the earth.

Raining Down Plagues

Clearly, these two prophets of God will be given great power and authority by God. But, if we understand verse 14 of Revelation 11 properly, we will be led to an even greater awe of the power of these two prophets. Note the announcement of verse 14: "The second woe is past. Behold, the third woe is coming quickly."

This *second woe* includes God's use of these two prophets to judge the earth, as presented in verses 3–13. But, this *woe* also connects the ministry of these two witnesses to the first six trumpet judgments[16] of Revelation chapters 8 and 9.[17]

In response to the first four trumpet judgments and in anticipation of the remaining ones, an angel in heaven introduces three *woes* to follow by this proclamation in Revelation 8:13. Then, following the fifth trumpet judgment, the author of Revelation makes this comment in 9:12 regarding the first woe: "One woe is past. Behold, still two more woes are coming after these things." Finally, immediately following the presentation of the two prophets, the apostle John tells us in 11:14 that the third woe is coming quickly.

The ministry of these two prophets of God is connected with the *woes* of the trumpet judgments of Revelation. In fact, the first six trumpet judgments are proclamations of God's displays of power through these two witnesses. They are a presentation of the plagues with which the two will strike the earth (11:6).

The first six trumpet judgments upon the earth, located in chapters 8 and 9, show us that a third of the trees will be burned up; all green grass will be burned up; a third of the sea will become blood; a third of the living creatures in the sea will die; a third of the ships will be destroyed; a third of the waters will become bitter, leading to many men dying from the water; insects will attack men with a sting so horribly painful that men will seek to commit suicide but will not be able to accomplish it;[18] and a calamity will kill a third of mankind.

The descriptions of these plagues portray the awesome measure of power God will grant these prophets. The demonstration of this miraculous power will be signs that these two prophets are indeed sent from God, and the world had better pay close attention to the message they will bring!

The God of Judgment

Since the two witnesses of Revelation 11 are prophets of God and thus represent God to the world, how will God be portrayed through them? Indeed, he will be portrayed as a God of judgment upon a rebellious world and clearly not as a sweet, grandfatherly type. This portrayal will be used by Satan to deceive the world into thinking that the God of heaven is an enemy of the people on earth and to lead them to worship Satan's man as their god—a man who will begin to rule the world at the very end of the first three and a half years of Daniel's seventieth week.

We might be tempted to ask, at this point, how God can be responsible for the kinds of judgments we have seen in this chapter and be a God of love at the same time. The answer is that these judgments are actually a demonstration of his love for mankind, for he will use them to draw people to him. God knows that people find their ultimate fulfillment and blessing in a relationship with him, whereas they experience destructive and tragic lives apart from him. Thus, if severe judgments are needed to draw people into a relationship with God, then to bring those judgments upon the earth will be a demonstration of great love toward people.[19]

As you may have noticed, we have not yet answered the question with which we began this chapter, which is this: If Jesus takes all believers off the face of the earth just prior to the final seven years before he returns to the earth, who will reach people with the gospel during that stretch of time? We have begun the answer with the introduction of two amazing prophets of God. But, the answer continues in the next chapter as we are introduced to the 144,000.

CHAPTER 7
144,000

A barber who believed in Christ for eternal life was so excited about receiving eternal life that he decided he was going to try to share this good news with each of his customers. The next morning, when his first customer came in and crawled into his chair, he approached him with his sharpened straight razor and began his approach into the gospel with: "Are you ready to die?"

No doubt that barber had the rapt attention of his customer. In a similar vein, the two future prophets of God will have the fully absorbed attention of Jews in southern Israel—particularly 144,000 of them.

A Fruitful Ministry

In the last chapter, we were introduced to two prophets of God who will powerfully prophesy to Israel from Jerusalem for the first half (1,260 days) of the future tribulation period. Among the fruit of their ministry will be 144,000 who believe in Christ and follow him as disciples. We can learn more about these key figures of prophetic fulfillment by exploring Revelation 7:2–8.

We have seen that the plagues brought upon the earth by the two prophets throughout the first half of the tribulation period will harm the earth, the sea, and the trees in significant ways.[1] Yet, an angel in Revelation 7 commands the other four angels not to harm the earth, sea, and trees until God has set his seal on the 144,000.

144,000 Jewish Servants

Having the seal of God placed on their foreheads means they belong to God as his servants. Of course, they cannot become God's servants until they enter into a relationship with God by faith in Jesus Christ.

From the verses above, we also learn that the 144,000 will be servants of God. This means they will serve God as faithful followers of Christ.

In addition, we note that the 144,000 will all be *Jewish*. This is shown by the announcement in these verses that they come from all twelve tribes of Israel—12,000 from each tribe.

How do the clues we have already received indicate that these 144,000 will become disciples of Christ through the ministry of the two prophets of God—and not through other believers? Let us add up the clues to discover the answer.

Disciples of the Prophets

First, the two prophets will be the only two believers in Christ at the very beginning of the tribulation period.[2] Second, the two prophets will be proclaiming the gospel in Israel (specifically Jerusalem), where the 144,000 are likely from.[3] Third, the 144,000 will believe in Christ at the very beginning of the tribulation. Therefore, by adding up all the clues, we can see that they will become believers in, and followers of, Christ as a result of the ministry of the two prophets of God.

144,000 Virgins?

More information about the 144,000 is presented in Revelation 14:1–6, where we learn that the 144,000 "are the ones who were not defiled with women, for they are virgins." However, it is possible that this description is metaphorical in nature.[4] For examples, note the following verses where the word virgin is used: "Therefore thus says the Lord: '. . . The *virgin* of Israel has done a very horrible thing' " (Jeremiah

18:13). "The *virgin* of Israel has fallen . . . . She lies forsaken on her land . . ." (Amos 5:2). "For I have betrothed you to one husband, that I may present you as a chaste *virgin* to Christ" (2 Corinthians 11:2, emphasis added in these verses).

The word *virgin* in these sample verses is used in a spiritual sense. It portrays those in a relationship to the Lord who are expected to remain faithful to him. This is likely the sense in which the 144,000 are stated to be virgins.[5] That is, they will be wholeheartedly faithful followers of the Lord Jesus Christ once they believe in him for eternal life.

Another key phrase describing the 144,000 in Revelation 14 is the phrase *not defiled with women*. This can be explained by the concept of fornication presented, for example, in Jeremiah 3:6: "The Lord said also to me in the days of Josiah the king: 'Have you seen what backsliding Israel has done? She has gone up on every high mountain and under every green tree, and there *played the harlot*' " (emphasis added). In this verse, the nation of Israel is pictured as playing the harlot in their relationship with God, referring of course to Israel's spiritual unfaithfulness to God.

Notice, also, the description in Revelation 17 of the city of Rome in the future tribulation period, and those who do business with her: " 'The great harlot [Rome][6] . . . with whom the kings of the earth committed fornication, and the inhabitants of the earth were made drunk with the wine of her fornication' " (Revelation 17:1–2). This great city (see Revelation 17:18) is pictured as a harlot, due to her great abominations against God, and all who take on her standards in order to do business with her are described as committing fornication with her.

This metaphoric depiction within the same book as the contrasting description of the 144,000 provides the same sense in which the 144,000 Jews will *not* be defiled with women. They will remain faithful to the Lord by resisting the seductions of the great harlot, Rome, with whom others will spiritually fornicate (by participating with her ungodly orientation).

Not only can the examples given above help us to understand the first sentence of Revelation 14:4, but we can better understand it when we connect it with the second sentence: "These are the ones who were not defiled with women, for they are virgins. These are the ones who follow the Lamb wherever he goes." Clearly, then, the statement that the 144,000 are "not defiled with women, for they are virgins" means they are faithful disciples of the Lord Jesus and are thus free from spiritually adulterous relationships with the pagan world system.

Firstfruits to God

Aside from learning that these 144,000 are faithful disciples of Christ, we also learn they will be "redeemed from among men, being firstfruits to God and to the Lamb." Since the concept of firstfruits in this verse stems from the Old Testament presentation of the first of all the harvest, then these 144,000 will be the first of many other Jews from Israel who will believe in Jesus for eternal life.

There is also a sense in which the harvest of the 144,000 being the firstfruits refers to the redemption of men. This means that the 144,000 are the very first of those in the tribulation period who will receive eternal life.

Pictures of Faithfulness

In verse 5, we also learn this about the 144,000: "And in their mouth was found no deceit, for they are without fault before the throne of God." In other words, they will speak the truth; they will not compromise God's word, including the gospel of Jesus Christ.

In Zephaniah 3, God announces that through his judgments upon the nations in the tribulation period, He will provide a remnant of Jews in Israel who have believed in Christ for eternal life. Here is how he describes them in verses 12–13: "I will leave in your midst a meek and humble people, and they shall trust in the name of the Lord. The remnant of Israel shall do no unrighteousness and speak no lies, nor shall a deceitful tongue be found in their mouth . . ." This description is similar to the description of the 144,000 in Revelation 14. Both passages describe a remnant of Jews in Israel as being very faithful to the Lord, which includes their not speaking deceit.

144,000 Evangelists

This faithfulness in following Jesus and only speaking truth shows *why* they will be used by God in a very special way to reach others during the tribulation period. Revelation 14:6 indicates *how* they will be used as God's instruments during that period of time—to reach the entire world with the gospel of Christ.[7]

Another indicator that the 144,000 will reach worldwide with their evangelistic efforts is this presentation from verses 9–14 in Revelation 7 which immediately follows the description of the 144,000:

> After these things I looked, and behold, a great multitude which no one could number, of all nations, tribes, peoples, and tongues, standing before the throne and before the Lamb, clothed with white robes, with palm branches in their hands, and crying out with a loud voice, saying, "Salvation belongs to our God who sits on the throne, and to the Lamb!" . . . So he [one of the elders in heaven in John's vision] said to me, "These are the ones who come out of the great tribulation, and washed their robes and made them white in the blood of the Lamb."

The ones described in these verses are Gentiles from all over the world who will believe in Christ for eternal life during the tribulation period. According to Revelation 7, it seems that the 144,000 will spread out throughout the earth during the tribulation period, reaching a multitude of Gentiles with the gospel of Christ.

The 144,000 will be special instruments to fulfill Jesus' words in Matthew 24:14: "And this gospel of the kingdom will be preached in all the world as a witness to all the nations, and then the end will come." According to this verse, the end will come when the 144,000 finish their ministry of evangelism. That means Jesus will return to end this age and to begin a new one: the kingdom age.

Trumpet Judgments and the 144,000

Clearly, the 144,000 will receive eternal life in the first half of the day of the Lord, since the two prophets of God, under whose ministry the 144,000 believe the gospel, will only minister during that time period. In fact, it is likely the 144,000 receive eternal life near the *very beginning* of the day of the Lord, since the trumpet judgments will be poured out on the earth during the ministry of the two witnesses.[8]

What do the trumpet judgments have to do with the 144,000? We have seen that the plagues brought upon the earth by the two prophets throughout the first half of the tribulation period will harm the earth, the sea, and the trees in significant ways. Yet, the angel in this passage commands the other four angels not to harm the earth, sea, and trees *until* God has set his seal on the 144,000—which refers to the point at which they believe in Jesus Christ. This would indicate that they will receive eternal life at the very beginning of the day of the Lord.

Departing Jerusalem

Undoubtedly, after the 144,000 believe in Christ for eternal life, they are taught from God's Word[9] for some time prior to going out as evangelists. This will be necessary in order to be fully prepared to make disciples of Jesus—to not only lead people to believe in Jesus for eternal life, but to also baptize and to teach them,[10] in order that they be devoted and effective followers of Christ in a most difficult age. Following that period of time, they will go out from Judea (southern Israel where Jerusalem is located) *before* the midpoint of the tribulation period. Two prophecies reveal the timing of their departure to participate in their worldwide evangelistic efforts.

The first revolves around Jesus' warning in Matthew 24:15, where he warns all Jews who are still in Judea at the time the abomination of desolation occurs, (which is at the very middle of the tribulation period), to flee into the wilderness, where they will be protected and taken care of for the final three and a half years.[11] Therefore, all Jews in Judea who will heed Jesus' warning will go into the wilderness, where they will remain until Jesus returns to the earth. And since all Jews in Judea at the midpoint of the tribulation period who heed Jesus' warning will go into the wilderness, where they will remain—and since the 144,000 will not remain in the wilderness, but will go into all the world to evangelize— then clearly, the 144,000 will have already left Judea prior to the abomination of desolation.

In Revelation 12 the second reason reveals itself. As mentioned above, chapter 12 pictures Israel fleeing into the wilderness, where she will remain for the remaining three and a half years. But, verse 17 shows that the 144,000 are not among this wilderness group: "And the dragon was enraged with the woman, and he went to make war with the rest of her offspring, who keep the commandments of God and have the testimony of Jesus Christ."

The wilderness group of Jews who will have fled for their lives at the abomination of desolation is pictured by the woman. In frustration at not being able to destroy these Jews, the Dragon—Satan—turns his efforts toward making war with "the rest of her offspring, those who keep the commandments of God and have the testimony of Jesus Christ."

If the testimony of Jesus Christ is the presentation of the gospel, then the identity of this group known as "the rest of her [Israel's] offspring" is the 144,000. Of course, the word *went* shows that Satan had to go elsewhere in order to "make war with the rest of her offspring," showing that they were not in the wilderness with the Jews who had been in Judea at the midpoint of the tribulation period. Thus, the 144,000 will have already left Judea *before* the abomination of desolation hits.

144,000 Examples for Us

Therefore, as we have seen, the primary fruit of the two witnesses who prophesy in Jerusalem during the first three and a half years of the tribulation period will consist of 144,000 Jews in Israel who will believe in Christ for eternal life and become his disciples. We have also seen that they will go out to the ends of the earth to evangelize the world.

As we think about the 144,000—and observe verses about them in the box below—think about how their examples might encourage us to become even more serious about following Christ from their example. Certainly, we should be encouraged by their example of great faithfulness of "following the Lamb wherever he goes"—that is, of complete obedience no matter what the cost might be. And, we should be encouraged to imitate their boldness in holding to the truth by proclaiming Christ to many others. In addition, they encourage us to remain faithful to Christ through our most difficult times, as they will continue in great faithfulness during the most difficult time in the history of the world.[12]

Below is a basic timeline regarding the 144,000 Jewish disciples of Jesus.

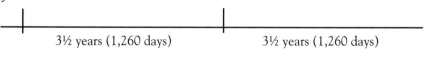

3½ years (1,260 days)	3½ years (1,260 days)
The conversion & training of the 144,000 Jews	The 144,000 Jews preach to the nations

While the 144,000 are being prepared to reach the world with the gospel, a man will arise in the Middle East to become a powerful king, affecting the entire world and bringing great persecution to believing Israel. In the next chapter, we will learn much more about him and his incredible rise to power.

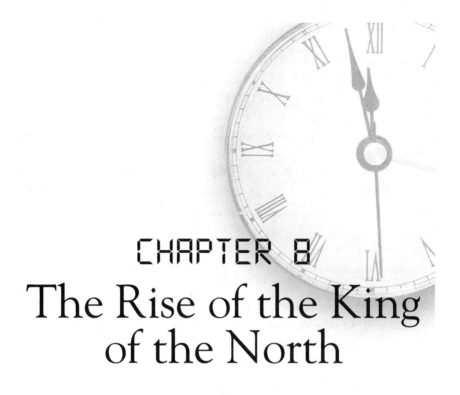

CHAPTER 8
The Rise of the King of the North

Grover Cleveland experienced a meteoric rise to power. He went from being a moderately successful Buffalo lawyer in 1881 to being elected president of the United States in three years! One of Cleveland's biographers, Horace Samuel Merrill, explained his political rise in this way: "He was lucky—almost unbelievably lucky!"[1]

It may have seemed that he was "unbelievably lucky," but the Bible declares that luck has nothing to do with anything—including a rise from seeming obscurity to great power. Instead, the only real explanation for anything of that sort is that God provided for it to happen.[2]

But, Grover Cleveland's amazing rise from obscurity to power will seem as nothing compared to the rise of a man from the seeming obscurity of a Middle Eastern country. Certainly, luck will have nothing to do with that rise. Satan will be behind it, but the same prophet of God who declared that God "removes kings and raises up kings,"[3] and who prophesies of this future king, indicates that his rise will be part of God's plan for the world.

What Have We Seen So Far?

In chapter 1 we saw that when the world believes it has achieved peace and security, sudden destruction will hit, from which there will be no escape.[4] However, immediately prior to this unexpected devastation, Jesus will remove all believers from the earth, an event referred to as the rapture of the church.

We have also seen that the rapture will occur on the same day as the sudden destruction, and at the same time a seven-year treaty between ten nations and Israel goes into effect. This treaty will begin the day of the Lord, a time when God will pour out his judgments upon a rebellious world.

In addition, we saw that on the very first day of this future tribulation period, two prophets will begin their three-and-a-half-year prophetic ministry to Israel from the city of Jerusalem. The fruit of their ministry will include 144,000 Jews who believe in Christ for eternal life and who will take the gospel worldwide to reach a multitude of Gentiles.

Out of the Abyss

In chapter 6, where we discussed the two prophets of God, we were briefly introduced to the beast, the future ruler of the world. Revelation 11:7 announced that at the end of the prophets' 1,260 day ministry, the beast will kill them—something no one could do before.[5] Moreover, this verse announced that the beast will ascend out of the bottomless pit to commit this heinous act.

The bottomless pit is a translation of a Greek word that is translated as *the abyss* in Romans 10:7, where we read: " 'Who will descend into the abyss?' (that is, to bring Christ up from the dead)." Here it is revealed that "the abyss" refers to the place of the dead. Before the ascension of Christ into heaven, all who died went to the abyss, or hades—though believers were separated from unbelievers by a large gulf.[6] After the ascension of Christ, only unbelievers went into the abyss following death. Therefore, when we read that he ascends out of the abyss, we understand that the beast will come up from the place of the dead to kill the two prophets. This means he will actually have died sometime prior to his assassination of God's prophets in Jerusalem.

As mentioned earlier, the beast will kill the two prophets exactly three and a half years to the day, or 1,260 days, into the tribulation period—at its exact midpoint. Revelation shows that the first half of Daniel's seventieth week consists of the 1,260 days of the prophets' ministry, and the second half consists of the forty-two-months' (1,260 days of a Jewish calendar) rule of the beast following the death of the two prophets. This indicates that the two prophets will most likely be killed following their final day of ministry right at sundown, which, from a Jewish standpoint, marks the end of one day and the beginning of another.

An Alter Ego

But, before this man becomes the beast, he is known as "the king of the North," as revealed in Daniel chapter 11. Six hundred years before the time of Christ, Daniel received an amazing vision of the future, which included the revelation of the death of Alexander the Great and the breakup of his kingdom into four distinct kingdoms.[7] One of these four kingdoms is referred to as the Seleucid kingdom, which covered an area now known as Lebanon, Syria, Iraq, and part of Iran. As this prophetic revelation traces the succession of Seleucid rulers, each is known as the king of the North.

Daniel's vision takes us through a continuous set of rulers, until the end of the rule of Antiochus IV (who died in 164 BC). Then, the vision leaps ahead more than two thousand years to a king ruling "at the time of the end" (verse 40). The description of this future king begins in verse 36: " 'Then the king shall do according to his own will: he shall exalt and magnify himself above every god, shall speak blasphemies against the God of gods, and shall prosper till the wrath has been accomplished; for what has been determined shall be done.' "

Another Identity

The description of this king is eerily similar to a description found in 2 Thessalonians 2. If we look closely, we will that the two passages above describe the same individual. Both portray one who exalts *himself* above every God, including the God of gods.

Verse 36 of Daniel 11 announces that the king will rule "till the wrath has been accomplished"—that is, until God is finished pouring out his wrath upon the earth during the day of the Lord. As 2 Thessalonians reveals, the king's reign will end with his destruction at the return of Christ,[8] which will put an end to the day of the Lord, the tribulation period.[9]

The War Is On

The description of the king of the North continues in Daniel 11. Then, in verse 40, we are informed of a new development: "At the time of the end the king of the South [Egypt] shall attack him; and the king of the North shall come against him like a whirlwind, with chariots, horsemen, and with many ships; and he shall enter the countries, overwhelm them, and pass through." This king will be attacked by Egypt, but he will retaliate with a powerful military response. And while on his way toward Egypt, he will conquer other Middle Eastern countries.

It is interesting to note that his conquest of other countries will be in *response* to an attack upon him; he is not presented as one who will initiate. This may indicate that his triumph over other countries is also achieved as a result of a response to their attacks against him. Possibly, the Middle Eastern Muslim countries will view him as a threat. Apparently, Egypt will—which is why it makes a preemptive strike upon the region he rules. It seems likely that while he retaliates due to the Egyptian attack, other countries will see that as an opportunity to make offensive gestures toward him as well. Therefore, it could be that this king will not be looking to conquer the area around him, but once attacked by other countries, he will know that he needs to aggressively retaliate—and conquer—in order to survive in his "neighborhood."

The Assyrian

To understand which countries the king of the North will conquer on his way toward Egypt, we need to discover his origin. Two passages will help us to begin to see this.

In a prediction that has yet to be fulfilled, the Lord announces in Isaiah 14:25–26 that he will "break the Assyrian" in the land of Israel. In addition, in Micah 5:5–6, the prophet predicts that Jews will rise up at the return of Christ against the Assyrian and his forces while he is in Israel. Since neither of these two passages has been fulfilled, we know they *will* be fulfilled in the future. As we look at them more closely, we will gain valuable clues that will show us how these apply to the king of the North.

Each of the above passages mentions a specific land: "I will break the Assyrian in my *land* and when the Assyrian comes into our *land*." Clearly, this is a reference to the land of Israel. After all, in the context, God, who is the speaker, refers to *his* land. The only land mentioned in Scripture as being uniquely his is the land of Israel—the land he prom-

68

ised to the patriarchs (Abraham, Isaac, Jacob, and their descendents) and the land in which the Lord will dwell in the future via the Messiah's reign (when he brings his kingdom to the earth).[10]

If we look again at those two passages above, we will see they both mention the Assyrian. The singular description indicates that these passages focus on a single Assyrian leader or ruler.

The verses in Micah 5 predict that Jesus will deliver Israel from the Assyrian. Though the reference does not specifically mention Jesus, the context[11] shows Jesus to be the one who will deliver Israel from the Assyrian, and this deliverance must necessarily occur at his return to the earth.[12]

These passages describe a future ruler who will enter the land of Israel. In Daniel 11:44–45, this man is identified as the king of the North who will enter Israel from Egypt, planting "the tents of his palace" (verse 45) at a place that has been identified as located "in the upper Kidron Valley to the northeast of the Temple Mount" in Jerusalem.[13] His removal (in these passages)—by the Lord Jesus Christ at his return—identifies him with the beast in Revelation 19:11–20 and with the Man of Sin in 2 Thessalonians 2:8. Thus, the king of the North, the beast, and the Man of Sin, are all descriptives of the same person, who is an Assyrian.

The King's Origin

So, from where does this Assyrian king of the North arise? We know that this king will arise from an area within the boundaries of the old Roman Empire.[14]

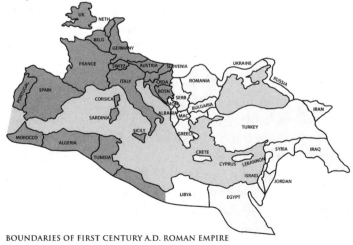

BOUNDARIES OF FIRST CENTURY A.D. ROMAN EMPIRE

In addition, as an Assyrian, of course, he will come from the area that belonged to the Assyrian Empire. Finally, as king of the North, he will belong to the territory within the boundaries of the Seleucid kingdom, which includes modern-day Lebanon, Syria, Iraq, and a small part of Iran. All of this means he will arise from the area of intersection of those three kingdoms, represented on the map below.

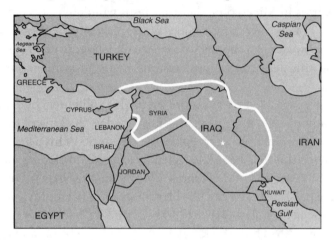

More specifically, since the capital of Assyria (Nineveh) resides in modern-day Iraq, it is very likely he will arise from that country. In fact, Iraq is also the country with the largest population of Assyrians in the world[15] and, interestingly, there has been a movement by Assyrians for recognized statehood in northwest Iraq, which could result in the beginning of an elevation of an Assyrian ruler. In addition, Daniel 11:41 states that Jordan,[16] which borders Iraq to the west, will fall to the king of the North, providing further evidence that the king's country of origin will be Iraq.

Conquest

If this king arises from Iraq, then we have an idea of what areas he will conquer[17] on his way to Egypt. He will conquer countries in the Middle East, which will most likely include Syria and Saudi Arabia.

In Daniel 8, this same king is pictured as a "little horn" that will grow "exceedingly great toward the south, toward the east, and toward the Glorious Land" (verse 9). This indicates that he will conquer countries that lie to the south—Saudi Arabia, and to the east—Iran. He will also enter into Israel (the Glorious Land).

When Will He Rise to Power?

So, when will this king begin his rise to power? Daniel chapter 8 tells us.

First, in verse 11 there is an announcement that he will take away the daily sacrifices. This will occur at the very midpoint of the tribulation period—when the seven-year treaty with Israel is broken. At that point he will enter the rebuilt temple and abominate it.[18]

Then, verses 13–14 show us *exactly* when he will begin his rise to power:

> Then I [Daniel] heard a holy one [an angel] speaking; and another holy one [angel] said to that certain one who was speaking, "How long will the vision be, concerning the daily sacrifices and the transgression of desolation, the giving of both the sanctuary and the host [Jews] to be trampled underfoot?" And he said to me, "For two thousand three hundred days; then the sanctuary shall be cleansed."[19]

The entire period of time that relates to the vision of this man and his power—from his rise in power till the cleansing of the sanctuary (the holy of holies in the temple where the Man of Sin will enter to be worshipped as god)[20] is presented as 2,300 days. However, the period of days from the removal of the sacrifices until the return of Christ is actually

1,260 days. This means the man will begin his rise in power 1,040 days (2,300 – 1,260) before he abominates the temple (when he enters it to be worshipped as God).

Another way of understanding this period of 2,300 days is to view it this way: The total number of days for the entire seven-year tribulation period[21] will be 2,520. If we subtract 2,300 days from 2,520 days, we arrive at the number of days following the rapture of the church and the start of the tribulation period, at which point he begins his dramatic rise toward worldwide authority—220 days following the rapture. Daniel 8 shows that he will be in a position of minor rule (as a little horn) by this period of time, so it is possible that the Christian who is paying very close attention to what is occurring in Iraq could *possibly* identify him prior to the rapture of the church. It is also likely that we will not know his identity before being taken into the air.

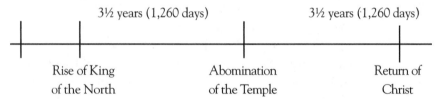

3½ years (1,260 days)		3½ years (1,260 days)
Rise of King of the North	Abomination of the Temple	Return of Christ

As we have seen, the king of the North is an Assyrian whose rise to power will begin two hundred twenty days following the commencement of the treaty with Israel. He will conquer the Middle East with a powerful military force while responding to an attack by Egypt. But, where will that lead, and how will he able to make such an amazing rise out of obscurity? Our answers will come in the next chapter.

CHAPTER 9
Conquest of the Middle East

*T*he *Exorcist*, one of the most profitable horror films of all time, opens with a powerfully symbolic archaeological site near Nineveh in Iraq. In his book, *Knowing Christ*, Craig Glickman describes the opening scene in this way:

> It is a remarkable site. The huge setting sun seems to rest like a gigantic fireball on the desert. A statue of an idol is on one side; the archaeological priest is on the other, and they face each other in conflict. In the foreground, two vicious dogs tear at each other's throats. And, quite, ingeniously, this symbolism is from the 'Greater Trump' card of the Tarot deck used by fortunetellers. It is said to symbolize the conditions of hell. The scene is ominous, dreadful, heavy, and oppressive with the weight of evil it signifies.[1]

The movie goes on to portray Satan's power in an impressive fashion. A twelve-year-old girl's life is taken over by one of Satan's emissaries—a demon. Religious leaders in the form of priests are unable to overcome this power and, instead, are shown to be humiliatingly weak in the presence of this demon. Finally, at the height of an exorcism performed on the girl, one priest dies of a heart attack, while another shouts at the demon to enter him. The demon responds to the invitation, at which point the priest throws himself through the bedroom window to his death in an attempt to keep the evil spirit from taking the girl's life. The film ends with Reagan, the formerly possessed girl, and her mother leaving that town to begin a new life.

As a result of the release of this movie in 1973, many people slept for a time with their lights on, fearing the power of Satan and his demons. But, what those individuals apparently did not realize is that it is God—not Satan or his underlings—who is sovereign. It is important to remember that God the Creator is infinitely more powerful than Satan, his creation—for Satan can only exhibit what power God allows him to have.

Making a Deal with the Devil

But, God has allowed Satan to make a deal. It is an arrangement Satan makes with a *former* king in order to become a *future* king—over the entire world!—*if* the king will worship him. As a result of this former king's acceptance of the transaction, Satan will grant him great power to rule and to make war. Interestingly, this future king, through whom Satan will show his power, will begin his rise from Iraq, the same country from which *The Exorcist* begins its presentation of the power of Satan.

In the last chapter we saw that, 220 days following the rapture of the church, this same king, who is Assyrian by heritage, will arise to power from the Middle East. We discussed the evidence that his origin will be the country of Iraq, which contains the ancient capital city of Assyria (Nineveh). This is the same Assyrian king whom Old Testament prophecies tell us will be conquered in the land of Israel by the Lord Jesus Christ when he returns to the earth. But, before that fateful event occurs, this king of the North will be a conquering king.

The King's Authority

We encountered the king of the North in Daniel 11, where we learned he will make an amazing rise out of obscurity. Let us return to chapter 11 to learn more about the background of this king, including how he makes such an astounding advance in power. We pick up the story about this king in verse 36: " 'Then the king shall do according to his own will: he shall exalt and magnify himself above every god, shall speak blasphemies against the God of gods, and shall prosper till the wrath has been accomplished; for what has been determined shall be done.' "

Much is revealed about this king in this verse. First, we see that he will do whatever he wants; there is no one who will stop him from getting anything he desires, including great power and authority.

We also learn that this king's authority will even go so far as to set himself above all gods, including the one true God, whom he verbally attacks. What is implied in this connection is that he will be worshipped as god.

This description is similar to the information regarding the same individual provided in 2 Thessalonians 2:4, where we find that he "opposes and exalts himself above all that is called God or that is worshiped, so that he sits as God in the temple of God, showing himself that he is God." Here we have the added detail that he will actually enter into the temple of God to be worshiped as God.

The King's Wrath

In returning to Daniel 11:36, we see that this king "shall prosper till the wrath has been accomplished." The "wrath" refers to the *indignation* this king will pour out on Israel during the last half of the tribulation period when Jewish followers of Christ will be fleeing from the king's armies.[3]

Though this wrath represents the king's vile persecution upon disciples of Jesus, it will be intended by God for his good purpose—for, God is in full control of what occurs. He will allow it to continue until its accomplishment of what he has determined—for Israel and for the preparation of his coming kingdom.[4]

God will use the wrath of the king to awaken the hearts of Israelites to the gospel, as well as to grow them spiritually after they have believed in Christ. In the same way that he uses trials and suffering for all believers, he will use the king's wrath for Jews who believe in Jesus Christ in order "to refine them, purify them, and make them white, until the time of the end" (Daniel 11:35). As Romans 8 teaches, God uses persecution and suffering in the lives of his children that they might "be conformed to the image of his Son" (Romans 8:29) so that, as a result of suffering with Christ, they may gloriously rule with him in his kingdom.

After all, this is the way God works. He seeks to not only bring people to believe in Christ for kingdom entrance, but also prepare them *after* believing for an even greater experience (reward) in his kingdom. But, suffering is required for conformity to Christ to be accomplished. Thus, God will allow the king to bring his wrath against Jewish followers of Christ until the wrath has been accomplished.

The King's Prosperity

So, until he is vanquished by Christ at his return, this king shall prosper. He "shall do according to his own will," experiencing great success in advancing his power and purposes in accomplishing what he desires. Though we mentioned in the last chapter that it seems he will be a responder—conquering in response to attack by others—when he does respond, he is able to accomplish whatever he chooses to accomplish. He will appear to be unstoppable![5]

This king will ascend to great power, placing himself above all gods—including the God of gods. But, unbeknown to him, he will be used ironically as a tool of God, for the benefit of Israelites, as he pours out his persecuting wrath upon them.

The King's God

In verses 37–39, we learn where he gets his power to make such an incredible rise from apparent obscurity. However, first, we learn that he will have nothing to do with the God of his ancestors, and he will not "regard . . . the desire of women."

The *desire of women* may be a reference to "the natural desire of Jewish women to become the mother of the promised Messiah, the seed of the woman promised in Genesis 3:15."[6] If so, this expression would be a reference to the Lord Jesus Christ, which would fit the description before and after the expression. And since Assyrians consider themselves Christian,[7] this meaning of the phrase makes even more sense: The Assyrian king will not regard the God of his ancestors (who are Christian), nor Jesus (who is God to his ancestors), nor any god. However, verse 38 announces that the king will have a god, but not one his ancestors have known as God.

We have encountered here what appears to be a contradiction.[8] On the one hand, this king will seemingly "elevate himself above all gods"; on the other hand, he will *have* a god—just not one his ancestors ever recognized as their God. So, how can he elevate himself above all gods, yet have a god at the same time? The answer is that he will worship a god who has not been *recognized* as a god. But, the god he worships will elevate him above every recognized god.

So, the question that remains is: What is the identity of this god? When we realize this king of the North will become the beast of Revelation,[9] we can begin to answer this question by first going to Revelation 13:4: "So they [the unbelieving world] worshiped the dragon who gave authority to the beast; and they worshiped the beast."

The Dragon will give authority to the beast to be worshiped as god by the world. If we discover the Dragon's identity, we will be able to solve the mystery of this king's god.

The identity of the Dragon is revealed in Revelation 12:9 and 20:2 as "that serpent of old, who is the Devil and Satan." This means that the king will worship Satan!

Honoring His God

This leads us back to verses 38–39 of Daniel 11, where we learn that this king will "honor a god of fortresses." The Hebrew word translated as *fortresses* in these verses is used earlier in Daniel chapter 11 (verse 31) to refer to the Jewish temple. This indicates that the fortresses of the god worshipped by the king of the North are temples erected to his god.[10]

According to verse 38, he will worship his god with "gold, silver, precious stones, and pleasant things." There is a good reason why he will worship his god in that way. The reason is displayed in a description of Satan found in God's address to Lucifer:

> "Thus says the Lord God: 'You were the seal of
> perfection, full of wisdom and perfect in beauty . . .
> every precious stone was your covering: The sardius,
> topaz, and diamond, beryl, onyx, and jasper, sapphire,
> turquoise, and emerald with gold. . . . You were the
> anointed cherub . . . . You were perfect in your ways

> from the day you were created, till iniquity was found in you. . . . Your heart was lifted up because of your beauty; you corrupted your wisdom for the sake of your splendor.' " (Ezekiel 28:12–15, 17)

From this passage, we learn that Lucifer was created in perfection and beauty. In addition, he was associated with beautiful, precious stones and pleasant things. Because he was created in radiant perfection and associated with the beauty of precious stones and pleasant things, it seems that he accepts those things as worship in tribute to his splendor.

Moreover, the king will "act against the strongest fortresses with a foreign god" (verse 39). This means he will advance and promote worship of his god by changing temples currently existing as places of worship of other gods to temples of worship to *his* god.

Mystery Solved

He will use these fortresses to advance his rule over many by causing people everywhere to worship Lucifer at these temples. The king will establish these places of worship everywhere (dividing the land with them) in order to make worship of Lucifer more accessible to more people, thus advancing not only the worship of Satan but also worship of the king (verse 39).

The king's worship of Satan—and his aggressive promotion of Lucifer worship—solve the mystery of this man's meteoric rise from apparent obscurity to king of the world in less than three years.[11] Satan will have made an offer this man could not refuse—an offer that was first made to the Lord Jesus Christ in Luke 4:5–8.

Satan's Authority to Grant Rule over the World

If Jesus would worship him, Satan would grant him rule of the entire world. The question that results from this, however, is: Did Satan possess the authority to make this offer? The answer is yes.

The authority to rule the world had been inadvertently handed over to Satan by Adam and Eve, who, upon being created, were given the authority by God to rule the earth.[12] The first man and woman then handed over to Satan the authority to rule when they gave in to the Devil's temptation in Genesis 3. As a result, Satan became "the ruler of this world."[13]

This means that before Christ won back the world through his death and resurrection, Satan could make the offer as a legitimate one. This is why when Satan tempted him, Jesus did not dispute his claim to be able to grant the authority to rule the world. After Jesus' death and resurrection, the offer could be made, but because it would no longer be legitimate, there would be no guarantee it would last. It could only last if Satan could do battle with Christ and win—which is what he will attempt to do (through the armies of the world) at Christ's return.

Therefore, the king's reception of Satan's offer, followed by his rigorous promotion of Lucifer worship, shows how he will make such a meteoric rise in power. His rapid ascension will occur due to Satan's powerful backing. In the next chapter, we will see the path the king will take to go from Middle Eastern ruler to king of the world.

CHAPTER 10
Entering the Glorious Land

N apoleon Bonaparte was one of the great military geniuses of all time. At the peak of his career, while he was emperor of France, he brought practically all of Europe to its knees. But, he did, at that time, make a disastrous military decision. He decided to invade Russia.

In the city of Wilna—on the border of Russia—there is a simple granite shaft. On the western side of that shaft (the direction from which Napoleon invaded Russia), there is an inscription that reads: "Napoleon Bonaparte passed this way in 1812 with 410,000 men." On the eastern face of the shaft, from which direction Napoleon retreated, there is this inscription: "Napoleon Bonaparte passed this way in 1812 with 9,000 men."

Great military leader though he was, he led hundreds of thousands of men to disaster and defeat. Invading the wrong land cost this leader significantly. That will be the grand mistake for the king of the North as well. He will invade the wrong land—Israel—and it will cost him significantly.

In our last two chapters, we learned about an Assyrian king who will arise rapidly in the Middle East from apparent obscurity to become king of the world. We discovered that his rapid ascent will occur due to Satan's powerful backing, as a result of a pact he will make with the Devil. This agreement will involve worshipping Satan and promoting Lucifer worship throughout all of the area he conquers.[1]

An Attack from the South

In this chapter, we return to Daniel 11 to complete that passage's description of the rise of this king of the North. According to verse 40, this king will defend himself from an attack launched by the leader of Egypt. However, as he responds, he appears to be very much on the offensive.

Unlike the king of the North's response toward Egypt, there is no mention of an invading army from Egypt. This indicates there will most likely not be a ground invasion in the attack upon the king. Based on the clues given, it appears that the leader of Egypt will launch a missile upon the king of the North.

In addition, we note that the king of the North will respond to this attack by taking his army down to Egypt. The Egyptian attack will probably not be a bombing run, since the king's likely response would be to shoot down those planes. Since we have ruled out ground forces from Egypt and an attack by planes, it seems Egypt's aggression against the king will consist of a missile launch from Egypt.

It is likely that the leader of Egypt will attack the king of the North perhaps believing that the growing power of the king of the North looms as a threat to the Middle East. If so, then Egypt may believe that the king must be dealt with by an offensive strike against him.

The King's Conquests

From the description in verses 40–43, the military strength of the king of the North will be immensely powerful, for his military invasion is presented "as a whirlwind" and as "overwhelming countries." These descriptions give the impression of an amazing military machine, which will achieve tremendous results. As an outcome of his campaign, countries will quickly and easily fall to him; they will be *overwhelmed*!

However, the country of Jordan (Edom, Moab, and the prominent people of Ammon) "shall escape from his hand." This means that the king will not overwhelm Jordan by sending his mighty army through it. The likely explanation for this is that Jordan will fear being conquered by this threatening king, so the small country will make a treaty to ally itself to him. It may also be possible that this not only means that the king will *not* defeat this tiny nation militarily, but it could indicate that the king's armies will not pass through that land. If so, then, for the king of the North to enter Israel but not to pass through Jordan on the way toward his invasion of Egypt, he would need to pass through (and *overwhelm*) Syria in order to get to Israel.

Verse 43 announces that "the Libyans and Ethiopians shall follow at his heels." Though Libya refers to the same country of Libya in existence today, Ethiopia actually describes the country of Sudan, north of present-day Ethiopia.

Just as Jordan will decide to join forces with the king of the North before being conquered, the same will be true of Libya and Sudan. Seeing the king overwhelm the Middle East and then Egypt, Libya and Sudan will decide it will be better to join him than to be destroyed by him.

We observed earlier that, according to Daniel 8, this king is pictured as a little horn that "grows exceedingly great toward the south, toward the east, and toward the Glorious Land" (verse 9). Since, as we have seen, he will originate from Iraq, the assertion of verse 8 implies the king will conquer countries that include Saudi Arabia (to the south) and Iran (to the east).

Israel's Treaty with Death

It appears, however, that the king of the North will *not* conquer Israel at this point, since the description in Daniel 11:41 reveals he will "enter" Israel rather than overwhelm or overthrow it, as he will with other Middle Eastern countries.

A passage that seems to explain this is Isaiah 28:14–15, which reveals a future scenario[2] describing a treaty (covenant) the leaders of Israel will make with another party. They will make this agreement in order to seek protection from the overflowing scourge.

The Hebrew[3] word for *overflowing* in the verses above is the same word that is translated as *overwhelm* in this statement in Daniel 11:40:

" 'At the time of the end the king of the South shall attack him; and the king of the North shall come against him like a whirlwind, with chariots, horsemen, and with many ships; and he shall enter the countries, *overwhelm* them, and pass through.' " This same Hebrew word seems to connect Isaiah 28:15 and Daniel 11:40 to the same person who will invade Israel—the king of the North.

Isaiah 28 prophesies that leaders of Israel will attempt to seek protection from the military force of the king of the North, who will pass through their land on the way to conquer Egypt. Apparently, these leaders will realize (as a result of a conflict breaking out between the king of the North and Egypt) that the king will feel the need to pass through Israel to counter-attack Egypt. Therefore, they will sign a protective treaty with the king.

This treaty will *not* be the same one as the treaty Israel will sign with ten nations initiating the day of the Lord. Instead, the treaty mentioned in Isaiah 28 will be used by the leaders of Israel to take refuge in lies and falsehood. Though the lies and falsehood could refer to lying to the king of the North when making this treaty with him, it is not likely they would risk lying to such a powerful force; thus, this will more likely be a secret treaty that will be *hidden* with lies. Due to the overwhelming power of the king of the North's military force, leaders of Israel will believe there is no recourse for the nation. They will try to protect themselves with this treaty.

A Mistake Realized

Isaiah 28:15 uses typical Hebrew synonymous parallelism to emphasize the extremely troubling nature of this treaty. After the leaders of Israel have cut this covenant with the king of the North, they will soon realize their mistake. They will see this is a treaty of death; it will be an "agreement with Sheol," the place of the dead.[4] These leaders will recognize too late that they cannot trust this man of Satan. This treaty that was meant to provide protection will end up costing Jewish leaders their lives and the lives of many others in the land of Israel.

Zechariah 13:8 reveals that two-thirds of all the Jews living in the land of Israel will lose their lives. Since the context of that prediction is within the last half of the tribulation period, then, in some way, the king of the North—who will become the beast by that point—will be responsible for their deaths. This means that the secret treaty of Isaiah 28 will become a treaty of death many times over!

Based on the same Hebrew word that connects the secret treaty to the king's conquest of many countries on his way to conquer Egypt, it seems this treaty is the agreement that allows the king to move his military machine through Israel in order to invade Egypt by ground forces. As we have seen, the result of the king's campaign into Egypt is that he will overwhelm and overthrow Egypt and take control over all its wealth.

In the last chapter, we learned that the king will honor his god, Lucifer, "with gold and silver, with precious stones and pleasant things" (Daniel 11:38), using those beautiful and extravagant items to worship him. In addition, the king will use these costly stones to promote Lucifer worship by the establishment of many temples to his god. All of this relates to the description of the king in the first half of Daniel 11:43: "He shall have power over the treasures of gold and silver, and over all the precious things of Egypt." His invasion of Egypt will provide him with great treasure in order to continue his worship of Satan and to advance Lucifer worship among the Egyptians, Libyans, and Ethiopians (northern Africa).

Troubling News

However, the king will not stay in Egypt long. In verses 44–45 of Daniel 11, we discover that troubling news will drive him to the northeast with great fury, for there we read:

> "But news from the east and the north shall trouble him; therefore he shall go out with great fury to destroy and annihilate many. And he shall plant the tents of his palace between the seas and the glorious holy mountain; yet he shall come to his end, and no one will help him."

Since the king is in Egypt when he receives troubling news from the east and the north, he will then return to Israel, the origin of that disturbing news. However, what will be going on in Israel at the time the king invades Egypt that might be so disturbing to him? And why might it disturb him?

The two prophets of God will be prophesying in Jerusalem at that time, and they will be reaching other Jews with the gospel. In addition, they will be commissioning the 144,000 to take the gospel to all the nations of the earth.

This will greatly trouble the king whose god is Satan. Satan seeks to continue his rule over this world, but he knows Jesus plans to return to rule this world as *his* kingdom upon the salvation of many Jews in Israel.[5] Moreover, the evangelization of the world will be troubling to the king, for it will cost him and his god many inhabitants and servants for their kingdom.

Invading Israel

As a result of this disturbing news, the king "shall go out with great fury to destroy and annihilate many." The word *many* in this verse is used elsewhere in Daniel to refer to the Jews in Israel. It is found most notably in Daniel 9:27, describing the seven-year treaty with Israel that initiates the day of the Lord. Based on the use of *many* in Daniel, it seems that when the king of the North hears the troubling news, he will go out to destroy and annihilate many Jews in Israel. Since the events of verses 44–45 take place near the end of the first half of the tribulation period, the many Jews whom the king attempts to destroy and annihilate are those warned by Jesus in Matthew 24:15 to flee for their lives. (Their flight will take place at the exact middle of the tribulation period.) This also fits the description of an army sent out by the beast in Revelation 12 to seek to eliminate those Jews fleeing Judea.

This helps us understand the Lord's proclamation in Zechariah 13:8 that two-thirds of all the Jews living in the land of Israel will be killed. Since that announcement appears in the context of the last half of the day of the Lord, it coincides with the king going out to annihilate many Jews in Israel.[6]

When the king arrives in Jerusalem, he will "plant the tents of his palace between the seas" (verse 45). *Between the seas* would mean between the Mediterranean Sea and the Dead Sea, which is where Jerusalem is located.

Another clue as to where he will plant the tents of his palace is found in the phrase *and the glorious holy mountain*. However, the word *and* is actually the Hebrew word meaning *at*, or *facing*. His palatial tents will actually face the glorious holy mountain, which is a reference to the Temple Mount.[7] This seems to indicate that he will set up camp in the Kidron Valley.[8]

The Timing of the Invasion

The timing of this seems to be the midpoint of the day of the Lord, or three and a half years into the tribulation period. At the point the king invades Jerusalem, the seven-year treaty the ten countries made with Israel will be broken.[9]

But, Daniel 11 does not go into that detail. Instead, we will have to look elsewhere for that chronology and other events related to his invasion of Jerusalem. However, chapter 11 ends by informing us that sometime after he takes his powerful army into Jerusalem, "he shall come to his end, and no one will help him." Though we are not given the time frame of his demise in this passage, we are told the king will come to his end without help from anyone, which coincides with his destruction at the return of Christ.[10]

As we mentioned at the beginning of this chapter, the king's climactic mistake will be his invasion of the wrong land—Israel. Verse 45 of Daniel 11 alludes to the tragic result of his consequential choice.

Daniel's vision ends with comfort for his readers. However, the king's end would not come for another three and a half years following his encampment in Jerusalem.

The king's encampment in Jerusalem brings us to the middle of the tribulation period—and to the point at which the king of the North becomes the beast. We will explore his "promotion" to become the beast in the next chapter.

The first half of the day of the Lord (1st 3½ years)	The king conquers

1   2   3 4

1 = Seven-year treaty begins
2 = Rise of king of the North
3 = Egypt conquered
4 = The king in Jerusalem

CHAPTER 11
The Beast from the Abyss

In 1883, the kind of wooden Indian that was seen in front of cigar stores was placed on the ballot for Justice of the Peace in Allentown, New Jersey. The candidate was registered under the fictitious name of Abner Robbins. When the ballots were counted, Abner won over incumbent Sam Davis by seven votes!

A similar thing happened in 1938. The name Boston Curtis appeared on the ballot for Republican Committeeman from Wilton, Washington, but Boston Curtis was a mule! The town's mayor sponsored the animal to demonstrate that people know very little about the candidates. He proved his point. The mule won!

But, neither of these anecdotes compares to the ultimate foolishness when men in the future will cast their ballots for the false candidate of all false candidates. This future candidate will be "elected" to be king over all the earth and the god of all of the world's unbelieving inhabitants.

A Look Back

So far in our exploration of the day of the Lord, we have seen that a brief period is coming in which the world will believe it has entered into "peace and security," but then sudden destruction will hit! At the same time, three other key events will converge: the rapture of the church will suddenly occur with Jesus coming in the air together with deceased believers in order to take believers with him; a seven-year treaty will begin between ten nations and Israel; and the three-and-a-half-year ministry of two powerful prophets of God to Israel will commence.

The fruit of the ministry of the prophets of God will include the conversion of 144,000 Jews who, after being taught by the prophets, will fan out to take the gospel to the ends of the earth. As a result of their evangelistic efforts, many Gentiles will believe in Christ during the latter three and a half years before Christ returns.

We have also seen that a man who is Assyrian by background will be empowered by Satan to rise from the Middle East to great power and authority. After vanquishing the entire Middle East,[1] he will move his military machine southward to conquer Egypt, and, as a result, Libya and Ethiopia will follow him as well.

While in Egypt, this king of the North will be disturbed by news coming out of Jerusalem. As a result, he will move his military machine northeast to deal with this troubling issue and will set up the tents of his palace in the Kidron Valley facing the Temple Mount. It will be there—in Jerusalem—where the king of the North will become the beast.

To this point, we have gained much insight about the king of the North from the book of Daniel. But, now we turn to Daniel's New Testament counterpart, the book of Revelation, which will inform us about the beast, including how the king of the North will become the beast.

The Beast from the Sea

So, let us begin our introduction to the beast with Revelation 13:1: "Then I stood on the sand of the sea. And I saw a beast rising up out of the sea, having seven heads and ten horns, and on his horns ten crowns, and on his heads a blasphemous name."

This verse reads like the introduction to a riddle. To apprehend its meaning, we will need to understand the terms within it.

The "sea" seems to be a reference to the Mediterranean, which borders Israel to the west.[2] The rising of the beast from the sea may then refer to one who comes out of the Mediterranean area, around which lay the old Roman Empire.[3]

The Rome Connection

Previously, we noted that the book of Daniel alluded to ten modern-day nations residing within the borders of what was once the Roman Empire. These nations will ratify and guarantee the terms of a seven-year treaty with Israel. It is this treaty that will start the clock ticking on the day of the Lord, the seven-year tribulation period.

Later, in Revelation 17, we discover that the beast will have a connection to Rome, which lies across the Mediterranean Sea from Israel. There, the woman pictured riding the beast is identified as " 'that great city which reigns over the kings of the earth' " (verse18), which could only be Rome.[4] Furthermore, we are told in Revelation 17 that the woman sits on seven hills (verse 9),[5] which again points to Rome as the identity of this city—for, Rome is famously known as the city of seven hills.

Therefore, 13:1 may refer to the beast's connection with the Roman Empire and, particularly, with the city of Rome. However, we previously saw that the king of the North, who will become the beast, will most likely arise from the country of Iraq. So, what is the beast's connection with Rome, and what is the meaning of the cryptic phrases, "having seven heads and ten horns, and on his horns ten crowns"? The answers begin for us in Revelation 17:8:

> "The beast that you saw was, and is not, and will ascend out of the bottomless pit[6] and go to perdition [destruction]. And those who dwell on the earth will marvel, whose names are not written in the Book of Life from the foundation of the world, when they see the beast that was, and is not, and yet is."

The Riddle of the Beast

Once more we seem to encounter riddles, particularly with this statement: "the beast was, is not, and will ascend out of the bottomless pit (the abyss)." There is only one way to understand this eerie phrase: The beast is a man who was once alive, but then died—prior to the writing of the book of Revelation in AD 68.[7] However, this deceased one will return to an eminently significant role within the realm of the living by emerging from the place of the dead.

This seems too strange to be true, but it is exactly what is prophesied in Revelation 17. Though the description in verse 8 still seems all too mysterious, it will become clearer as we move through the next few verses.

An Astonishing Connection with a Roman Emperor

The next verse makes this proclamation: "Here is the mind which has wisdom: The seven heads are seven mountains [hills] on which the woman sits." As we have already seen, the woman represents the city of Rome, which sits on seven hills.

Understanding the identity of the woman as the city of Rome will enable us to identify the kings presented in verse 10. There we encounter another cryptic statement: "There are also seven kings. Five have fallen, one is, and the other has not yet come. And when he comes, he must continue a short time."

No doubt verse 10 is speaking of seven specific kings. Five of those kings had died ("have fallen") by the time the book of Revelation was being written, and another king ("one is") was ruling at the time John was writing the book. The final one of the seven kings had not yet ascended to the throne ("the other has not yet come").

The announcement regarding these seven kings is connected with the proclamation about the city of Rome in the previous verse.[8] This means there is a relationship between the kings and Rome, which is this: These kings were Roman emperors that ruled from that great city.[9]

The beast's relationship with those kings is presented to us in verse 11: "And the beast that was, and is not, is himself also the eighth, and is of the seven, and is going to perdition [destruction]." Astoundingly, this statement declares that this man was once a Roman emperor; *he is of the seven*! This reinforces what we mentioned earlier—that this man was once alive, but then died, as portrayed by this phrase: "the beast that was, and is not."

But, not only was this man a Roman emperor from the first century, but amazingly, we discover that he will become a *future* Roman ruler, for John discloses that he is also the eighth king and is going to perdition. This information reveals that he will *come back* from the dead, since it is presented in a future sense.[10] Of course, verse 8 had already clarified this with the pronouncement that he "will ascend out of the bottomless pit and go to perdition," showing he will come back from the dead before he goes to his destruction.

One of the First Five

Clearly, verses 8–11 are telling us that the beast was a Roman emperor, since he was one of the seven. More specifically, he was one of the first five emperors. We know that because verse 8 shows that the beast is a man who once lived but was no longer alive at the writing of Revelation. Regarding the seven kings, John presents that "five have fallen, one is, and the other has not yet come." This demonstrates that the first five kings had died by the writing of the book of Revelation, while the sixth one was ruling while Revelation was being written. This means that since the beast had died prior to the writing of Revelation, and since at the writing of Revelation only the first five of the Roman emperors had died, then the beast must be one of the first five.

In case you are curious regarding the identities of the first seven Roman emperors, here is a listing of them:

1. Caius Octavianus Caesar (Augustus) (27 BC-AD 14)
2. Tiberius Claudius Caesar Augustus (Tiberius) (AD 14–37)
3. Gaius Julius Caesar Germanicus (Caligula) (AD 37–41)
4. Claudius (AD 41–54)
5. Nero Claudius Caesar (Nero) (AD 54–68)
6. Servius Sulpicius Galba (AD 68–69)
7. Otho (AD January–April 69)

As we look closely at verse 10 once again, we can see that Revelation was written in AD 68, for here is what it states: "There are also seven kings. Five have fallen, one is, and the other has not yet come. And when he comes, he must continue a short time." The fact that the apostle announces there *were* seven kings indicates he was referring to the first seven Roman emperors.

This means that the emperor in power at the time of the writing of Revelation would have been Galba, who died in January of 69. This fits perfectly the announcement of verse 10 regarding the seventh king that "when he comes, he must continue a short time." As the list above shows, the seventh emperor, Otho, reigned only three months. That certainly fits the description of *a short time*! This presents more evidence that the seven kings of Revelation 17 refer to the first seven Roman emperors and, therefore, the beast—the man who will rule the world in the future—was actually one of the first five.

Ten Kings Submitting to the Beast

We have identified the seven heads mentioned in Revelation 17:9 as seven hills upon which the city of Rome sits and as the first seven Roman emperors. We also saw those seven heads mentioned back in chapter 13 verse 1, which stated that the beast will have "seven heads and ten horns, and on his horns ten crowns."

Notice that in addition to the seven kings, "ten horns" are introduced. The identity of these ten horns is revealed in 17:12: " 'And the ten horns which you saw are ten kings who have received no kingdom as yet, but they receive authority for one hour as kings with the beast.' " Therefore, these "ten horns" are ten kings who will rule with the beast in the future. And since, as we will see, the beast will rule for only three and a half years, these ten kings will rule with the beast for a short time ("one hour").

We have been introduced to seven kings and to ten kings, but how are they different? The seven kings were Roman emperors who ruled in the *past*, while the ten kings will rule with the beast in the *future*, as indicated by this explanation: "who have received no kingdom as yet."

The World Worships the Beast

As we return to Revelation 17:8, we see what kind of response people will have toward the beast: "And those who dwell on the earth will marvel, whose names are not written in the Book of Life from the foundation of the world, when they see the beast that was, and is not, and shall be present." As declared in this verse, people will *marvel*. They will be amazed at the beast!

Those responding in that way are those whose names are not written in the Book of Life. They are people who have never believed in Jesus Christ for eternal life. The fate presented in Revelation 20:15 of these same individuals is that "anyone not found written in the Book of Life was cast into the lake of fire." They will be swept away in amazement at the beast. In fact, Revelation 13:4 proclaims they will worship him. But, why? As we explore chapter 13 a little further, we will see the reason for this.

Verse 1 pictures this man as "having seven heads and ten horns, and on his horns ten crowns." As already noted, this description coincides with the presentation of him in chapter 17 of Revelation, in which the seven heads refer to the first seven rulers of the Roman Empire (of which he is one) and the ten horns allude to the ten kings who will rule under his authority in the last half of the day of the Lord.

But, another important piece of information about the beast is presented at the end of verse 1 when we are told that "on his heads [there is] a blasphemous name." This aligns with the description of the king of the North we saw in Daniel 11, where we learned "the king shall do according to his own will: he shall exalt and magnify himself above every god and shall speak blasphemies against the God of gods" (verse 36). Revelation 13:1 also makes the connection of the beast with the king of the North. In addition, verse 6 of Revelation 13 shows this connection when it proclaims that the beast "opened his mouth in blasphemy against God."

We have seen that the king of the North will begin his rise in power 220 days after the day of the Lord begins, while the beast will make his first appearance 1,260 days into the day of the Lord. The only way to harmonize this information is to see that this individual will begin as the king of the North and will later become the beast.

Verse 2 of Revelation 13 further connects the beast with the king presented in the book of Daniel by likening him to a leopard, a bear, and a lion. Though these three appear in reverse order to their appearance in Daniel 7, they are the same three animals. These animals picture three empires—Babylon as a *lion*,[11] Medo-Persia as a *bear*,[12] and Greece as a *leopard*[13] —all of which are presented to be in power prior to the rule of the beast. By identifying the beast with the three animals of Daniel 7, Revelation is letting us know his rule would include the strengths and characteristics of those former empires. In addition, he will rule over all of the land area (and more) those three empires ruled.

Authority from the Dragon

We receive this fascinating information in verse 2: "The dragon gave him his power, his throne, and great authority." Previously, we saw that Revelation 12:9 revealed the Dragon's identity as "that serpent of old, called the Devil and Satan, who deceives the whole world." As we discovered of the king of the North in Daniel 11, the beast also will obtain "his power, his rule, and his great authority from Satan" (Revelation 13:2). This is the secret of his astonishing rise to power and to being worshipped by the world as a god.

As a reminder of why Satan would give the beast his power, his throne, and great authority, we will look again at Luke 4:5–8:

> Then the devil, taking Him up on a high mountain, showed Him all the kingdoms of the world in a moment of time. And the devil said to Him, "All this authority I will give You, and their glory; for this has been delivered to me, and I give it to whomever I wish. Therefore, if You will worship before me, all will be Yours." And Jesus answered and said to him, "Get behind Me, Satan! For it is written, 'You shall worship the Lord your God, and Him only you shall serve.' "

In one of three temptations of Jesus by Satan described in depth in the Gospels, the Devil offered him authority to rule all the kingdoms of the world. If only Jesus would worship Satan, the Devil would grant Jesus the opportunity to rule the world.

But, Jesus turned down the offer, choosing to trust the Father's path toward rule, which involved enduring the suffering and shame of the cross. Having been spurned by his number one choice to be ruler over his kingdom, Satan will then make this same offer to the man who will become the beast, and the beast will accept it. As a result, the Dragon will give him his power, his throne, and great authority.

Augustus?

Depending on which of the first five Roman emperors the beast is, Satan may have made the offer to him soon after Jesus turned it down. Let us imagine that the identity of the beast is Caesar Augustus. He was the first Roman emperor, the architect of the Roman Empire, and by far the greatest administrator of all the emperors.[14] Satan may have already gone into the place of the dead (the abyss) to make the offer to him. The offer would be attractive enough to most on its own merits, but

THE BEAST FROM THE ABYSS

because Augustus is a dead unbeliever, the offer to come back and rule the world would be hard to turn down. In fact, if one such as Augustus had the high ambition of ruling the world, this offer would be the perfect complement to that of escaping the torment of hades.[15]

Resurrection from the Dead?

Earlier, when we looked at Revelation 17, we saw the beast described as having seven heads, referring to seven hills (Rome) *and* to the first seven Roman emperors. But, we learn in the vision recorded in 13:3 that the apostle John "saw one of his heads as if it had been mortally wounded, and his deadly wound was healed." Later, in verse 14 of the same chapter, we see that a false prophet tells "those who dwell on the earth to make an image to the beast who was wounded by the sword and lived."

In putting these two verses together, we learn that one of the heads of this coming world ruler will receive a deadly wound from a sword. The phrase translated *deadly wound* literally indicates *slain to death*. As a result of being physically attacked with a sword, someone is killed.

But, after experiencing this deadly wound, this man will live![16] Since it appears he is put to death, it also seems that he rises from the dead! This seems to explain this response in Revelation 13 verse 3: "And all the world marveled and followed the beast."

The World Follows the Beast

Note two important things about this response. First, people *marveled* as a result of the appearance of this man's resurrection from the dead! Second, not just a few will be carried away by that apparent resurrection—*all the world* will respond in that way!

Obviously, the presentation of the wounding and healing of this man will be highly impressive. However, it must also be true that the man who will experience this apparent death and resurrection will be equally impressive to the world. For in order for the entire world to be impacted in such a way by anyone—even one who appears to rise from the dead—that individual will have to be known by the world; he will have to be a very important man in order for the whole world to be acquainted with him. And he will be.

What is fascinating is that though the whole world will follow the beast as a result of his resurrection, God's Word seems to indicate that it is not the beast who is killed—though it may be the beast who rises from the dead. If this sounds like a complicated riddle, then you are following the logic so far. Hang with me while I walk us through this riddle, and I believe you will soon understand how to solve it.

The Beast Slain

Returning to John's statement in Revelation 13:3, we note that he proclaimed: "I saw one of his [the beast's] heads as if it had been mortally wounded." This is a rather odd way of stating that he had seen the beast killed. Clearly, this does not refer to the beast; instead, it is *one of his heads*. As we saw in Revelation 17, *heads* represent rulers. This means that the one slain by a sword is a ruler connected with the beast. This victim is not the beast himself but is connected with the beast, just as the heads in Revelation 17 were rulers connected with the beast.

But, unlike the heads in chapter 17 who lived in the first century, the one described as slain in chapter 13 is not from the first century; he will be alive up until the middle of the seven-year day of the Lord. This is demonstrated by the response of people to his death and apparent resurrection. There has never been a recording in history of the entire world following one man. This means that this picture will be fulfilled in the future.

Though this man will *not* be the beast, he will be a ruler. And interestingly, though he is not the beast, his apparent resurrection causes this incredible response from the world: "So they worshiped the dragon who gave authority to the beast; and they worshiped the beast" (Revelation 13:4).

Who *Really* Gives the Beast His Authority to Rule?

As we previously learned, this man will worship Satan, though he may call him something like Lucifer, which has a better connotation.[17] In addition, he will promote Lucifer worship to the world. The promotion of this worship will be part of the deal Satan strikes with him, and to fulfill his part of the bargain, Satan will give this man authority to rule the world. But, though the deal may provide for the man to rule as long as he continues to worship Satan and to promote worship of him, according to Revelation 13:5, he will actually rule for forty-two months, which translates into three and a half years.

If the deal between Satan and this man is for him to rule as long as he promotes Lucifer worship, then why does verse 5 proclaim he is given authority for only forty-two months? Who has given him authority for only forty-two months, if Satan apparently gives him authority for as long as the man worships the Devil? It is God, the only one in control of all things, who will actually give this man authority to rule for that limited amount of time.

Would God Grant Authority to a Satan Worshipper?

Some readers may object to the thought that God would grant authority to a Satan worshipper, a man who will be anti-Christian, and who will even be guilty of putting Christians to death. However, if we take stock of some specific verses in connection with this topic, we will see that this indeed is true.

For example, Daniel, functioning as a prophet of God, informs us of this about God: "He removes kings and raises up kings" (Daniel 2:21). It is God, and God alone, who grants authority and rule.

This is illustrated by Jesus' answer to Pontius Pilate after Pilate asked him, "Do you not know that I have power to crucify you, and power to release you?" (John 18:10). In response, Jesus proclaimed, "You could have no power at all against me unless it had been given you from above" (verse 11). Once more—and this time from the lips of Jesus—we learn that God alone grants authority to individuals, even to someone such as Pontius Pilate, who handed Jesus over to be crucified.[18]

This same thought is echoed by John the Baptist in John 3:27: "A man can receive nothing unless it has been given to him from heaven." Everything anyone possesses—including any authority he or she may have—is due to God having granted it.

Even evil authorities possess what they have because God has decreed it. In all of this, as wicked as this future king, the beast, may be, and as wicked as the deal between him and Satan may be, God is in full control of it all—and God will use all of this for his good plan.

No Purpose of God Can Be Hindered

As Job learned and expressed to God, "I know that you can do everything, and that no purpose of yours can be withheld from you" (Job 42:2). No one can hinder the good purposes of God—not even Satan, after all his efforts. In fact, Satan—in all of his conniving—plays right into God's hands, accomplishing exactly what God has decreed according to his perfect will.

This is an important lesson to keep in mind, especially as we observe in our next chapter Satan's attempt to destroy all believing Jews who live during the last half of the tribulation period.

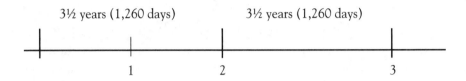

1 = The rise of the king of North
2 = The king becomes the beast
3 = The return of Christ

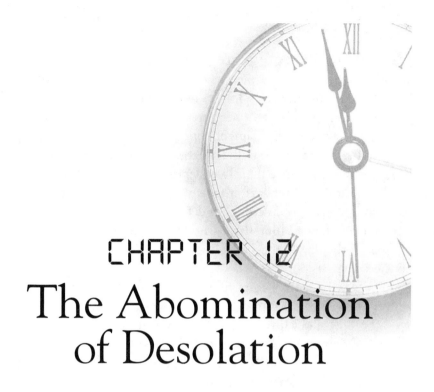

CHAPTER 12
The Abomination of Desolation

D r. E. Schuyler English once told of a man on Long Island who was able to satisfy a lifelong ambition by purchasing a very fine barometer. When he unpacked the instrument, he was dismayed to find that the needle appeared to be stuck, pointing to the section marked "Hurricane." After shaking the barometer vigorously, the man wrote a scorching letter to the store from which he purchased the instrument, and on his way to his office in New York the next morning, mailed the protest. That evening he returned to Long Island to find not only the barometer missing, but his house, as well!

In hindsight, of course, it was foolish for that man to ignore the clear warning of impending danger from a trusted instrument. But, it would be even more foolish to ignore the warning of impending danger from the trusted Son of God.

Jesus' Warning to Future Jewish Believers

In Matthew 24, Jesus warns of coming danger during the day of the Lord. Specifically, in verses 15–16, he presents a clear admonition for Jewish believers in Christ: "Therefore when you see the 'abomination of desolation,' spoken of by Daniel the prophet, standing in the holy place . . . then let those who are in Judea flee to the mountains." They need to heed this warning, since their lives depend on it.

This warning of biblical prophecy points to an act committed by a man who, himself, is described in detail in the Bible. Because there is so much detail about him, those who believe in Jesus Christ for eternal life during the day of the Lord should recognize him when he appears on the scene.

The April 22, 1974 edition of *Time* magazine ran this letter to the editor:

> A man who does not make value judgments could be dangerous. A man who does not ask who is right may operate with a blank and pitiless conscience. If the same man happens to be amassing ever greater power and popularity, watch out, world! A brilliant mind, a passionate ego and an imagination unfettered by any moral absolutes concoct the ultimate delusion: Your savior has come—fall down and worship him.[1]

This warning sounds a lot like the man associated with the abomination of desolation. As we have learned, the future will reveal a man known in the Bible as the king of the North who will become the beast, seen by the world as its savior and even as its god. As we have seen, this Assyrian will be empowered by Satan to arise to great power and authority from the Middle East. After vanquishing the Middle East and northern Africa, he will move into Jerusalem, where he will become the beast, the ruler of the world.

Assassination and Resurrection of the Beast

Shortly after moving his powerful army into Jerusalem, and setting up the tents of his palace facing the Temple Mount, the king of the North will suffer an assassination attempt by someone with a sword. As a result, he will be mortally wounded. However, in what appears to be a miracle, his deadly wound will be healed! (Revelation 13:3). As Revelation 13:14 announces: he "was wounded by the sword and lived."[2]

The response to the healing from his apparent deadly wound is pictured in this way in Revelation 13:3–4:

> And all the world marveled and followed the beast. So they worshiped the dragon who gave authority to the beast; and they worshiped the beast, saying, "Who is like the beast? Who is able to make war with him?"

From the world's viewpoint, it will appear as if the king received such a wound that he *should* have died, but is miraculously healed. Or, it may appear that he *does* die and rises from the dead.[3] It will be at this point that the king of the North will become the beast, when the spirit of a departed Roman emperor from the first century[4] arises from *the abyss*, the place of the unbelieving dead, and enters this man.

Overcoming the Prophets of God

Following his healing, the beast will decide to take on the two prophets of God prophesying in Jerusalem and eliminate them. This is described in Revelation 11:7: "When they [the two prophets] finish their testimony, the beast that ascends out of the bottomless pit [the abyss] will make war against them, overcome them, and kill them."

We learned in an earlier chapter that these two prophets will be given great power and authority by God. In fact, here is what we find about them in Revelation 11:5: "And if anyone wants to harm them, fire proceeds from their mouth and devours their enemies. And if anyone wants to harm them, he must be killed in this manner."

This description tells us that others will attempt to kill them before the beast is successful. After all, this information would not even appear in the Bible if no one *will* try to harm and kill them.

The Death of the Prophets: God's Plan?

Revelation 11:5 shows how difficult it will be to kill these two prophets. In fact, it will seem to be impossible! God will grant the prophets such amazing power throughout their three-and-a-half-year prophetic ministry to Israel that no one will be able to harm them. And anyone who is foolish enough to try to eliminate these pesky prophets will be killed by them.

Since no one else will be able to bring harm to these prophets, how is it that the beast will be able to overcome them and kill them? The answer can be found by taking a close look at the very beginning of Revelation 11:7. God will allow the beast to kill them when "they finish their testimony" to Israel, but and not one day before! When their God-appointed ministry ends—on the exact day God has determined—he will then allow the beast to kill his prophets.

Would God Allow Deception?

Why? It will be part of God's plan to allow the hardened of heart to be handed over to their own deception. This is explained in 2 Thessalonians 2:9–10: "The coming of the lawless one is according to the working of Satan, with all power, signs, and lying wonders, and with all unrighteous deception among those who perish, because they did not receive the love of the truth, that they might be saved."

The context of these verses describes the day of the Lord, the seven-year tribulation period. Specifically, verses 9–12 present the deception that will occur during that future era and the identity of the recipients of that deception.

The deception is presented from vantage points. First, Satan will deceive by "all power, signs, and lying wonders, deceiving those who perish, because they did not receive the love of the truth."

The one who authored the book of Revelation—the apostle John—is the same one who penned this well-known verse in John 3:16 that reveals the identity of those who perish. Here John announces that those who believe in Jesus Christ for everlasting life will *not* perish. This means that those who perish—the ones Satan will deceive during the tribulation period—are those who have never believed in Jesus for eternal life.

The deception mentioned in 2 Thessalonians 2 is also presented from another vantage point in verses 11–12: "And for this reason God will send them strong delusion, that they should believe the lie, that they all may be condemned who did not believe the truth but had pleasure in unrighteousness."

What did we just read? God will send strong delusion to unbelievers in the tribulation period! This is an amazing and disturbing statement!

Why Would God Do That?

We can begin to understand this revelation by observing *which* unbelievers God will target for deception. God will not send strong delusion to all unbelievers, only those "who did not believe the truth." More specifically, they will be handed over to deception "because they did not receive the love of the truth, that they might be saved."

The "love of the truth" refers to the gospel. Because they did not receive it—by believing in Jesus Christ—they were not saved. But, that is the point—that is the reason why God will send them strong delusion. These are unbelievers who were presented with the truth of the gospel of Jesus Christ, and they did not believe. Their hearts were hardened to it. Therefore, it is as if God will say to them, "All right, have it your way. Since you have chosen deceit by not receiving the love of the truth, I will hand you over to strong delusion, that you should believe the lie."

How God Works

This is not at all unlike how God works. For example, Romans chapter 1 warns about people "who suppress the truth in unrighteousness" (verse 18) by pursuing a sinful lifestyle (verses 20–32). As a result of their choice of pursuit, God says, "Have it your way," by handing them over to their sinful pursuits (see verses 24, 26, 28). This demonstrates the fulfillment of Proverbs 14:14, in which the wicked will have the fill of his ways.

God is sovereign, meaning he is in complete control of *all* things. That also means that if the beast overcomes and kills the two prophets of God, it is because God has allowed it according to his perfect plan. As we have seen, God will allow this apparent tragedy in order to hand over to deceit those who have hardened their hearts against the gospel.

Remember that the two prophets will be perceived by the unbelieving inhabitants of the tribulation period as their enemies; after all, they will "torment" the world with their plagues.[5] For example, like Elijah of old, "these have the power to shut heaven, so that no rain falls in the days of their prophecy" (Revelation 11:6). Due to their power to bring judgment, the earth will experience a three-and-a-half-year drought. Furthermore, this may mean that the last day of rainfall anywhere upon the earth will be the day before their ministry begins, and upon their deaths, rain will come for the first time in 1,260 days! This, of course, will bring great celebration upon the planet.

The World Deceived to Worship the Beast

Though others will attempt to "remove" the prophets, no one will be successful; in fact, everyone who attempts to harm these men of God will be killed by them. All of this will make the men seem unconquerable—that is, until the beast overcomes them.

What, then, will the unbelieving world think of the beast when he overcomes the two prophets of God and kills them? Those of the world will believe he is more powerful than the God of the prophets. In fact, they will see him as their god.

Abominating the Holy Place

From clues given to us in the Bible, we can know what the beast will do immediately after he kills the two prophets. At the end of three and a half years, which is 1,260 days on a Jewish calendar, there will be an end to sacrifice and offering (Daniel 9:27). This means something will occur in the exact middle of the day of the Lord—the seven-year tribulation period—to cause the cessation of Jewish sacrifices in the temple. On the very day he kills the two witnesses,[6] he will enter the temple.

The apostle Paul describes that act in 2 Thessalonians 2:3–4 by explaining that the day of Christ—the last half of the tribulation period—will begin when the Man of Sin enters into the temple of God. With that act, he will be declare he is God.

Jesus also describes that same act in this way: "Therefore when you see the 'abomination of desolation,' spoken of by Daniel the prophet, standing in the holy place . . ." (Matthew 24:15).

The "holy place" in this verse refers to the holy of holies in the temple. However, God directed in the Old Testament that no one was to enter the temple except the high priest—and only once a year.[7] And even then, the priest had to undergo preparation by offering up a sin offering for himself in order to enter the temple.[8] Any other entrance into the holy of holies would be an abomination and was not allowed by the Lord.

The Sign of Desolation

Therefore, in Matthew 24:15, the "abomination of desolation" refers to the beast abominating the temple by entering it against God's regulations. "Desolation" refers to what will occur once he abominates the temple. Thus, the abomination of the temple by the beast will signal that he is about to bring desolation to Israel.

This is indicated by Jesus' admonition in the verses following verse 15 of Matthew 24:

> "Therefore when you see the 'abomination of desolation,' spoken of by Daniel the prophet, standing in the holy place . . . then let those who are in Judea flee to the mountains [hills]. Let him who is on the housetop not go down to take anything out of his house. And let him who is in the field not go back to get his clothes. But woe to those who are pregnant and to those who are nursing babies in those days! And pray that your flight may not be in winter or on the Sabbath. For then there will be great tribulation, such as has not been since the beginning of the world until this time, no, nor ever shall be."

The Recipients of Jesus' Warning

Jesus' command in these verses is for Jews in Judea to flee to the hills. These are the Jews from the region in which Jerusalem is located who have believed in Christ for eternal life.

So, why is Jesus speaking to Jews in Judea, and why would they be there? These Jews will believe in Christ due to the ministry of the two prophets of God who will be prophesying in Jerusalem. In all likelihood, they will remain in Judea (specifically, Jerusalem) to be taught God's Word by the two prophets. Therefore, they will be there when the prophets are killed and the beast abominates the temple.

Run!

Observe Jesus' exhortation to his future audience. By the most serious of warnings, he is calling for believing Jews residing in Judea at the time of the abomination of the temple to flee Judea immediately!

It will be critically important that those particular Jews *not* hesitate to obey Jesus' command at that point. If they *do* hesitate, they will lose their lives.

Then, almost inexplicably after that powerful exhortation, Jesus adds this warning: "But woe to those who are pregnant and to those who are nursing babies in those days!" Why would He tack on this detail? What does it add to the warning he has already given?

This statement adds emphasis. In it, Jesus announces that those who are pregnant or who are nursing babies will not be able to leave Judea quickly and could therefore be caught by the beast's armies. He is emphasizing the haste with which these Jews will need to escape Judea.

In addition, Jesus gives this somber warning: "And pray that your flight may not be in winter or on the Sabbath." Taking flight in winter would be slower due to inclement weather. Fleeing on the Sabbath would be equally difficult because travel would be limited due to Israel's observance of the Law during the tribulation period, limiting travel on the Sabbath. The point of this warning is to stress the importance of haste in getting out of Judea when the beast abominates the temple, because desolation of the Jews will immediately follow.

From the exhortation to flee immediately, to the warning about not even taking the time to enter the house from the roof, to the woe attached to being pregnant when it is time to take flight, to the prayer of the Jews not to have to attempt their exodus on the Sabbath, there could not be a stronger emphasis put on the absolute necessity for them to flee Judea immediately.

Great Tribulation

As we have noted, the abomination of desolation initiates the final half (three and a half years) of the seventieth week of Daniel 9:24–27, the final seven years of a 490-year prophetic period regarding Israel. To put it another way, the abomination of desolation begins the final three and a half years before the return of Christ to the earth, which will be a time of unparalleled persecution of Jews who are disciples of Jesus.[10] No other period of Jewish persecution in human history can measure up to the intensity of persecution that will be heaped upon Jewish followers of Jesus at that time.

A Picture of the Warning from Revelation 12

The flight of believing Israel is pictured with different detail in Revelation 12. In verse 1, Israel is being described in this way: "Now a great sign appeared in heaven: a woman clothed with the sun, with the moon under her feet, and on her head a garland of twelve stars." The description of the woman in this verse refers us back to Genesis 37:9–10, where we learn, through a God-given dream by Joseph that this is an allusion to Israel.

Then, in verses 2–5 of Revelation 12, a special child is introduced:

> Then being with child, she cried out in labor and in pain to give birth. And another sign appeared in heaven: behold, a great, fiery red dragon . . . . His tail drew a third of the stars of heaven and threw them to the earth. And the dragon stood before the woman who was ready to give birth, to devour her Child as soon as it was born. She bore a male Child who was to rule all nations with a rod of iron. And her Child was caught up to God and His throne.

Clearly, this describes the Lord Jesus Christ. These verses present three eras for this child—his birth,[11] which occurred at the beginning of the first century; his rule over the nations, which will occur following his return to the earth; and his present position in heaven—seated at the right hand of the Father.[12]

An Intense Spiritual Battle

But, these verses also present an intense spiritual battle. At the birth of Christ, the Dragon shows up. In Revelation 12:9 he is identified as "the great dragon . . . that serpent of old, called the Devil and Satan, who deceives the whole world." This is the one who, as the highest of all angels created, rebelled against God and, in addition, "drew a third of the stars of heaven and threw them to the earth."

Since angels are called "stars" in Scripture,[13] this description likely refers to Satan's influence of a third of the angels to rebel against God with him. In fact, it is more than likely that *stars* refer to rebellious angels, as verse 7 reveals that the stars connected with the Dragon in verse 4 are actually his angels.

In Revelation 12, the spiritual battle of the ages is pictured by the Dragon being present at the birth of Christ to destroy him. Though Jesus was not destroyed at that time, his family had to escape to Egypt in order to save him from the wrath of Satan working through King Herod. Later, Satan worked through Judas and the religious leaders to put Jesus to death.

However, as verse 5 proclaims, Israel "bore a male Child who was to rule all nations with a rod of iron. And her Child was caught up to God and His throne." Though Satan sought to destroy this child (so he could hold onto his kingdom), ultimately, he failed. This child, Jesus, ascended to heaven forty-three days following his death, where he awaits his future rule. He has been given the kingdom over the earth that Satan so desperately has desired for himself, and will ascend the throne when he returns to the earth.

Satan's Pursuit

Because the child escaped the clutches of Satan, the infuriated Dragon turned his attention toward the woman who "gave birth" to the Son—Israel. His persecution toward Israel has a long history behind it and will continue into the future, as verse 6 of Revelation 12 shows: "Then the woman fled into the wilderness, where she has a place prepared by God, that they should feed her there one thousand two hundred and sixty days."

In connection to the war in heaven between Satan with his angels and Michael with his angels,[14] this passage portrays the flight of believing Jews at the midpoint of the tribulation period. At that point, in which the beast kills the two prophets of God and commits the abomination of desolation, Jews in Jerusalem who have believed in Christ for eternal life will flee into the surrounding hills located in the wilderness area of Israel. Their flight to escape the beast will occur in obedience to Jesus.[15]

The time period of 1,260 days mentioned in Revelation 12:6 refers to the last half of the day of the Lord. Notice in the verse that *they* will feed her (believing Israel) throughout that era of time. Though the context of this verse does not reveal the identity of "they," we will later see that God will use Gentile Christians to meet her needs.

Verse 6 is sandwiched by pictures of the Dragon (Satan) before and after. As we have seen, the Dragon attempted to destroy the child when he came to the earth (the first time), and he will battle with the angels of God in heaven. Between these two presentations of the Dragon, we see the flight of the woman in verse 6.

Since the beast will receive his authority from Satan—due to his allegiance to him—we can see that the beast's attempt to destroy Jews is

THE ABOMINATION OF DESOLATION

Satan-inspired. The clues of Revelation 12 verify that understanding.

As we will see in our next chapter, Satan's full-fledged effort to destroy the Jews will occur following the outbreak of war in heaven.

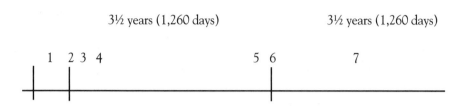

1 = The world will proclaim "peace and security!"

2 = The rapture of the church; sudden destruction, which will end the period of "peace and security"; the beginning of a seven-year treaty between ten nations and Israel; the beginning of the day of the Lord; the two prophets of God begin their three-and-a-half-year ministry to Israel

3 = The conversion of 144,000 Jews

4 = The rise of the king of the North

5 = The 144,000 take the gospel to all the nations

6 = The king of the North becomes the beast, the ruler of the entire world

7 = God provides for the Jews who have fled into the wilderness for 1,260 days

CHAPTER 13
War in Heaven

T en-year-old Carla wrote this brief letter to her pastor:
>Dear Pastor,
>Are there any devils on earth? I think there may be one in my class.
>Carla

The answer to Carla's question is yes and no. The Devil is portrayed in the New Testament as "a roaring lion, seeking whom he may devour" (1 Peter 5:8). So, in a sense, he is on the earth. Yet, oftentimes he does not dwell on the earth. In fact, surprisingly, the Bible tells us that he currently has access to heaven, where he dwells *day and night* in his operation to target Christians for destruction.[1] But, the time is fast approaching when the Devil will be expelled from heaven, at which point he will come to the earth with a fury. His removal from heaven will be the result of a great war that will take place there.

War Breaks Out

At the time the beast assumes authority from Satan to begin his reign, a war will break out in heaven. This cosmic conflict is described in Revelation 12:7–9. We are not told what initiates this conflict. It may simply be that God gives Michael the archangel[2] and his angels the command to expel Satan and his minions from heaven because it fits God's perfect timing of events to accomplish his kingdom plan. The result is that Satan will be barred from heaven—forever! Never again, after this, will Satan be able to approach God's presence to accuse believers in Christ.

Satan Is Where?!

Many Christians are surprised to learn that Satan will be cast out of heaven *in the future*, since most people seem to believe he was kicked out of heaven long ago. However, Scripture presents a different picture. Notice the view given to us by Job 1:6 and 2:1 regarding Satan's current access to the presence of God:

> Now there was a day when the sons of God[3] came to present themselves before the Lord, and Satan also came among them. . . . Again there was a day when the sons of God came to present themselves before the Lord, and Satan came also among them to present himself before the Lord.

A popular view regarding Satan's current abode is that he is in hell; others believe he was long ago relegated to the earth. Certainly, most people believe he was cast out of heaven when he rebelled against God—before the creation of the world.[4]

However, these verses from Job show that Satan certainly did have access into God's presence in heaven—well after the creation of the world. According to the book of Job, Satan came before God to accuse the most righteous man on the earth at that time—Job. Satan's accusation was that Job only worshipped God because he blessed him. Furthermore, the Devil charged that if God would allow Satan to bring trials upon Job, Job would turn against God.

The Accuser

Compare this with Revelation 12:10, the verse that immediately follows the verses describing the war in heaven: "Then I heard a loud

114

voice saying in heaven, '. . . the accuser of our brethren, who accused them before our God day and night, has been cast down.' "

Take note of what we see regarding Satan in verse 10 that is similar to the verses we observed in Job: he accuses believers before God. Notice how often he is described as participating in this activity: he accuses believers all the time—*day and night*.

This picture of Satan shows the parallel between Revelation 12:7–10 and Job 1:6; 2:1. These verses show that Satan continues his accusation against believers, as well as demonstrate that he still has access to the presence of God in heaven.

Cast Out of Heaven

In addition to the evidence that Satan *continues* to have access to heaven, the depiction of Satan being cast out of heaven in Revelation 12 is presented in the context of the future tribulation period. Specifically, it is related to the timing of Israel fleeing into the wilderness where believing Jews receive provision by God for 1,260 days (Revelation 12:6). This means that the ousting of Satan from heaven will occur at the exact middle of the tribulation period.

As we have seen, one result of this war in heaven is that Satan and his angels are cast out of heaven forever. Another result is seen in the context of verses 12–17 of Revelation 12, particularly in this realization regarding Satan in verse 12:

> "Therefore rejoice, O heavens, and you who dwell
> in them! Woe to the inhabitants of the earth and the
> sea! For the devil has come down to you, having great
> wrath, because he knows that he has a short time."

Satan's Fury

Notice the contrast presented in this verse: the inhabitants of heaven are called to rejoice, while the residents of earth will experience woe. When Satan is cast out, heaven will rejoice. However, because Satan will then bring his fury to the earth, woe will be pronounced upon the planet.

As a result of being cast out of heaven, Satan will come to the realization that he has only a short time. We can better understand the phrase "he knows that he has a short time" if we understand the meaning of the verses (13–17) that follow that phrase. Beginning with verse 13, we see this: "Now when the dragon saw that he had been cast to the earth, he persecuted the woman who gave birth to the male Child."

As we learned earlier, the woman represents Israel—more specifically, the multitude of Jews who will believe in Christ for eternal life. The Dragon is identified in this passage as "that serpent of old, called the Devil and Satan" (verse 9). Therefore, verse 13 presents Satan's response once he is cast out of heaven: he will persecute the believing Jews.

Satan Knows God's Timetable

This means that when Satan is cast out of heaven in the exact midpoint of the future tribulation period, he will see that, according to God's timetable, he will only have 1,260 days (three and a half years) until Jesus will return to the earth to establish his kingdom. Now, it may seem odd to learn that Satan knows God's timetable, but he does. Not only does Satan know God's Word, he knew it well enough to quote from Psalm 91 during the temptations in which he sought to get Jesus to worship him. (When was the last time you quoted from Psalm 91?) And in order to have any chance of tempting Jesus by quoting God's Word to the One who is the living Word of God, he has to know it well. However, he does not believe it.

Satan knows what God has said in his Word. He understands, for example, God's prophetic plan and the timetable in conjunction with that plan. However, though he knows God's plan, he does not believe the inevitability of Jesus taking the kingdom from him and ruling over the earth himself in the future. Satan does not know the certainty of his own defeat. He still believes he can defeat God's plan and hang onto this world as his kingdom.

Thus, Satan understands God's plan, but he does not believe it. He also knows God's timetable, meaning he realizes that if God *does* kick him out of heaven in the future, he will only have three and a half years left until Jesus' return. So, when he is banished from heaven, he will work furiously to accomplish his plan of halting Jesus' return to rule. How will he do that?

Israel's Cry to the Lord

In Zechariah 13:8, set in the context of the future tribulation period, God predicts Israel will respond to him in this way: " 'They will call on My name, and I will answer them. I will say, "This is My people"; and each one will say, "The Lord is my God." ' " Israel as a whole will finally call upon the Lord, and he will answer.

In the next chapter of Zechariah, verses 1 and 2 describe the situation of Jerusalem at the time Israel cries out to the Lord. The scenario will occur during the seven-year day of the Lord, but more specifically, this describes what awaits Jerusalem at the very end of that era. This will be a living nightmare for the city of God as it faces devastation while being overrun by all the nations of the earth.

A Demonic Gathering

We learn from Revelation 17:13–14 that this horrific situation for Jerusalem originates when demons are sent out by Satan, the beast, and the false prophet. These unclean spirits will be "performing signs, which go out to the kings of the whole world, to gather them to the battle of that great day of God Almighty." The battle mentioned here is the one that will occur at the return of the Lord Jesus Christ to the earth, which is that great day of God Almighty.

As Revelation 16:16 announces, demonic spirits will "gather them [the kings of the whole world] together to the place called in Hebrew, Megiddo."5 Megiddo is a city in the northern sector of Israel, very close to Jesus' boyhood home, Nazareth. Both Megiddo and Nazareth overlook the plain of Jezreel (Esdraelon), where significant biblical battles took place, such as the great victory of Barak over the Caananites (Judges 4 and 5) and of Gideon over the Midianites (Judges 7). It is a perfect place for the armies of the world to gather together, but it will not be the location of the future battle of the armies of the earth.

Cutting Off the Path of the King

Instead, once the armies are gathered and coordinated, they will stream down into the Kidron Valley, which separates the Mount of Olives from the Temple Mount. However, the Kidron Valley will not be a large enough area to contain the vast amount of troops to be gathered at that time. The multitude of troops will spill over into the surrounding areas, which include Jerusalem. As a result, "the city shall be taken, the houses rifled, and the women ravished."6 That will be the scenario when Israel cries out to the Lord.

This is how God will answer: "Then the Lord will go forth and fight against those nations, as He fights in the day of battle. And in that day His feet will stand on the Mount of Olives, which faces Jerusalem on the east."

As a result of believing Israel calling out to the Lord, Jesus will return to the earth in order to deliver Israel and to establish his kingdom. It is the establishment of God's kingdom upon the earth that Satan desires to stop. He knows that if that occurs, he will lose his rule over the world.

Therefore, Satan knows that when he is cast out of heaven, he will have only three and a half years remaining to stop the culmination of God's plan. One way to do that is to halt the portion of God's plan in which Jesus returns to the earth.

Satan's Plan to Stop Jesus

In Satan's mind, the way to stop Jesus' return is to eliminate the Jews—especially those who have believed in Jesus for eternal life. Here is the thought behind this reasoning: if there are no believing Jews left alive on the earth, there will be none to call out to the Lord for deliverance (salvation). And if there are no Jews to call out to the Messiah for salvation, God's Word will not be fulfilled.[7]

In addition, Satan will believe he has triumphed over God if he can eliminate the Jews, for if he accomplishes that, he will have thwarted God's plan. Satan apparently believes that if he can eliminate Jews who might be open to the Lord, he can put a halt to God's plan to send Jesus to the earth. If there is no Israel to repent, and no Jews to call out to the Lord, the condition for fulfillment of God's promise will not be met, and Jesus will not return to the earth. In that case, Satan will be able to retain this world as his kingdom.

Specifically, Satan may be thinking about God's promise communicated through the apostle Peter in Acts 3:19–21. Israel is portrayed in the Old Testament as a son of God[8] who drifted far from his Father. As a result of presenting Israel as being in a family relationship with him, God calls Israel back into fellowship (a *close* relationship) with him throughout the Old Testament, the Gospels, and the book of Acts.[9] That call back to fellowship with God is called repentance.[10]

Though Jews need to believe in Jesus Christ for eternal life in order to *individually* enter into a relationship with God, the nation (the son of God) is called to repent.[11] And if Israel does that, God promises that he will send Jesus back to the earth to establish his kingdom. Israel will then experience forgiveness of sins and times of refreshing.

God's Plan to Deliver Israel

God has a plan for believing Israel, as Revelation 12:14 portrays. To understand this plan, some metaphors in this passage need to be explained. The first of these is found in this extended metaphor: "the woman was given two wings of a great eagle, that she might fly into the wilderness to her place."

Since the book of Revelation is founded upon the Old Testament, it only makes sense that the source of the meaning of this metaphor will be found there. Two passages in particular, Exodus 19:4 and Deuteronomy 32:9–12, present this same metaphor as God's deliverance of Israel from her enemies in connection with the wilderness. In both passages, the eagle's wings represent God's care for Israel.

Exodus 19:4, in particular, provides a close comparison with Revelation 12:14, for both describing God's deliverance of Israel in the wilderness from Israel's enemies. While Exodus 19 describes God's deliverance of Israel from the pursuing Egyptians, Revelation 12 presents Israel's deliverance from the beast's pursuing army.

We also learn in 12:14 that after the Lord delivers Israel into the wilderness from her persecutor, Israel will be "nourished for a time and times and half a time, from the presence of the serpent." Thus, these believing Jews in the future will have their needs met for three and a half years (*a time*: one year; *times*: two years; and *a half a time*: one half year). Verse 6 (in the same chapter) clarifies the time frame for us in this way: "Then the woman fled into the wilderness, where she has a place prepared for God, that they should feed her there one thousand two hundred and sixty days."

A Miraculous Protection

Verse 15 presents another extended metaphor calling for explanation: "So the serpent spewed water out of his mouth like a flood after the woman, that he might cause her to be carried away by the flood." The word *flood* in this verse refers to a flood of troops.[12] This means that, at the command of the beast, Satan (the serpent) will send out an army to hunt down the Jews who had fled into the wilderness.

However, while Satan will seek to destroy Israel, God will have a ready plan available for her deliverance, as we see in verses 16–17 of Revelation 12:

> But the earth helped the woman, and the earth opened its mouth and swallowed up the flood which the dragon had spewed out of his mouth. And the dragon was enraged with the woman, and he went to make war with the rest of her offspring, who keep the commandments of God and have the testimony of Jesus Christ.

The portrayal in verse 16 is not unique; it has happened before. In Numbers 16:28–33, following a rebellion by Korah and others who sought to overthrow Moses' authority, "the earth opened its mouth and swallowed them." When the earth *opened*, the rebellious men fell into it and were covered by the ground. Just as will occur with the armies of the beast in the future, they were *swallowed* by the earth!

Remember that the book of Revelation is a thorough-going Jewish book; it is built almost entirely upon the foundation of the Old Testament. Therefore, that this event literally occurred once before points to it happening again—in the future.

Thus, Revelation 12:15 is communicating this: When Satan (via the beast's command) sends out a flood of troops after the Jews fleeing into the wilderness, God will cause the ground to literally open up and swallow the troops. This is also similar to what God did with the Egyptian army that pursued the Israelites, whom God had borne with eagle's wings—he caused the water to swallow the troops.

A Well-Timed Earthquake

This phenomenon of the earth swallowing the troops may be explained by an event described in Revelation 11:13, which will occur right after the two prophets of God ascend into heaven (three and a half days following their deaths). Here is the description: "In the same hour there was a great earthquake, and a tenth of the city fell. In the earthquake seven thousand people were killed, and the rest were afraid and gave glory to the God of heaven."

It seems that this earthquake is the explanation for the miraculous swallowing of the troops while in pursuit of Jews on the run. The timing certainly works. Because this earthquake will occur three and a half days following the abomination of desolation, it will, therefore, take place while the Jews are fleeing into the wilderness.

The location works as well. We know that the center of this earthquake will be close to Jerusalem since, as a result of this quake, a tenth of the city fell.[13] Therefore, it seems God will frustrate this plan of Satan to capture fleeing Jews by using a well-timed earthquake to cause the ground to open up and swallow the pursuing troops.

Satan's Response of Rage

When the troops sent by the beast are eliminated, Satan will respond in this way: "And the dragon was enraged with the woman, and he went to make war with the rest of her offspring, who keep the commandments of God and have the testimony of Jesus Christ" (12:17).

Satan will be enraged because of the physical deliverance of the believing Jews who had fled into the wilderness. The sending out of the troops from Jerusalem to capture and eliminate Jews who are followers of Jesus will be Satan's big hope to hang onto his kingdom. But, when that plan is frustrated, he will turn from his pursuit of the Jews in the wilderness to pursue another group of believing Jews.

We have already seen the group of Jews described as those "who keep the commandments of God and have the testimony of Jesus Christ." There are two clues to their identity in this description. The first is their faithfulness to God, displayed by the description that they "keep the commandments of God." Thus, this is a group of Jews who are very faithful.

The second clue to their identity is the announcement that they "have the testimony of Jesus Christ." This testimony is the verbal announcement of the gospel.

Putting these two clues together, we can see which group of Jews Satan will pursue once he realizes God will protect the Jews in the wilderness. He will pursue the 144,000, previously described as very faithful to God, and who will go worldwide with the gospel, which is the testimony of Jesus Christ.

The Great Escape

In the fourteenth century, Robert Bruce, next in line to the Scottish crown, led the fight to gain independence from England. At one point in the conflict, the English were about to capture him, but he escaped into the forest, so they put bloodhounds on his trail.

Within minutes, the hounds, tracing Bruce's steps, came to the bank of a small river, but they went no farther. The English soldiers urged them on, but the trail was broken; the stream had carried away the scent. A short time later, the crown of Scotland rested on the head of Robert Bruce.

In the same vein, Israel will be pursued into the wilderness and will also escape. And because of their faithfulness to Christ, they, also, will end up with crowns resting on their heads—ruling with Jesus in the kingdom of God.

In this chapter, we have seen that a future war will break out in heaven in which the archangel Michael and his angels will do battle with Satan and his angels. Michael and his angels will triumph in that war, resulting in Satan and his angels being cast out of heaven forever! When Satan is cast to the earth, he will realize that he has a short time left before Jesus returns. As a result, he will attempt to wipe out believing Jews on the earth during the last half of the tribulation period.

However, the focus will immediately change because of a very unusual and amazing occurrence. In our next chapter, we will return to God's two prophets to see this extraordinary happening—one meant to challenge and to encourage us as followers of Jesus.

CHAPTER 14
An Astounding
Turn of Events

In the summer following my seventh-grade year, I worked for a seed corn company detasseling corn. One day, while working in a field, a fellow junior higher was working beside me. For some reason, he made a crack about the mother of a girl working nearby, poking fun at her physical stature because she was pregnant.

The girl thought *I* had made the comment, so, from that day onward, she wouldn't have anything to do with me. In fact, it was worse than that; she turned her family and friends against me. I didn't even know why at the time, but I knew I was being persecuted for something I didn't even do. Yet, no matter how hard I tried to find out why, it was to no avail. Finally, after more than two years, I discovered the reason—and the other boy confessed that it was *he* who had made that remark. At long last, I was exonerated!

From that experience, I discovered that it is no fun to be misunderstood or to be disliked for something I did not do. In addition, I found that it is an exhilarating experience to finally be vindicated.

The Bible tells us that Christians who seek to be followers of the Lord will be misunderstood and hated by the world. After all, Jesus himself was misunderstood and hated. However, there is a sense in which he experienced the exhilaration of vindication in dramatic fashion by his resurrection.[1]

The Two Misunderstood Prophets

According to Revelation 11:2–6, there will be two prophets of God who will be misunderstood and hated. However, they too will be vindicated in a very dramatic fashion.

These two will begin their ministry in Jerusalem on the very day a treaty between Israel and ten other nations goes into effect. In addition, that will be the same day in which the rapture of the church will occur.

These two prophets will prophesy for 1,260 days—exactly three and a half years on a Jewish calendar.[2] As indicated earlier, this is a period of time known as the first half of the day of the Lord, or the first half of the tribulation period.

On day 1,260 of their ministry, this is what will occur, as described in Revelation 11:7: "When they [the two prophets of God] finish their testimony, the beast that ascends out of the bottomless pit [the abyss] will make war against them, overcome them, and kill them."

This verse presents some key details. For example, we not only learn that the two prophets of God are killed by the beast, but we learn *when* they are killed, which tells us something important about God.

They are killed when they *finish* their testimony—and only then. This reveals that God is in complete control. After all, the two prophets are not killed one day before their assignment from God is finished. He will not allow anything to occur to them until his plan for them is completed.

This principle should bring us great comfort and encouragement. Because God is in control—and because he is perfectly good—God will not allow anything to occur to us that is outside his good plan and his perfect timing for us.

Their Killer: The Beast from the Dead

Verse 7 presents another important detail to us. The beast will ascend from the abyss. But, what is the abyss?

An essential clue comes to us from Romans 10:7. This verse uses the same Greek word as the one translated as *bottomless pit* in Revelation 11:7. However, Romans 10:7 translates that word as *the abyss* in this context: " 'Who will descend into the abyss?' (that is, to bring Christ up from the dead)."

When Romans 10:7 describes bringing Christ up from the dead, it speaks of descending into the abyss (bottomless pit) to do so. That means the abyss is the place of the dead. It also means the beast will ascend from the place of the dead. This reveals that the beast has lived before, has died, and will come back—to kill the two prophets.

To underline this understanding of the beast, an angel in Revelation 17:8 announces this: "The beast that you saw was, and is not, and will ascend out of the bottomless pit and go to perdition [destruction]." This announcement means he was once alive, but had died prior to the writing of the book of Revelation, (which was most likely written in AD 68). Therefore, when Revelation 11:7 announces that the beast ascends out of the bottomless pit [the abyss], it means a particular man will come back from the dead in order to "make war against them [the two prophets], overcome them, and kill them."[3]

Why the World Will Hate These Prophets

According to Revelation 11:6—the verse preceding the announcement of the beast ascending from the abyss—these two prophets will be given power by God "to shut heaven so that no rain falls" in the three and a half years of their prophecy and to make waters unusable and undrinkable and "to strike the earth with all plagues as often as they desire."

Through these prophets, God will bring plagues upon the earth, including a three-and-a-half-year drought. He will use these plagues to demonstrate his judgment against sin, but also to draw people to himself. However, the inhabitants of the world will perceive the two prophets as villains and the beast as a hero when he "makes war against the prophets, overcomes them, and kills them."

Following the deaths of the prophets, this scene is presented in Revelation 11:8–9:

> And their dead bodies will lie in the street of the
> great city which spiritually is called Sodom and Egypt,

where also their Lord was crucified. Then those from the peoples, tribes, tongues, and nations will see their dead bodies three-and-a-half days, and not allow their dead bodies to be put into graves.

The Beast's Triumph over the Prophets

The beast will not allow the bodies of the two prophets to be buried. Instead, he will cause their bodies to lie in the street for three and a half days. The intent behind this gross act will be to bring shame to the prophets. But, this will also be his way of declaring his triumph over the God of these prophets. He will seek to convince the world that his defeat of these powerful prophets of God shows that he is even more powerful. It will likely be communicated to the world that, though their God was able to protect them from others who attempted to overcome them, he was not able to protect them from the beast. And by causing the bodies to remain lying in the street, the beast will present a striking reminder that he, and not the God of the prophets, is the all-powerful god.

This reminder will not be missed, for "those from the peoples, tribes, tongues, and nations will see [the] dead bodies" of the prophets. This viewing will prepare them to worship this man as God. For, as we see in Revelation 13:8, "all who dwell on the earth will worship him, whose names have not been written in the Book of Life of the Lamb slain from the foundation of the world."

Likely, Satan and the beast will intend for those bodies to remain in the street to decay and putrefy in order to thoroughly discredit the prophets and the God they represent. However, God will allow the bodies to stay in the street for only three and a half days.

God's Use of Three and a Half Days to Send a Message

This three-and-a-half-day period is mentioned twice within this passage (verses 9 and 11). In the Bible, repetition of a word, phrase, or concept is for the purpose of emphasis in order to drive home a concept. Repetition draws attention to a concept, showing its importance within a particular context. It is God's way of saying, "Don't miss this! I am communicating to you something of importance that I want you to grasp."

Of course, God wants us to catch the meaning of these three and a half days, but it is likely he especially wants another audience to grasp their meaning. That audience would be Jews in Israel who have believed in Christ for eternal life during the first half of the tribulation period. More than likely, God wants those Jewish believers to apprehend the symbolism of that time period.

So, what might be the significance and meaning of the three and a half days in which the bodies of the prophets lie in the street? Here is a hint: What other three and a half have we already encountered in our study of the day of the Lord? The tribulation period is divided into two halves of three and a half years each. God is communicating that the three and a half days of apparent triumph by the beast will represent and signal the three and a half years of exhibited triumph by the beast that will follow. This also means that it will signal three and a half years of persecution that are ahead for Jewish followers of Jesus. Just as the two godly Jewish followers of Jesus were persecuted and experienced three and a half days of supposed defeat by the beast, other godly Jewish followers of Jesus will be persecuted and experience three and a half years of apparent defeat. But, the operative word here is *apparent*, for all faithful followers of Jesus will experience ultimate and eternal vindication—and victory.

A Spiritual Wasteland

This context describes the city in which the prophets' dead bodies lie as "the great city which spiritually is called Sodom and Egypt, where also their Lord was crucified." This city is, of course, Jerusalem. These prophets of God will be put to death in the same city in which their Savior was crucified.

At the time the apostle John recorded the book of Revelation, Jerusalem was such a spiritual wasteland that its judgment was imminent.[4] It will be a spiritual wasteland once more following the deaths of the two prophets and the flight of believing Jews into the wilderness. As a result of the deaths of these prophets of God, this will be the response of the earth-dwellers: "And those who dwell on the earth will rejoice over them, make merry, and send gifts to one another, because these two prophets tormented those who dwell on the earth" (Revelation 11:10).

Surprise!!!

As mentioned earlier, most people on the earth at that time will view the prophets as the source of all of the plagues and torment during the first three and a half years of the tribulation period. Due to the amount of torment the unbelieving world will endure at the hands of these two prophets, they will be so excited about the deaths of these two prophets that they will celebrate and even give gifts to one another.[5]

But, just when the world—and the beast—believe their problems are solved and that they have triumphed over God's two prophets, an immensely surprising event occurs in verses 11 and 12. After thee and a half days, the two prophets rise from the dead and ascend into heaven!

Details in these verses capture the drama of this scene: "The breath of life from God entered them, and they stood on their feet . . . and they heard a loud voice from heaven saying to them, 'Come up here.'" Clearly, these details are present for emphasis and dramatic effect. Each detail causes us to slow down a bit to visualize what this scene might look like.

Can you imagine what will go through the minds of the enemies of these prophets at this point? The very multitude that had just been excitedly and triumphantly celebrating the defeat of the two men who had caused the world such torment up to this point will watch their corpses rise, stand on their feet, and respond to the invitation from heaven by physically ascending into the air and out of sight.

Then, to twist the knife: "In the same hour there was a great earthquake, and a tenth of the city fell. In the earthquake seven thousand people were killed, and the rest were afraid and gave glory to the God of heaven."

As if there is not enough drama with the resurrection and ascension of the two prophets of God, a devastating earthquake will hit. A tenth of the city of Jerusalem will be destroyed and seven thousand people will die.

This is clearly a specific judgment of God upon Jerusalem. The primary reason for this judgment was revealed back in verse 8 when the city was described as "the great city which spiritually is called Sodom and Egypt, where also their Lord was crucified." At that time, Jerusalem will be spiritually bankrupt in the eyes of God because it persecuted and killed God's prophets. In addition, the beast will have desecrated God's temple by this point in time. Thus, it will almost beg for God's judgment to be brought upon it. And the Lord will comply.

In response to these dramatic developments, those who see the ascension of the prophets and who survive the earthquake will give "glory to the God of heaven." While, at first glance, it appears from this that they will believe in Christ for eternal life, there is no mention of that. However, they certainly are affected by the dramatics from God and do give him glory.

It is possible that they direct glory to the God of *heaven*, rather than simply to *God*, because they continue to perceive that the beast is the God of the *earth*. Thus, this hints at a future showdown between the God of heaven and the God of the earth.[6]

Vindication

Consider for another moment that the enemies of these prophets of God will see them stand on their feet and ascend into heaven. What will this scene declare to the adversaries who had been cheering the deaths of the prophets? It will announce the ultimate triumph of the God of the prophets over the beast and his followers, and it will vindicate God's prophets.

The apparent triumph of the world and its immoral values over God and his Word provides an apparent message for us. The message is: Though we will experience apparent defeat by the world, we will experience ultimate vindication one day when God, through Jesus Christ, demonstrates his triumph over the world system. Our *apparent* defeat appears whenever we, as Christians, are attacked by the world in print, in word, or in the media. In addition to attacking Christians as if they were fools, the world tends to attack the truthfulness of the Bible or the historicity of Jesus. However, we can trust that God will indeed ultimately vindicate us and his Word.

The Coming Earthquake

As we have seen, there will be a devastating earthquake in Jerusalem in connection with the resurrection of the two prophets of God—three and a half days following the midpoint of the day of the Lord. As we consider that future cataclysmic event, there is evidence that God has already given Israel a clear warning.

On January 15, 2001, *The Internet Jerusalem Post* ran an article by David Rudge and Yoav Appel that told of an Israeli government statement that predicts an earthquake within the next fifty years, with estimated apocalyptic damage of 10,000 dead, 22,000 injured, and a $50 billion bill! According to Dr. Avi Shapira, head of the Seismological Institute of the Geophysical Division, the question is not "one of *if*, but *when*." He indicated the quake could measure at least seven on the Richter scale!

The resurrection of the two prophets of God will be a setback for the beast. However, as we will see in the next chapter, he will set his course to control the world and to cause all to worship him.

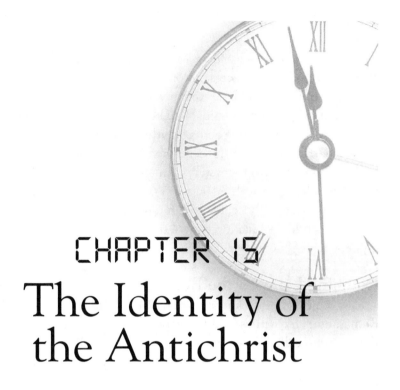

CHAPTER 15
The Identity of the Antichrist

I n September of 1975, the Associated Press ran an article dealing with an investigation in the Waldrop, Oregon area. The inquest involved reports that approximately twenty people sold their property and left the area with a man who claimed to be from outer space. Sheriff detective Ron Sutton said he received a report of one man selling his five-thousand-dollar fishing boat for five dollars, and another of a van that had been given away.

"One hippy is said to have given away his guitar," said Sutton. "To him, that meant everything."

On September 14, 1975, about three hundred people attended a meeting at a motel in this hamlet of about eight hundred people. The message delivered at this meeting was that in the next ten years, people from earth would be taken to another world and a better life. Before they went, they would need to sell their worldly goods and discard their personal relationships. Those attending the meeting were told that there was a camp in Colorado that would prepare them for departure in a UFO.

Oregon state police officer Mel Gibson stated that one man gave away one hundred fifty acres, all of his farm equipment, and three children. The children and land were given to friends.

"It's strange," Gibson said. "I've been around here for about twenty years, but I've never come across anything like this."

Quite strange indeed! It seems amazing that a group of people could be duped into believing a mystery man—to the extent that they give their complete allegiance to him! However, that is an extremely small scale example of what will occur in the future when a false prophet will convince the world's population to give their complete allegiance to another mystery man—one who will receive his authority directly from Satan.

Catching Up with the Beast

At the exact midpoint of the day of the Lord, the soul of a deceased Roman emperor will ascend from the place of the dead and enter into the Assyrian called the king of the North. This will occur after the king has conquered the Middle East and northern Africa and has entered into Jerusalem.

When we examined Revelation 13, we observed that this future ruler will receive all of his authority and rule from Satan. Moreover, we saw that he will receive an apparent mortal wound, but then will appear to rise from the dead, which is the point at which the spirit of the departed Roman emperor will enter his body. In response to the beast's apparent resurrection from the dead, the entire world will worship him and his god, Satan, who will grant the beast his authority.

This newly crowned world ruler will speak against (blaspheme) God and all that belongs to God. His great arrogance will manifest itself as he proclaims himself as God and speaks evilly of the Creator of the universe.

To add to his arrogance, it will be granted to him to make war with believers in Jesus Christ (the saints)[1] and overcome them. He will appear to defeat those who belong to God as he persecutes them through pursuing, arresting, and putting them to death.

God's Allowance of Evil and Suffering

However, the phrase *it was granted to him* presents a far different story than the façade of this king dominating God by conquering his people. Instead, because God is sovereignly in control of all things, then it is *God* who will grant this perceived victory to the beast over believing Jews. This phrase shows that the beast will make war and appear to conquer believers in Christ during that time period only because God will allow it—and only because doing so will be one aspect of accomplishing his plan. So, while the beast convinces the world that he has full power over the earth, God shows us it is *he*—and he alone—who is in control.

This thought is difficult for some to digest. However, God only allows what is according to his perfectly good plan. Because he will greatly and eternally reward those who faithfully suffer for Christ, he will use the beast's persecution of believers for their good. And, as we saw earlier with God's two prophets, God will ultimately and eternally vindicate followers of Christ who experience apparent defeat at the hands of their enemy. This is partly why God has allowed the suffering and deaths of his prophets in the past.

Furthermore, persecution grows the faith of believers in order to conform them more to the image of God's Son.[2] This also leads to great reward in God's kingdom.

Moreover, persecution glorifies God. For example, persecution of God's people heaps up judgment for the persecutor. In the case of the beast, it will build to a crescendo so that when God *does* judge, he will dynamically demonstrate his justice and righteousness, as well as his power and authority. This will lead to him being glorified forever by those in his kingdom.

The Beast's Authority

In addition to the beast being granted the power to overcome some of God's people, we are told that authority was given him over every tribe, tongue, and nation. As verse 8 declares: "All who dwell on the earth will worship him, whose names have not been written in the Book of Life of the Lamb slain from the foundation of the world."[3]

We have already seen the source of the beast's authority. As verse 2 announces: "The dragon gave him his power, his throne, and great authority." But, as we have also seen, ultimately the beast will have that authority over the world because God has granted for him to have it.

And his authority will be extensive! He will rule over every tribe, tongue, and nation! The entire world will be in the palm of his hand.

But, of course, this does not mean that every person on the planet will be under his control—only those whose names have not been written in the Book of Life will worship the beast. Let's compare this with Revelation 20:15, which states: "And anyone not found written in the Book of Life was cast into the lake of fire."

The lake of fire refers to eternal separation from God, and since the book of Revelation specifically tells us that the lake of fire will be the habitation of Satan and the beast,[4] we can know the identity of those whose names have not been written in the Book of Life. They are those who have not believed in Christ for eternal life.[5]

We learn in Revelation 14:9–11 of the fate of those who will worship the beast:

> "If anyone worships the beast and his image, and receives his mark on his forehead or on his hand, . . . He shall be tormented with fire and brimstone in the presence of the holy angels and in the presence of the Lamb. And the smoke of their torment [in the lake of fire] ascends forever and ever; and they have no rest day or night, who worship the beast and his image, and whoever receives the mark of his name."

Those Who Will *Not* Worship the Beast

If we look closely at what these verses are saying, we will learn something very important about who will worship the beast and who will not. We learn that only those who will *never* believe in Christ for eternal life will worship the beast.

We see this truth by observing that the promise in these verses is to anyone and everyone who worships the beast by receiving his mark on their person. The result of worshipping the beast is to experience the eternal destiny of the lake of fire, which involves torment forever apart from God.

This promise cannot include anyone who has believed in Jesus Christ for eternal life. After all, Jesus guarantees that anyone who has believed in him for eternal life will not experience condemnation,[6] which includes eternal separation from God. Once one believes in Jesus Christ, he then already possesses *everlasting* life,[7] which can never be lost.[8] Or, to put it another way, once one believes in Christ, he is born into God's family as one of his children,[9] and he cannot become spiritually unborn any more than any person can physically. Neither can he become un-resurrected once he receives resurrection life.[10] Nor can *anyone* (includ-ing himself) spiritually pluck him away from God's eternal grasp;[11] once he receives eternal life, he cannot spiritually perish.[12]

This means God will protect believers from worshiping the beast. Faithful believers, of course, will choose not to worship the beast. How-ever, while unfaithful believers could be tempted to give their loyalty to the beast to try to protect themselves and their families, God will not allow it. Since elsewhere we learn that unfaithful believers will not physically survive the tribulation period, it seems God will use the tim-ing of their deaths to prevent them from succumbing to the mark of the beast. In other words, they will be put to death before they can give their allegiance to the beast.[13]

The Beast's Helper

As we continue in Revelation chapter 13, we find that the beast has a helper, who is introduced in verse 11: "Then I saw another beast com-ing up out of the earth, and he had two horns[14] like a lamb and spoke like a dragon."

The word *earth* in this verse is the same word for *land*. If it were translated as land, instead of earth, it would be a clear reference to the land of Israel.[15] In fact, the word *land* seems to be a preferable translation because of the Jewish orientation of the book of Revelation. If so, this tells us that this second beast is Jewish.

Though this may not seem believable, there is a historical precedent for this possibility. It is found back in the second century BC, where there was a ruler over the land of Israel who seemed to be evil incarnate. He was called Antiochus IV, but the book of Daniel refers to him as the king of the North. If this sounds familiar, it should. In fact, a descrip-tion of him appears in the very same chapter as the future king of the North—in Daniel chapter 11.

He was not only purposefully placed in the same chapter as the fu-ture king of the North, his description immediately precedes that of the future king who will become the beast. Though he appears in verses 21–35, and the future king is described in verses 36–45, there is no apparent break between the two descriptions; they appear to flow together. At first reading, one might think verses 36 and those following continue to describe the same king—that is, until arriving at verse 40 and the mention of "the time of the end" (the end times). The reason for this apparent confusion of identity is very purposeful. By presenting Antiochus IV as sliding into the description of the future king of the North, it demonstrates that the king of verses 21–35 is a type, or symbolic forerunner, of the king of verses 36–45. That means that the *future* king of the North will bear similarities to the king of the North from the second century BC.

Antiochus IV was a Gentile king in the land of Israel, just as the future king will be. The *past* king of the North persecuted faithful Jews, as will the future king of the North. Antiochus IV abominated the Jewish temple by entering the holy of holies, as will the future king.

The similarities between the two kings do not stop there. In fact, there appears to be one more fascinating similarity. Antiochus IV had the Jewish high priest, Onias III, killed because he would not work with the king to cause the Jews to worship him. He replaced that high priest in 171 BC with the priest's wicked brother, Jason, because of Jason's allegiance (and bribe) to Antiochus. At that point, the king of the North had a Jew in a very influential position in Israel to advance his cause among the rest of the Jews.

It seems that a similar scenario will occur once more. Once the future king of the North becomes the beast, a Jew will step in as his "high priest," so to speak. Only, this Jew will be given great, miraculous power by Satan in order to advance the cause of this king; he will cause others (including other Jews) to worship the king. Interestingly, he is also described in Revelation 13 as a beast—but a beast from the land rather than from the sea.

The Character of the Second Beast

It is likely that both he and the king will be described as beasts because of their character. By being connected with the same moniker (beast), they are portrayed as being on the same level and working for the same cause. Though they will have differing roles, both of them will receive authority from Satan to advance his "kingdom" work.

The apostle John pictures this beast from the land as having two horns like a lamb but speaking like a dragon. This means that he will come across to the world as meek and mild like a lamb, but he will speak the message of Satan. Like some religious leaders today, he will be soft-spoken, speaking the language of love and unity and acceptance. However, his teaching will be Satan-inspired. Again, like much religious teaching today, it will go against the gospel of grace, contradicting the free offer of eternal life by believing in Jesus Christ alone for it. Furthermore, like much religious teaching today, he will encourage people to worship a different god than the God of the Bible.

The False Prophet

Jesus illustrates this concept regarding the second beast by this exhortation to the multitude in Matthew 7:15: "Beware of false prophets, who come to you in sheep's clothing, but inwardly they are ravenous wolves." What did Jesus mean by this? He meant that false prophets may appear harmless, like one of the sheep (that is, a believer in Christ); however, they are not as they appear.

Jesus' warning is appropriate to the second beast for more than one reason. We get further insight into this beast when we observe what he is called later in the book of Revelation. After chapter 13, he appears three more times. First, he appears in this interesting scene in 16:13: "And I saw three unclean spirits like frogs coming out of the mouth of the dragon, out of the mouth of the beast, and out of the mouth of the false prophet." In context, this verse describes Satan, along with the first and second beasts, sending out demons to gather the kings of the earth and their armies to prepare to battle against Christ at his return.

We learn more about the second beast in 19:20, where we not only see the destiny of this man, but we find out about his power, his role, and his character. In regard to his power, we learn he is able to work miraculous signs. His role, revealed through his power, is to cause people to worship the first beast. His character is revealed by the role he plays— deceiving the world so they will worship the first beast, meaning that even though he will be the world's foremost religious leader, he will be extremely deceitful.

Finally, one other verse in Revelation displays the second beast's destiny. In Revelation 20:10, we see that God has ordained his eternal experience—that of torment in the lake of fire forever and ever!

All three of these verses we just visited reveal something else about the second beast. Notice what he is called in each: "the false prophet" (16:13), "the false prophet" (19:20), and "the false prophet" (20:10). It is as if God is seeking to drive home a point to us.

He is called the false prophet because, like prophets of God, he is able to do miraculous signs. But, unlike *true* prophets, he deceives people; he does not bring God's message to the world. And, in each case, he is called *the* false prophet because he will be the *ultimate* false prophet—the false prophet of all false prophets.

Interestingly, prophets in Scripture were Jewish.[16] His description as a false prophet may indicate he will imitate Jewish prophets of old, which may lend more evidence to the view that he is Jewish.

Indeed, Jesus warns Jewish believers in the tribulation period about being deceived by false prophets.[17] It is more likely Jewish believers would be tempted to be deceived if there were Jewish false prophets and, especially, if *the* false prophet—the one who can do miraculous signs—were Jewish.

Who *Really* Is the Antichrist?

Though many Christians refer to the coming world ruler (the one we have been calling the beast) as the Antichrist, we may need to re-evaluate that title in light of Revelation 13 and the places where the word *Antichrist* appears. The only writer in the Bible who uses the term Antichrist is the apostle John—the same individual who wrote the book of Revelation. He uses the term only in 1 John and 2 John.

The biggest clue to the meaning of the term can be found in 1 John 4:1–3, where the apostle John is warning of false prophets—those who deny that Jesus Christ has come in the flesh. According to these verses, false prophets in the world are a preview of the ultimate false prophet, who is the Antichrist. This would indicate that the Antichrist is *the* false prophet. Therefore, the Antichrist is not the world ruler, but is instead the false prophet.

The Role and Abilities of the Antichrist

We have seen that the second beast is the false prophet, the Antichrist. In Revelation 13:12, we learn that the false prophet will demonstrate the same authority as the first beast. In addition, he will cause the world to worship the first beast.

Verse 13 shows us how he will seek to accomplish that purpose: "He performs great signs, so that he even makes fire come down from heaven on the earth in the sight of men." By making fire come down from heaven, he will imitate a great Old Testament prophet by the name of Elijah. In 1 Kings 18:38, Elijah called upon the Lord who, in response to Elijah's prayer, brought fire down from heaven. Ironically, the fire called down by Elijah was meant to eliminate idolatry, while the fire that will be called down by the false prophet is meant to promote idolatry—via worship of the image of the beast.[18]

The Miraculous Deception of the Antichrist

The false prophet's ability to deceive is portrayed in verses 14–15 of Revelation 13:

> And he deceives those who dwell on the earth by those signs which he was granted to do in the sight of the beast, telling those who dwell on the earth to make an image to the beast who was wounded by the sword and lived. He was granted power to give breath [a spirit] to the image of the beast, that the image of the beast should both speak and cause as many as would not worship the image of the beast to be killed.

There definitely seems to be something very upside down about what is presented in verses 14–15. People will create an image and will then worship their creation. It, of course, makes sense for creation to worship its creator, but not for a creator to worship his creation.

Earlier we saw that the false prophet will be able to perform a miracle by making fire come down from heaven. But, that is not the only miracle he will perform. As we see in verses 14–15, he will give "life" to the image after it is built. The result of granting it "life" is that the image will speak and cause any who will not worship the image to be killed.

It is interesting that the passage does not give us an explanation of this "miracle." Apparently, God wants us to get the feel of how the world could be deceived by this miracle. If the explanation were readily available in the passage, we would not grapple with it as much, and we would not see as well how the world could be fooled.

There is a simple explanation of this miracle. It is most likely a case of demon possession of an inanimate object, which, interestingly, is the only case of demon possession in all of prophecy. Though this will probably be accomplished by demon possession, the world will believe this is truly a miracle—the miracle of the talking image.

What is even more significant than the image being able to speak is that it is able to bring about the deaths of any who do not worship it. Again, we are not given an explanation of how this will occur, but, apparently, the demon possessing the image will be given the power to kill.

The fact that miraculous signs will be associated with the false prophet aligns with the description we see in Revelation 19:20 when the beast and the false prophet are captured by Jesus at his return: "Then the beast was captured, and with him the false prophet who worked *signs* in his presence, by which he deceived those who received the mark of the beast and those who worshiped his image" (emphasis added).

In connection with this, there is the description in 2 Thessalonians 2:9–10 that explains that the "power, signs, and lying wonders" of the Antichrist will stem from Satan, and will be made evident to the world by the false prophet. The authority Satan will give the beast is the power to make war (Revelation 13:4) and to rule the world, but the authority Satan will give the false prophet is the power to work great signs and wonders.

Division of Power

Based on this thought, the question then becomes: Why does Satan divide up the power that he gives to these two? In other words, why would he not give all the power to one man? Apparently, Satan will not trust all that power to one man, as he may believe that one man with all that power will be tempted to rebel against him. It is also possible he will be able to better control them by dividing up the power. That way, each needs the other, and they each will need Satan.

As we have seen, the false prophet will play a vital role in causing the world to worship the beast. In connection with that, he will be the one to institute the mark of the beast—but more on that in the next chapter.

CHAPTER 16
The Mark of the Beast

D uring World War I, the German treasury was low in gold. Its budget was unbalanced. Inflation went sky high.

In 1919, the German mark was worth twenty US cents, or four marks to the dollar. Within four years it plunged in value to seven thousand marks to the dollar in January, one hundred sixty thousand to the dollar in July, and one million to the dollar in August.

Panic and madness swept the country. People carried suitcases of money to buy a sausage. And the mark kept falling—until, when in November of that year, 4.2 trillion marks were needed to equal one dollar in buying power.

The value of every pension was wiped out. All security was gone. Then the people were ready to listen to anyone who could voice their bitterness. Enter Adolph Hitler.

In a 1979 *Time* magazine article entitled, "Inflation: Who Is Hurt Worst?" forty-three-year-old Arthur Garcia seemed to speak out of great frustration for a number of people. One could understand why, because at the time, he was supporting a wife and five children on a salary of $19,000 as a worker in US Steel's South Chicago mill. In the article, he was quoted making this statement: "You really want to revolt, but what can you do? I keep waiting for a miracle—for some guy who isn't born yet. And when he comes, we'll follow him like he was John the Baptist."

What Will Taking the Mark Mean?

This is no longer 1979, but signs are evident that both the US and the world's economies are shaky. Things could happen quickly, setting the stage for the world to receive a man who will control the global economy in the way described in Revelation 13:16–17. This man will be the one described in Revelation as the false prophet and the Antichrist who will cause everyone to receive a mark[1] on their right hand or on their foreheads. This will not be an addition to the role he will play, but part of it.

According to verse 12 in the same chapter of Revelation, the Antichrist "causes the earth and those who dwell in it to worship the first beast." The *first* beast is the one we have been calling the beast. He is the one who will be given the authority to rule the world for forty-two months (Revelation 13:5).

So, what is the real significance of taking the mark of the beast? What does it have to do with worshipping the beast? The book of Revelation provides us with the answer to these questions in verses 9 and 11 in chapter 14. In both of these verses, receiving the mark of the beast is connected with worshipping the beast. Of course, both verses also mention the worship of his image in conjunction with worshipping him, but this is just a way of emphasizing the worship of the beast. In addition, worshipping the image shows us one way people will worship him—by bowing to the physical image of the beast.

The connection between taking the mark of the beast and worshipping him (his image) is also made in 16:2: "So the first [angel] went and poured out his bowl upon the earth, and a foul and loathsome sore came upon the men who had the mark of the beast and those who worshiped his image." This verse describes a specific judgment of God during the last half of the future tribulation period upon those who possess the mark of the beast and who worship his image.

Three chapters later, in 19:20, the connection is once more made between taking the mark of the beast and worshipping him. These verses reveal that the beast and the false prophet will meet their ends by being captured at the return of Christ to the earth and being "cast alive into the lake of fire." By this revelation, we also discover something else: Those who *received* the mark of the beast prior to this scene are the same ones who *worshiped* his image up to this point.

Our final example of this connection in the book of Revelation is found in 20:4. There the apostle John describes his vision of seeing those martyred for their faithfulness to Christ during the day of the Lord ruling in the future kingdom of God upon the earth: "Then I saw the souls of those who had been beheaded for their witness to Jesus and for the word of God, who had not worshiped the beast or his image, and had not received his mark on their foreheads or on their hands."

Clearly, in each of the examples we just viewed, there is a relationship between receiving the mark and worshipping the beast. But, the relationship between the two actions seems fuzzy unless we understand a particular grammatical concept.

In the verses we cited, the two actions are connected by the word *and*, which makes it seem as if they are two different and distinct acts.[2] However, *and* is used here as simply a connector, joining the act of taking the mark of the beast with that of worshipping the beast. This means that to take this mark of the beast is to commit to worship him as God. It further indicates that all who receive this mark will realize that when they do so, they are vowing to worship the beast.

The Identification of Those Who Will Worship the Beast

So who are they? Which individuals will vow to worship the beast during the last half of the tribulation period?

They are identified in Revelation 13:16 as "small and great, rich and poor, free and slave." These phrases employ merisms. A merism is a figure of speech in which polar opposites, or contrasts, are used to show the *total* of the opposites, including everything and everyone in between. This means that these phrases are used to emphasize that *all* unbelievers on the earth will receive the mark of the beast. The three contrasting pairs of "small and great, rich and poor, free and slave" emphasize that no one is exempt, no matter what their social, class, financial, or freedom status might be.

Motivation for Taking the Mark of the Beast

So, what will be the major motivation for receiving the mark of the beast? In order for everyone to buy into the concept of taking the mark, there must be a powerful motivation—one that will unite all classifications of people around the globe. The motivation for receiving the mark and vowing to worship the beast will be this: one will not be able to buy or sell without it. That is certainly a very powerful motivation for anyone who does not have faith in God to provide for their needs.

Think about what this will mean for those who choose not to receive the mark. They will not be able to purchase any of the necessities of life such as food, clothing, and shelter, let alone anything else. Neither will they be able to sell anything. In other words, individuals who refuse to worship this world ruler will seem to make the choice to starve themselves and their families.

Those Who Will *Not* Take the Mark of the Beast

But, as powerful as the motivation will be to take the mark, there will be those who will not do it. We get a glimpse of that thought from Revelation 13:8, which announces who will receive the mark, and by so doing, it also proclaims who will not: "All who dwell on the earth will worship him [the beast], whose names have not been written in the Book of Life of the Lamb slain from the foundation of the world."

All who do not believe in Christ for eternal life will worship the beast, meaning they will receive the mark of the beast. In making that statement, the apostle John implies that believers in Christ will *not* receive the mark.

We are given an even clearer statement about who will not take the mark of the beast from Revelation 14:9–11. In this passage, the wrath of God and the eternal torment described are two different experiences, though both are experienced by those receiving the mark of the beast. The wrath of God is something that is experienced temporally—during one's present, mortal life[3]—while the other experience mentioned in Revelation 14:9–11 occurs eternally. Therefore, one who receives the mark of the beast will experience God's temporal judgment during the last half of the tribulation period[4] *and* eternal torment in the lake of fire.

This shows that *all* unbelievers will receive the mark of the beast, while *no* believer in Christ will receive the mark. How is that shown?

144

Revelation 14 declares that "anyone who worships the beast . . . shall be tormented with fire and brimstone . . . forever and ever."

The Bible clearly teaches that when one believes in Christ for eternal life, he has eternal life.[5] Because it is *eternal*, it cannot last merely ten, twenty, or thirty years and then be lost—or it would not be eternal. Therefore, the proclamation of Revelation 14—that all who receive the mark of the beast will experience eternal torment—shows that a believer in Christ will not receive the mark of the beast.

Why Believers Will Not Take the Mark of the Beast

How is it that *no* believer will receive the mark? Obviously, faithful believers will choose not to worship the beast. But, will not unfaithful believers—those who might drift from God—be tempted to take the mark? It will take great faith to refuse to take the mark because, humanly speaking, that will seem to mean a certain but slow death for them and their families. Will not those believers whose hearts are lukewarm—or worse—be tempted to receive the mark of the beast in order to provide for themselves and their families?

The answer to that question is yes; undoubtedly, some believers will be tempted to receive the mark of the beast. But, God can certainly protect them from taking the mark. One way he can do that is by causing their deaths before they can take that very wrong and disastrous step.

It is not unheard of for God to take the lives of believers because of their unfaithfulness. This occurred, for example, in Acts 5, when Ananias and Sapphira lied to God; it also happened when some of the Corinthian Christians got drunk at the Lord's Supper. In addition to illustrating its possibility, God has clearly warned about its occurrence to believers again and again.[6] Specifically, Jesus implied that God will take the lives of believers during the last half of the tribulation period by this announcement in Matthew 24:13: "But he who endures to the end shall be saved."

There are two key words that must be understood in this verse in order to grasp what Jesus is saying here. One of those is the word *saved*.

Oftentimes when Christians see this word, they have a knee-jerk reaction to the understanding that it refers to being saved from hell. However, the vast majority of the uses of *save* or *salvation* (its noun form) in the Bible have nothing to do with salvation from hell. To discover the meaning of this word, one simply needs to look nine verses later in the same chapter—to verse 22. There the word *save* clearly refers to physical deliverance. In other words, it shows us that the meaning of *save* in verse 13 relates to saving the physical life.

The word *endures* in verse 13 is a word that is used in the New Testament referring to Christians remaining faithful to Christ through difficult times. Of course, the ultimate difficult time for believers will be the last half of the tribulation period. Therefore, the statement, "he who endures to the end shall be saved," means this: the Christian who remains faithful to Christ through the difficulties of the tribulation period will physically survive the tribulation.

This also implies that unfaithful believers will not survive the tribulation period. Since God is in control of life and death, this statement by Jesus further indicates that God will take the lives of unfaithful Christians during the tribulation period. This adds to the evidence that though some unfaithful believers may be tempted to receive the mark of the beast, one way God may protect unfaithful believers from taking it is to take their lives before they can take the mark.

The Incredible Examples of Faithful Jewish Believers

To begin to appreciate what faithful Jewish believers in Christ may have to endure during the last three and a half years before Christ returns, let us return to Jesus' warning and exhortation to them in Matthew 24:15–21 of the abomination of desolation, which refers to the beast entering into the holy of holies of the temple of God. Upon this act, (which will follow his murder of God's two prophets), the beast will abominate the temple and begin his desolating activity.

The desolation will begin when the beast sends his armies out to round up believing Jews for the purpose of putting them to death. Understanding this truth enables us to see why Jesus would command the response he does to the Jewish believers addressed in this passage. Jesus warns that when the abomination takes place, the desolation will immediately follow. That is why, when the beast enters into the temple in Jerusalem, his future Jewish followers should leave immediately—without delay of any kind. In fact, they are to leave so quickly that they are not to even take the time to enter into their homes to retrieve any of their belongings. This means that if they are to preserve their physical lives, they will not be able to take anything but the clothes on their backs.

Undoubtedly, the two prophets of God will teach the Jewish believers about this warning and exhortation by Jesus in Matthew 24, but, in addition, he will impart to them much more information about the great tribulation—the three and half years of persecution they will experience. Due to the Jewishness of the book of Revelation, the information the two prophets will impart to their Jewish audience during their 1,260 days of ministry will definitely include teaching from that book.

This means that these Jewish believers will know what is coming, including the knowledge that they will not be able to buy or sell anything without having the mark of the beast. So, to heed Jesus' command to flee Jerusalem and Judea at the abomination of desolation—with only the clothes on their backs—will take great faith in him. They will have to believe that the Lord will miraculously provide for them for three and a half years, while taking no provisions with them into the wilderness!

These future Jewish believers serve as great examples for us to follow. Can you imagine being in their shoes—trusting God for all of their needs, with no visible means of obtaining those needs, while knowing their situation will continue for three and a half years? Imagine losing your job, your house, your bank account, your retirement—all of your possessions—and realizing that, as you are completely wiped out in the present time, your situation will not change for more than three years!

But, while knowing all of that up front, they will still make the incredible—and wise—choice to obey Jesus when the beast enters into the temple. Their examples of trusting God can strongly encourage us to trust him in any challenging area of our lives, including the areas of God's provision for finances, parenting, marriage, work, and health issues. And we can be particularly encouraged to trust God against all odds by knowing that God will not let them down when *they* rely on him, and neither will he let us down when *we* trust him.

Understanding the Positioning of the Mark

As we return to the presentation of the mark of the beast in Revelation 13, the question that arises is: Why would the mark go on the right hand or on the forehead? Answering this may move us into speculation, but there are clues in Scripture to guide us toward the answer.

The Old Testament presents the right hand as a metaphor for strength and power.[7] The right hand was also used for making a vow or a commitment, as illustrated in Isaiah 62:8, where the Lord vows by his right hand that in the future he will no longer give Israel's crops to her enemies.

From these Old Testament examples, we can see that the future mark placed on the right hand signifies that one is vowing to give his strength—his very being—to serve and worship the beast. However, some unbelievers will also receive the mark of the beast on the forehead. So, what is the meaning in its placement on that particular part of the anatomy?

The Bible presents examples of placing a turban on the head of the High Priest, with the message "Holiness to the Lord," to remind the priest and all of Israel that the priest is set apart to serve God alone.[8] In Revelation, the 144,000 are shown to be set aside for special service to God with a seal on their foreheads,[9] while faithful believers will have the eternal reward of having the name of God placed on their foreheads to demonstrate that they are set aside for very special and honored service to God forever.

This all seems to indicate that those who receive the mark on the forehead will be setting themselves apart for service to the beast—and to him alone. Therefore, whether individuals in the last half of the tribulation period receive the mark on the right hand or on the forehead, the act seems to symbolize that the individual so doing is committing to give himself wholeheartedly to serve and worship the beast.

666

In looking again at verse 18, we see this: "Here is wisdom. Let him who has understanding calculate the number of the beast, for it is the number of a man: His number is 666."

In response to this verse, many have attempted to calculate the number of the beast in order to identify him. As Zane Hodges explained, "this may well be a misguided exercise."[10] He went on to surmise this:

> Perhaps—but only *perhaps!*—the Beast's name can be expressed in Hebrew or Greek characters and the numeric values of the letters will yield the sum of 666. It is equally possible that the "number of his

name" is his own registration number in this system and that the sum of its digits is 666. After all, the King will no doubt have the most affluent account available to anyone on earth. In that case, a digit series like 100-544-22 (sum = 666) would fit. Perhaps all other registration numbers will involve variations of these digits (like 510-144-12 [sum = 666 again]). Or perhaps 666 may be interfaced with other digits (examples, 76-76-76, or 561-464-262). The alternative registration format could involve the actual letters of his name followed by, or interfaced with, other letters or digits: (Name)-5271-3460, or TC(N)-FY(A)-GP(M)-(E), where NAME stand for whatever letters his name may actually have. In other words, the actual letters of this man's name could precede a series of numbers (or letters), or the letters of his name could be scattered out and mixed with other letters (or with numbers).[11]

Mr. Hodges then expressed this resulting thought: "Obviously, men will not be able to really identify this King until he is actually on the scene and has begun to fulfill the prophecies of Scripture."[12]

Though we cannot calculate his identity at this time, God is communicating something about the beast by giving us his number in Revelation 13:18. What might be his point in the use of 666? In other words, what might the number 6 represent, and why is it repeated in this fashion?

God seems to be announcing by this number that the beast is merely a man. The number 6 is representative of man, who was created on the sixth day of creation. In addition, while the number 7 is the number of God—the number of perfection—the number 6 falls short of God. Hence, it represents man in two ways—by his creation and by his status before a perfect God. The repetition of the number 6 emphasizes that, though this man is worshipped by the world as God, he is merely a man—for his number "is the number of a man." There is only one God, and this man is not he!

As we have seen, this system, represented by the effort to cause all humanity to receive the mark of the beast, will seemingly make things even more difficult for Jews who believe in Christ during the last half of the tribulation period. However, in our next chapter, we will see by way of a parable of Jesus the importance of those Jews remaining faithful to Christ to the very end.

CHAPTER 17
Ten Virgins

A college student sent the following terse e-mail to his mother: "Mom, have failed everything. Prepare Dad."

The next day the student received this reply: "Dad prepared; prepare yourself!"

As important as it was for that student to be prepared to meet his father, it is far more important for believers in Christ to be prepared to meet their Lord. The New Testament often exhorts us to prepare ourselves for the return of Christ, and Jesus told more than one parable to drive home that important concept.

One of those parables is recorded in Matthew in order to prepare Jews who will believe in Jesus during the tribulation period, but, so that we would not feel left out, Jesus included a warning for us, as well. Moreover, this same parable, located in Matthew 25:1–13 provides us with a clearer understanding of Jewish believers and God's role for them during the tribulation period upon the earth.

The Background of This Parable

This parable is part of Jesus' Olivet Discourse—so called because he gave this extended teaching to his disciples on the Mount of Olives. Located just east of Jerusalem, this is the very mountain upon which he will return to the earth.[1]

In the discourse, Jesus taught about what will take place during the tribulation period in response to questions by the disciples. However, though Jesus utilized their questions to teach his first-century disciples about the day of the Lord, he was actually directing this material—particularly the warnings within it—to Jewish disciples who will live through the future calamitous time he was describing.

This last point will be important to keep in mind as we seek to understand the parable. In fact, if we do not grasp that truth, we will miss the point Jesus is communicating.

The Introduction of the Parable

With that in mind, we will begin our look at this revealing parable with verse 1: " 'Then the kingdom of heaven shall be likened to ten virgins who took their lamps and went out to meet the bridegroom.' "

This verse is an introduction that provides us with some major pieces of information about the story. In this statement, Jesus announces that this parable will illustrate the kingdom of heaven in some respect. Based on the message of this parable, this means it will reveal different experiences of (rewards for) believers in the future kingdom of God based on their respective foolish or wise responses as indicated in this parable.

In addition, in verse 1 we are introduced to the characters of this story—ten virgins and a bridegroom. We are also informed of the first action of the parable—that of the virgins taking their lamps and going out to meet the bridegroom. This information gives us a major clue to the background of this story, which can help us understand it better.

The Jewish Wedding Ceremony

This first verse shows us that this story stems from, and revolves around, a Jewish wedding ceremony, as described below:

> In late afternoon or early evening, the bridegroom would set out from his home with a group of his companions, one of whom would function like our

best man. The groom would then go out to a predetermined meeting place, such as the house of the bride,
where he would meet the bride with her ladies in waiting. The two wedding parties would merge, and they
would return to the house where the wedding supper
would be held, usually at the home of the bridegroom,
where the father would preside. If the father happened
to be a wealthy man, he would provide a large amount
of food and festive entertainment, which might involve some young virgin girls.

These virgins would wait at the home of the groom until the wedding party would approach. They would then light their torches and go
out to meet the wedding party. Then, they would light the pathway back
to the house where the wedding supper was to be held. When the party
was seated, these virgins would perform the torch dance—a series of patterns and movements with the torches. This dance would continue until
their torches went out.[2]

The parable in Matthew 25 is about these virgins. But, since the
parable as a whole is based on the Jewish wedding ceremony described
above, we can gain even more insight into this story through other passages that reveal the identities of the characters and events associated
with it.

Identity of the Characters

The first step in understanding the parable is to determine who the
characters represent. Ephesians 5:23–25 provides us with great insight
into their identities by an analogy that identifies the bride of Christ as
the church and the bridegroom as Christ himself. The church is the universal body of believers, consisting of everyone who has believed in Jesus
Christ for eternal life from its inception—the day of Pentecost in the
first century, as presented in Acts 2—until its removal from the earth at
the rapture of the church.

This is an important understanding, for it can reveal who the virgins
in our parable are *not*, as well as who they are. Because of much misun-
derstanding of this particular parable, it is necessary to point out that in
the Jewish wedding ceremony the virgins are not the bride. Therefore, if

the bride is the church, then the virgins in our parable cannot represent those who make up the church. Again, this would mean that the virgins cannot be identified as believers in Christ during the period of time that began at the first century and will extend until the rapture.

So, who *are* these virgins? Since this parable is part of a unit of teaching on the future tribulation period,[3] then it must involve characters who will live during that period of time. God's focus during that era is upon Israel, and since this parable is based on a Jewish ceremony, it makes sense that these virgins represent Jews in the land of Israel during the day of the Lord.

In addition, since the parable makes no statement about the need for faith in Christ for eternal life, and because it deals with a "kingdom of heaven" truth, the virgins in the parable must represent those who already have received eternal life. This means they represent Jewish believers in Christ during the tribulation period.

Finally, as we saw earlier, the church will be taken off the earth via the rapture *before* the tribulation period begins. Furthermore, those participating in a Jewish wedding ceremony are Jewish. This means the virgins represent Jewish believers during the tribulation period.

Interestingly, the 144,000 Jewish believers are described as "virgins,"[4] adding to the concept that the virgins in this parable are Jewish believers in the tribulation period. However, the virgins in the parable refer to *all* Jewish believers in the tribulation period, not just the 144,000 that represent one segment of all Jews who will believe in Christ during the day of the Lord.

The Bridegroom's Home

Based on the description of the Jewish wedding ceremony we saw earlier, the bridegroom returns home, where he is met outside his home by the virgins. And, as we have noted, Jesus Christ is the bridegroom of the parable. However, this still leaves some questions to be answered, such as: Where is his home? To what city will he return? And where might the virgins, the Jewish believers, meet him when he returns? To help us answer these, we will turn to two Old Testament passages— Zechariah 14:2–4 and Jeremiah 3:17.

Zechariah 14:2–4 reveals that the city to which the bridegroom will return is Jerusalem. This is reinforced by Jeremiah 3:17 as it presents

Jerusalem to be the habitation of Jesus when he rules upon the earth: " 'At that time [after Jesus returns to the earth] Jerusalem shall be called the Throne of the Lord, and all the nations shall be gathered to it, to the name of the Lord, to Jerusalem.' "

Thus, Jesus will return to Jerusalem in order to rule from there. The virgins, then, will meet him outside of Jerusalem at the Mount of Olives.

To help us understand this parable even better, we need to remember that Israel and Jerusalem are the earthly home of the bridegroom, the Lord Jesus Christ. Some two thousand years ago, he left that home to find his bride. When he meets his bride, catching the Christian church up in the air, he will return to his home (Jerusalem) with her. When he returns to set up his kingdom, he will be met on earth by those who have believed in him and have gone forth to meet him. These are the virgins of our parable.

The Virgins and Their Lamps

Now, let us continue in our parable by looking at verses 2–5:

> "Now five of them were wise, and five were foolish. Those who were foolish took their lamps and took no oil with them, but the wise took oil in their vessels with their lamps. But while the bridegroom was delayed, they all slumbered and slept."

Here we learn a bit more about these virgins. The Lord calls five of them wise, while he identifies the other five as foolish. In addition, we learn why five are considered wise; it is because they took extra oil for their lamps.

The lamps in the ancient Jewish wedding ceremony were actually torches that consisted of long poles or sticks, with rags wrapped around one end. The rags were dipped in oil and lit. However, they would burn only for about fifteen minutes, so they had to be repeatedly soaked in oil in order to be able to continue to burn. This helps us see the importance of taking extra oil for the lamps—in order to keep them burning. Certainly, the virgins would want their lamps burning at the arrival of the bridegroom; it would be shameful for them if they met the bridegroom with unlit lamps. Therefore, those who prepared well by obtaining extra oil would be viewed by the bridegroom as wise, while others would be seen as foolish.

A Time to Rest

At this point, the parable mentions that "while the bridegroom was delayed, they all slumbered and slept." While at times in Scripture slumbering is a metaphor for spiritual dullness, it is not presented as a bad thing in these verses. After all, *all* of these virgins slumbered and slept while they waited for the bridegroom—even the wise virgins. Had sleeping during this time been wrong, *wise* virgins would not have slept.

The folly is not found in going to sleep, since the wise ones did so as well. If the groom and wedding party are not going to be there until sometime after midnight, then the virgins might as well rest while they wait.

Earlier in this two-chapter unit (Matthew 24 and 25) on the tribulation period, Jesus told a parable in which a servant is condemned because he says in his heart, "My lord delays his coming" (Matthew 24:48). That earlier parable (verses 45–51) illustrates the current time before the rapture of the church in which there is no prophetic event between us and the coming in the air of Christ. Thus, we are to look for Jesus' coming for us as imminent; it could occur at any time.

However, the parable of the ten virgins is about the revealed prophetic program of the future day of the Lord. Those knowledgeable of that era will include Jews who believe in Christ during the first half of the tribulation period and who will be taught by God's two prophets in Jerusalem. They will realize that, during the unfolding of the seven years, there will be a period of time before the Bridegroom will come for them. They will understand there will be an opportunity to rest and to conserve their strength prior to the midpoint of the day of the Lord.

Earlier, in Matthew 24:6, Jesus makes an announcement regarding the first half of the tribulation period that, ultimately, is for Jewish believers living during that period of time: "And you will hear of wars and reports[5] of wars. See that you are not troubled; for all these things must come to pass, but the end is not yet." By this declaration, there is an indication that Jesus tells them to relax (rest) during the first half. He does it by indicating that they are not to allow events during the first half to disturb them; therefore, in that sense, they can be at rest because the end is not yet.

The Midnight Cry

With that in mind, look at verse 6: " 'And at midnight a cry was heard: "Behold, the bridegroom is coming; go out to meet him!" ' "

The word *midnight* is actually translated from two Greek words that literally mean *in the middle of the night*. The concept of night is a natural reference to the day of the Lord, for that future period is described in Scripture as a time of "darkness and gloominess," of "thick darkness" (Zephaniah 1:15), and of "darkness, and not light," as "very dark, with no brightness in it" (Amos 5:18, 20). In verse 6 of the parable of the ten virgins, Jesus refers to a cry in the middle of the night, which alerts the virgins to get ready to meet the bridegroom.

Remember that chapters 24 and 25 of Matthew are all one teaching unit. In chapter 24, Jesus provides us with a powerful exhortation based on a Satanic-inspired event occurring at midnight of the day of the Lord. There we see that the cry in the middle of the night is the announcement resulting from the abomination of desolation, occurring at the midpoint of the seven-year period of darkness upon the earth—midnight.[6] When the beast kills the two prophets of God, undoubtedly, the word will spread like wildfire. And following the beast's triumph over God's prophets, he will seek to present a complete domination of the God of Israel by his abomination of the temple of God. At this point, the cry will go out to believing Jews in and around Jerusalem that they need to flee for their lives into the Judean hills—immediately! The cry will reach down through the streets of Jerusalem and into the homes of believers, and it will travel into the fields outside of the city. Those believing Jews who are faithful followers of Jesus will heed the cry and will flee from Jerusalem into the mountains, where they will have the best chance of escaping the pursuing armies of the beast.

The Importance of Having Reserves of Oil

The exhortation in 25:6 that pictures what Jesus exhorts in 24:16–20 is this: "Go out to meet him!" At that point, there is a sense in which Jewish believers will be leaving the home (Jerusalem) of the Bridegroom to go out to meet him just as the ten virgins go out from the groom's home to meet the wedding party. However, there will still be three and a half years left until the actual return of the Bridegroom, so extra oil will become very important, as we see in verses 7 and 8.

In Luke 12:35–37, Jesus exhorted his followers to keep their lamps burning, being ever watchful of his return from the wedding. The burning lamps portray continued faithfulness to Christ. Those who keep their lamps burning until his return will be greatly rewarded by him.

This illustrates the importance of having extra oil for their lamps. That oil will keep the lamps burning until the Bridegroom returns. This gives us insight as to the meaning of the lamps going out. Clearly, that means that their faithfulness to Christ begins to fade.

Unfortunately, there will be believing Jews in the tribulation period whose lamps will go out. Note, for example, what Jesus says about this in Matthew 24:12–13: "And because lawlessness will abound, the love of many [Jewish believers in Christ] will grow cold. But he who endures [remains faithful through difficulties] to the end [of the tribulation period] shall be saved [physically delivered]."

Both Jesus' description (verse 12) and exhortation (verse 13) are focused upon believers in him. For example, the word translated *endures* is used elsewhere in the New Testament of Christians remaining faithful to Christ through difficult times, and certainly, unbelievers would not be exhorted to endure in their unbelief. Instead, they would be commanded to believe in Christ for eternal life.[7]

When Jesus speaks of love, it can only be love as defined from God's point of view. One of the clearest descriptions of biblical love is found in 1 John 4:7–11 where God shows us that love—*true* love—is sourced in him. In fact, God is love; therefore, the believer in Christ who does not love is not in fellowship with God. But, this kind of love is not feeling-oriented; instead, this passage illustrates God's love for us by his willingness to send his Son into the world to die for us in order to atone for our sins.

Therefore, when Jesus speaks of love, it is that which is sourced in God, and it is displayed by those born of God when they sacrificially give of themselves for one another. Jesus' description of love that *will grow cold* during the tribulation period is the love of believers—in this case, Jewish believers—that has waned because they have been influenced by the environment of lawlessness all about them. And since Jesus defined love as obedience to his commands[8]—which includes believers loving one another[9]—then his description of love growing cold indicates that some Jewish believers will drift into unfaithfulness during the day of the Lord. In other words, their lamps will go out.

What Is This Oil?

It is important to understand that the oil in our parable does not refer to eternal life. Verse 9 will help us to see that: " 'But the wise answered, saying, "No, lest there should not be enough for us and you; but go rather to those who sell, and buy for yourselves." ' " Note that this oil is something the virgins need to buy, while eternal life is a free gift that has already been purchased by Christ.

Therefore, to what does this oil refer? It refers to the cost believers must pay to gain the spiritual reserves needed to keep their lamps burning for Christ during difficult times.

We also need to pay the cost to obtain the spiritual reserves necessary to keep our lamps burning for Christ through dark and difficult times. But, how do we "buy" those reserves? We buy them by making efforts to grow in our relationship with God through spending regular time in his Word (the Bible), through daily prayer, through weekly worship of God, through serving God by serving believers, and through obedience to the Bible in other areas as well. Spiritual growth is costly, because it takes effort and sacrifice on our part; but by paying the price, we buy the oil of spiritual reserves needed to keep our lamps burning through dark and difficult times.

According to the parable, the wise virgins cannot provide oil for the foolish ones lest they not have enough to keep *their* lamps burning until the bridegroom comes. No believer can provide spiritual reserves for another believer. Each Christian must pay the cost for his own reserves.

The Meaning of the Shut Door

As the parable continues, we find this:

> "And while they went to buy, the bridegroom came, and those who were ready went in with him to the wedding; and the door was shut. Afterward the other virgins came also, saying, 'Lord, Lord, open to us!' But he answered and said, 'Assuredly, I say to you, I do not know you.' "

The Jewish wedding ceremony included joyful festivities, such as a supper where only honored guests were welcome to experience the joyful privilege of dining with the bridegroom in a special manner. Jesus illustrates this in Luke 12:35–37, where we see that a significant reward awaits those who keep their lamps burning till the Bridegroom returns. They will have the privilege of sitting down at the table of the Bridegroom where he will serve *them*! Thus, they will experience the amazing joy of being highly honored by him.

Understanding this reward enables us to realize the meaning of the shut door to the foolish virgins. Though these foolish ones will be granted entrance into the kingdom, the door will forever be shut to them of the opportunity to experience very unique and special joy, honor, and privilege in the kingdom.

The announcement, "I do not know you," by the bridegroom to the foolish virgins refers to being shut out of the special privileged intimacy, joy, and honor that wise virgins will obtain as a reward. It is very different from the announcement Jesus will make to unbelievers in the future when he declares, "I never knew you; depart from Me, you who practice lawlessness!" (Matthew 7:23) In fact, Jesus chooses a different Greek word for *know* in Matthew 25:12 than he does in Matthew 7:23, likely to portray a different meaning. While in 7:23 Jesus' address to unbelievers indicates he has never had a relationship with them, his presentation in 25:12 to believers shows he does not have *intimacy*, or fellowship, with them.

Jesus' Exhortation to Us

Jesus then concludes the parable with this exhortation in verse 13: "Watch therefore, for you know neither the day nor the hour in which the Son of Man is coming."

Though this parable is ultimately for Jewish believers during the day of the Lord, Jesus provides a statement of application to us in this verse. His exhortation to us is this: we are to keep our lamps burning in faithfulness to him, for we do not know when he will come for us. As we have previously seen, Jesus' appearing in the air for believers at the rapture of the church could occur at any time! Therefore, it is important for us, who are on this side of the day of the Lord, to keep our lamps burning, for we do not want to be caught with unlit lamps at his coming for us.

As we have seen, these ten virgins represent Jewish believers who will live during a most difficult time—the tribulation period. In the next chapter, we will explore the difficulty of life during that time by examining the tribulation judgments and God's purpose for them.

CHAPTER 18
Tribulation Judgments

Toward the end of the nineteenth century, Swedish chemist Alfred Nobel awoke one morning to read his own obituary in the local newspaper: "Alfred Nobel, the inventor of dynamite, who died yesterday, devised a way for more people to be killed in a war than ever before, and he died a very rich man."

Actually, it was Alfred's older brother who had died. A reporter had made a "grave" mistake.

But, this had a profound effect on Nobel. He decided he wanted to be known for something other than developing the means to kill a large number of people efficiently and acquiring wealth, as a result. So, he initiated the Nobel Prize, the award for scientists and writers who foster peace. Nobel declared, "Every man ought to have the chance to correct his epitaph in midstream and write a new one."

This is why God brings temporal judgment. As Pastor Ray Stedman stated in a 1974 sermon,

> Judgment is *not* God's way of saying, "I'm through with you." It is not a mark of abandonment by God,

but it is the last loving act of God to bring you back, the last resort of love. C. S. Lewis said, "God whispers to us in our pleasures; He speaks to us in our work; but He shouts at us in our pain." Every one of us knows that there have been times when we would not listen to God, would not pay any attention to what His word was saying, until one day God put us flat on our backs or allowed us to be hurt badly. Then we began to listen."

This is one of God's purposes for bringing judgment upon the earth during the tribulation period.

In this chapter, we will pause from our chronological approach of prophetic events in order to get an overview of God's judgments throughout the seven-year time frame. Hopefully, this overview will give us a better understanding of the day of the Lord and encourage us to trust God even more, as a result.

The Pattern of Tribulation Judgments in Revelation

Since the clearest presentation of how these judgments fit into the tribulation period appear in the book of Revelation, that is where we will go to understand them. Note the pattern of the judgments below as they are presented in the book of Revelation:[1]

Judgments	Heavenly Prelude	Judgments 1 - 6	Earthly Parenthesis	Judgment 7	Earthly Postlude
Seals	4:1 - 5:14	6:1 - 17	7:1 - 17	8:1	
Trumpets	8:2 - 6	8:7 - 9:21	10:1 - 11:14	11:15 - 19	12:1 - 14:20
Bowl	15:1 - 8	16:1 - 12	16:13 - 16	16:17 - 21	17:1 - 18:24

The left column represents the three series of judgments presented in Revelation, while the rest of the chart shows the pattern of the judgments. You will notice that before each series of judgments, there is a scene that takes place in heaven, labeled on the chart as "heavenly prelude". Then, the first six judgments occur. These six judgments are followed by a scene upon the earth which, in itself, is not part of the judgments. Then, the seventh judgment occurs.

After the seventh seal judgment, there is no concluding portion to this section, because the seventh seal judgment is simply a dramatic silence.[2] However, following the other two series of judgments, there is a postlude that takes place upon earth.

Some Christian Bible teachers have concluded that these three series of judgments occur in a telescopic fashion—that is, the first series (seal judgments) concludes, then, out of the first series' seventh judgment, comes the next series (trumpet judgments), and out of that series' seventh trumpet judgment comes the next series (bowl judgments). However, the clues in Revelation present a different picture. God, who is very purposeful, has a distinct purpose for the arrangement of these judgments, so let us examine the evidence to determine how the judgments are presented and the purpose for their presentation.

The Seal Judgments and the Return of Christ

The first piece of evidence deals with the ending of each series of judgments in respect to the return of Christ to the earth. Compare the ending of the seal judgments, found in Revelation 6:12–17, with the description Jesus gives in Matthew 24:29–31:

Matthew 24:29-31	Revelation 6:12-17
"Immediately after the tribulation of those days the sun will be darkened, and the moon will not give its light; the stars will fall from heaven, and the powers of the heavens will be shaken. Then the sign of the Son of Man will appear in heaven, and then all the tribes of the earth will mourn, and they will see the Son of Man coming on the clouds of heaven with power and great glory. And He will send His angels with a great	I looked when He opened the sixth seal, and behold, there was a great earthquake; and the sun became black as sackcloth of hair, and the moon became like blood. And the stars of heaven fell to the earth, as a fig tree drops its late figs when it is shaken by a mighty wind. Then the sky receded as a scroll when it is rolled up, and every mountain and island was moved out of its place. And the kings of the earth, the great men, the rich men, the

Matthew 24:29-31	Revelation 6:12-17
sound of a trumpet, and they will gather together His elect from the four winds, from one end of heaven to the other."	commanders, the mighty men, every slave and every free man, hid themselves in the caves and in the rocks of the mountains, and said to the mountains and rocks, "Fall on us and hide us from the face of Him who sits on the throne and from the wrath of the Lamb! For the great day of His wrath has come, and who is able to stand?"

What similarities do you see in these two descriptions? Notice that both include: cosmic, cataclysmic events such as the sun and moon becoming dark and stars falling from the sky; the word *shaken* describing the occurrence in the heavens; and a signal that Jesus is about to return.[3] In fact, these two descriptions portray the same scene.

According to Jesus in Matthew 24, this scene will occur at the end of the tribulation period upon the earth. Therefore, based on the comparison of these two similar passages, the next expected event to occur following the sixth seal judgment is the return of Christ to the earth.

The Trumpet Judgments and the Return of Christ

In revealing the seventh trumpet judgment in Revelation 11:15–18, the seventh angel heralds the eternal kingdom of God and Christ, announcing that it has replaced the kingdoms of this world. This statement clearly shows the arrival of the kingdom at the end of the tribulation period.

Adding to this statement regarding the return of Christ, comes this one by the twenty-four elders to the Lord: "You have taken Your great power and reigned." This announcement by the elders portrays the arrival of God's reign upon the earth. The use of the past tense ("reigned") shows that in this vision of the future, the Lord's rule upon the earth has begun. So, this too pictures the arrival of God's kingdom upon the earth with the revelation of the seventh trumpet.

In addition, one more indicator that the seventh trumpet reveals the return of Christ to the earth is presented in this statement by the elders:

"The nations were angry, and Your wrath has come." This quote is drawn from Psalm 2, which portrays the anger and rebellion of the nations, followed by God's response of wrath upon them by sending his Son to the earth to judge these enemies of God. This judgment is then followed by the Son ascending his throne and ruling over the earth. Therefore, the arrival of God's wrath indicates the return of Christ to the earth.

Finally, at the revelation of the seventh trumpet, the elders declare that the time has come for the Lord to reward his faithful servants. Since the rewarding of Christians—at the judgment seat of Christ—will take place following the return of Christ to the earth,[4] this statement shows that the next expected event is the return of Christ to the earth. In fact, we have seen that the revelation of the seventh trumpet in Revelation 11:15–18 leads to the return of Christ to the earth to judge the nations and to establish his kingdom rule.

The Bowl Judgments and the Return of Christ

The third series of judgments in Revelation is represented by the bowl judgments. Coming on the heels of the bowl judgments is a description of the judgment of the city of Rome[5] (chapters 17–18). This is followed by the return of Jesus to the earth to judge (19:11–21) and to establish his kingdom (chapter 20).

Therefore, each of the three series of judgments in the book of Revelation takes the reader right up to the very same prophetic—and climactic—event. It is the return of Christ to the earth.

The Similarity of the Endings of Each Series of Judgments

There is even more evidence that shows that each of the three series of judgments will end at the same time. The similarity of descriptions following the culmination of each series of judgments presents this evidence. Note the endings of each:

Seal Judgments	Trumpet Judgments	Bowl Judgments
Then the angel took the censer, filled it with fire from the altar, and threw it to the earth. And there	Then the temple of God was opened in heaven, and the ark of His covenant was seen in His temple. And	And there were noises and thunderings and lightnings; and there was a great earthquake, such a mighty

Seal Judgments	Trumpet Judgments	Bowl Judgments
were noises, thunderings, lightnings, and an earthquake (8:5).	there were lightnings, noises, thunderings, an earthquake, and great hail (11:19).	and great earthquake . . . And great hail from heaven fell upon men, each hailstone about the weight of a talent. Men blasphemed God because of the plague of the hail, since that plague was exceedingly great (16:18–21).

At the end of each series of judgments in Revelation, there are noises, thunderings, lightnings, and an earthquake.[6] The similarities indicate that all three series of judgments end at the same time—just before Jesus returns to the earth.

Building to a Climax

Thus, to build up to the climactic focus of the book of Revelation, the author, with great dramatic effect, uses the first series of judgments (the seal judgments) to take us right up to the return of Christ—then he backs off. Then, through the second series of judgments (the trumpet judgments), John once again takes us to that climactic event, Christ's return—but he backs off again. Finally, through the third series of judgments (the bowl judgments), John once more builds up to the return of Christ to the earth—but he follows that with a two-chapter delay (17–18), which heightens the anticipation of the climax. Thus, this building of anticipation toward the climax of the book is done through the three series of judgments that culminate at the same time.

This all shows how significant the return of Christ to the earth is. It will be climactic to God's prophetic plan, and it will be the turning point of our eternal experience.

But, even though the judgments all end at the same place—just prior to the return of Christ to the earth—their time focus is not the same. In other words, one series of judgments may take place throughout the entire seven-year period, while another may occur primarily within the first half of the tribulation period, etc. Let us examine this a little more closely.

The Time Frame of the Seal Judgments

It has been convincingly argued that the first seal (Revelation 6:2) portrays the return of Christ in the air, commonly referred to as the rapture of the church.[7] If this is true, then the seal judgments begin at the very beginning of the tribulation period.[8]

The fifth seal, however, pictures the persecution and martyrdom of believers during the tribulation period. But, the question that arises is: When does this occur? The answer to this question begins with understanding that the persecution of Christians by being put to death during the tribulation period begins with Jewish believers.

Remember at what point in the tribulation period Jewish believers in Christ are commanded by Jesus to flee to escape persecution? It is at that point in the tribulation period that the martyrdom of the fifth seal would occur. They are told to flee at the midpoint of the tribulation period—after the beast kills the two prophets of God and after he enters the temple of God to announce he is God. And, it is only at that point that Jesus calls for them to flee in order to escape persecution. This indicates that persecution in the tribulation period does not occur until the midpoint onward. It means that the fifth seal, which pictures the martyrdom of believers, occurs within the second half of the tribulation period.

Thus, the fifth and sixth seal judgments occur in the latter three and a half years prior to Jesus' return to the earth.[9] This shows us that the seal judgments provide an overview of the entire seven-year period of the tribulation upon the earth.

The Time Frame of the Trumpet Judgments

On the other hand, the trumpet judgments are attached to the ministry of the two witnesses of Revelation 11. We can see that by the "woes" mentioned in connection with the trumpet judgments. For example, at the end of the fifth trumpet judgment, it is announced: "One woe is past. Behold, still two more woes are coming after these things" (9:12). After the sixth trumpet judgment is described, and immediately following the presentation of the ministry, death, resurrection, and ascension of the two witnesses (11:2–13), this proclamation is given: "The second woe is past. Behold, the third woe is coming quickly" (11:14).

This means that the "woes" are attached to the ministry of the two witnesses, which indicates that the ministry of the two witnesses is attached to the trumpet judgments. In fact, the trumpet judgments are likely the very plagues that the two witnesses bring upon the earth during the three and a half years of their ministry (11:6). This connection to the two witnesses shows us that the trumpet judgments take place during the first half of Daniel's seventieth week, the first 1,260 days of the tribulation period.

The Time Frame of the Bowl Judgments

The introduction of the bowl judgments in Revelation 16:2 tells us when they occur: "So the first went and poured out his bowl upon the earth, and a foul and loathsome sore came upon the men who had the mark of the beast and those who worshiped his image." So, when does this first bowl judgment occur? It occurs during the last half of the tribulation period. We know that because the mark of the beast, which is presented in this verse, is not initiated until the beast assumes his place of rule over the earth—at the very midpoint of the day of the Lord. After all, the beast will only rule the world for the last forty-two months[10] of the tribulation period.

Therefore, the time frame covered by the seal judgments consists of the entire seven-year period, while the trumpet judgments occur primarily within the *first* half of the tribulation period, and the bowl judgments take place within the *last* half of Daniel's seventieth week. The timelines appearing below illustrate the timing of these tribulation judgments.

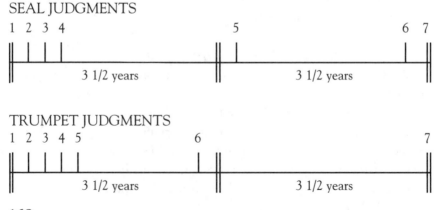

SEAL JUDGMENTS

1 2 3 4   5   6 7

3 1/2 years   3 1/2 years

TRUMPET JUDGMENTS

1 2 3 4 5   6   7

3 1/2 years   3 1/2 years

BOWL JUDGMENTS

God's Purposes for These Judgments

The return of Jesus to establish his kingdom upon the earth is the climax of the book of Revelation.[11] However, before his kingdom is established, God will accomplish a few things. First, he will glorify himself by judging the world for its wickedness.

Through the plagues God will pour out upon the planet, he will also demonstrate that he is infinitely more powerful than the god (Satan) the world will worship through the beast.[12] As Exodus 12:12 shows, this was one of the purposes of God's judgments upon Egypt, which resulted in Israel's deliverance from bondage at the time of Moses. The final plague was the killing of the firstborn of each household in Egypt.

In the ten plagues he released upon Pharaoh and the Egyptians, God powerfully attacked—and "conquered"—the Egyptian gods. In a number of ways, those judgments typify the judgments during the tribulation period.[13] This leads us to understand that by the plagues God will pour out upon the earth during the day of the Lord, he will attack and "conquer" the god worshipped by all who have not believed in Christ for eternal life.

But, there is something else God will seek to accomplish prior to the return of Christ to the earth. He will seek to bring many to believe in Jesus Christ for eternal life. As we have seen, he will utilize the 144,000 to fulfill this prophetic statement by Jesus: "And this gospel of the kingdom will be preached in all the world as a witness to all the nations, and then the end will come" (Matthew 24:14). God will use the cataclysmic crises he will bring upon the world to awaken many people to the gospel, as illustrated in this way in Revelation 7:9: "After these things I looked and behold, a great multitude which no one could number, of all nations, tribes, peoples, and tongues, standing before the throne and before the Lamb, clothed with white robes."

The Judgments and Israel

However, God will have a particular focus upon one group of people that he will seek to bring to himself, and then he will use this people group to reach many others for Christ. This national people group is connected to the tribulation period in, for example, Jeremiah 30:7: "Alas! For that day is great, so that none is like it; and it is the time of Jacob's trouble, but he shall be saved out of it."

Jacob is another biblical name for Israel, since, as a result of Jacob's all-night struggle with God in Genesis 32, God gave him the name Israel,[14] which may mean "having power with God" or "God's fighter."[15] And, in the context of Jeremiah 30:7, God is speaking of the future great tribulation—the three and a half year time frame during which believing Jews will experience great persecution. Or, to put it in the vernacular of Jeremiah 30:7, Israel will experience trouble like never before.

Jesus certainly must have had that verse in mind when he declared to his Jewish followers living at that time that "then there will be great tribulation, such as has not been since the beginning of the world until this time, no, nor ever shall be" (Matthew 24:21). Though Israel has experienced much trouble throughout its history, the future era described by Jeremiah 30:7 and Matthew 24:21 will be the climax of Jacob's trouble. But, the good news is that Israel shall be saved out of it; that is, the Messiah will return to deliver Jacob.

In both of these verses, the Lord indicates that Israel will be the special focus of that era. It will be a time of great trouble for the Jews, but their trouble will lead to the initiation of the kingdom of God upon the earth.

Israel and Repentance

Peter speaks to this same people group in Acts 3:19–21,[16] where he calls for Israel to repent. Repentance is defined in the Bible as a movement toward fellowship with God, producing good works. This is demonstrated, for example, by the people of Nineveh in response to the preaching of Jonah. Jesus declared that they "repented at the preaching of Jonah" (Luke 11:32), and when we go to Jonah 3:10 to see what repentance is, we find this: "Then God saw their works that they relented from their evil way." As a result, God withheld the judgment he had announced through Jonah—the destruction of Nineveh, with the resulting loss of much life. But, notice in this connection that there is nothing mentioned about eternity, hell, or eternal life. Neither is there any statement about believing in Christ. For repentance, in itself, does not deal with any of those issues. It is a movement from wickedness toward fellowship with God.

To add to this explanation, we can see the promotion of works in regard to repentance with the ministry of John the Baptist. His ministry involved calling the nation of Israel to repentance. We can see that in Matthew's recording of John's message in 3:3: "Repent, for the kingdom of heaven is at hand!" It is also presented by linking his baptizing ministry with repentance.[17] And it is shown by John the Baptist calling for those responding to his preaching to "bear fruits worthy of repentance" (Luke 3:8), which were all about good works in one's life.[18]

In the parable of the prodigal son in Luke 15:11–32, repentance is illustrated by a son who had traveled far from his father, wasting what his father had given him in foolish living, and then, when he had hit bottom, confessing his sin and coming back to his father. The result for the son is joyous fellowship with his father.

This parable shows the desire of God for Israel. From early on in the Old Testament, God considered Israel his son.[19] Since Israel the son has traveled far from his Father, the Father has been calling his son to repentance—to come back into joyous fellowship with him. Thus, God desires the nation to repent; but he also desires for individual Jews to receive eternal life by believing in Christ for it.

Repentance is not necessary for receiving eternal life,[20] but in cases like Israel, which is portrayed as a stubborn son of God, repentance seems necessary in order to awaken Jews to believe in Jesus Christ for eternal life. Though John the Baptist called the nation of Israel to repent, he also sought individual Jews to believe in Jesus Christ.[21]

While many people may receive eternal life without repenting, in the tribulation period, Israel will repent nationally; and then many will believe in Christ individually. This is because repentance for Israel is a national event, while receiving eternal life is an individual one.

As we also see in Peter's declaration to Israel, if the nation as a whole would repent and turn to the Lord, God would send Jesus back from heaven in order to establish his kingdom upon the earth. However, it seems that before the nation of Israel turns to the Lord in repentance, individual Jews will believe in Jesus as the Christ (Messiah), the giver of eternal life. The nation will turn to the Lord at the very end of the tribulation (more on that in a later chapter), but, prior to that, the vast majority of the Jews alive in the land of Israel will have believed in Christ for eternal life.

Other Benefits of These Judgments

Not only will God use these judgments to lead people to receive eternal life by believing in Jesus Christ for it, he will also use them to increase the faith of believers during that time. He will do so, just as he encouraged and increased the faith of the Israelites through the judgments upon Egypt through Moses,[22] as he revealed his reality and power[23] through the plagues.

Now, the question that arises concerns the benefit for us of understanding these judgments. To help answer that in a personal way, complete the following statement: These judgments demonstrate God's love, power, and wisdom, which encourage me to trust him even more because _____.

As we have seen, God will use the day of the Lord to bring Israel into a harmonious relationship with himself. When this occurs, Christ will return to establish his long-awaited kingdom upon the earth. Satan understands this connection, which is why—as he sees Jews from Israel responding to the Lord—he and the beast will prepare for Jesus' return. He will do so by gathering the nations to war, as we will see in the next chapter.

CHAPTER 19
Gathering to War

Since 3,600 BC, the world has known only 292 years of peace! During this period there have been more than 14,350 wars in which 3.65 billion people have been killed. The value of the property destroyed is equal to a golden belt around the world nearly one hundred miles wide and more than thirty-three feet thick.

In addition, since 650 BC, there have also been 1,660 arms races, only 16 of which have not ended in war. The remainder ended in the economic collapse of the countries involved. Man seems to have an endless capacity for conflict!

But, there is coming the conflict to end all conflicts, one that will be far different than any war that has ever occurred on the planet. This one will consist of the armies of the entire planet gathering against the army of heaven.

Satan's Plan to War against Jesus

The gathering will occur toward the end of the tribulation period to prepare for war against Jesus at his return.[1] It will be Satan's attempt to stop Jesus from assuming his reign over the earth. After all, Satan currently rules the world[2] and will do whatever possible to maintain the earth as his kingdom.

But, how is it that Satan can still believe that he can win against the Lord? After all, Satan knows the Bible; in fact, he knows it well enough to quote it to Jesus in an attempt to tempt him to do evil.[3] And because Satan knows the Bible this well, he knows God's plan for the future, as revealed in Scripture.

However, Satan's condemning sin is pride.[4] Pride blinds one to the truth and gives one an inflated view of one's abilities. It is what moved Satan to rebel against God. And it is what causes him to refuse to believe that God will inevitably establish his kingdom upon the earth. His blinding pride, coupled with a lofty ambition (to be like God),[5] will move Satan to gather the nations to war. Due to his arrogance, even though he has seen God fulfill his word over and over again, Satan still believes he can somehow thwart God's future kingdom plan. He still believes he can win!

While it is true that Satan's blinding pride and lofty ambition will lead him to do whatever he can to hold onto this world as his kingdom, he could accomplish nothing if God did not allow him to do so. Not only will God *allow* him to gather the armies of the world together to war against Jesus, he will even *enable* that to occur! Here is the way it will develop.

Preparing the Way

As we discussed in the last chapter, God will pour out upon the earth a series of judgments, called bowl judgments,[6] during the last half of the day of the Lord.[7] When the sixth bowl is opened, this is what is revealed in Revelation 16:12: "Then the sixth angel poured out his bowl on the great river Euphrates, and its water was dried up, so that the way of the kings from the east might be prepared."

Verse 12 mentions the drying up of the Euphrates River in order to provide for the kings from the East and their armies to cross over it. As you can see from the map below, the Euphrates, which is about 1800 miles long, begins in Turkey, flows across Syria, and then through Iraq to the Persian Gulf. It is scarcely fordable at any time of the year and has always been a separation between people on the east of it and people to the west of it. Historically, it has been a great hindrance to military movements.

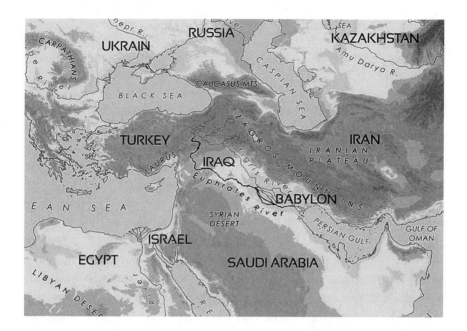

What will the drying of the Euphrates accomplish? It will enable armies from other parts of the Middle East to gather in the northern part of Israel.

We can see why Satan would want to take advantage of the drying of the Euphrates—in order to gather the nations to war against Christ. However, by drying up the Euphrates, God will be lowering the drawbridge, so to speak. He will be welcoming the nations to come together to attempt to war against his Son. But when they do, he will judge them. This will be another case of Satan falling right into God's trap.

Gathering the Armies to War

Then, verses 13–15 of the same chapter describe three demons being sent out by Satan, the beast, and the false prophet. They will go worldwide, performing miraculous signs, to deceive the kings of the earth and to move them to send their armies "to the battle of that great day of God Almighty."

That battle is what many have termed the "battle of Armageddon." Where do they get that term? It stems from verse 16 of Revelation 16, where we see this description: "And they gathered them together to the place called in Hebrew, Armageddon."

However, the battle of Armageddon is a misconception. Though Armageddon has become known as the place where the final battle of the world takes place, Scripture does not announce that as the place of a great battle. The battle will actually take place near the Mount of Olives, just outside Jerusalem.

Instead, verse 16 refers to Armageddon as the place where the armies of the earth will gather. Neither verse 16 nor anywhere else in the Bible refers to the battle of Armageddon.

Though most Bible versions present Armageddon as the area where the armies of the earth will gather, that is most likely not even the place of gathering. "Armageddon" means the *hills of Megiddo*. But, the hills would not be a good strategic location for the gathering of a massive number of troops, particularly if the assembly is for the purpose of preparation and organization for a battle to be held elsewhere. It would be more likely that such a large gathering would take place in a vast plain. In fact, the original text of Revelation may have read "Megiddo," instead of Armageddon.[8]

Megiddo overlooked the Valley of Megiddo, also known as the Jezreel Valley. So to gather at Megiddo would mean to assemble in the valley, at the base of the ancient city, between Megiddo and Nazareth.[9]

The Timing of the Battle

We noticed in verse 15 that the demons will gather the armies of the world to the battle of that great day of God Almighty. The "great day of God Almighty" will occur on the day Christ returns to the earth, at which time God will display his almighty power through the Lord Jesus. This will be the when this battle takes place—the showdown between Satan and his armies and the Lord Jesus Christ and his army. Thus, Satan will deceive the kings of the earth to send their armies to assemble at the Valley of Megiddo, which will be the beginning of their preparation to do battle with the Lord at his return to the Mount of Olives. This battle will be the culmination of the day of the Lord.

Psalm 2 describes this gathering for us in verses 1–3:

> Why do the nations rage, and the people plot a
> vain thing? The kings of the earth set themselves,
> and the rulers take counsel together, against the Lord

and against His Anointed [Messiah, or Christ], saying, "Let us break Their bonds in pieces and cast away
Their cords from us."

Notice what occurs in these verses. The kings of the earth will
gather their people against the Lord and his Anointed one. The word
anointed is the Hebrew word *Messiah* and the Greek word *Christ*. Since
there has never been a time in which the kings of the earth have gathered together against Christ, then, obviously, this fulfillment will occur
in the future. In fact, the initiation of this rebellion is described in
Revelation 16:12–16 with the culmination presented at the return of
Christ in Revelation 19:11–21. There we see Christ do battle with the
kings of the earth and their armies who have gathered to make war with
him (19:19).

The gathering of the kings of the earth against Christ, as presented
in Psalm 2, did *not* occur when Christ was upon the earth the first time.
This, of course, means that these verses portray the rebellion of the kings
of the earth against the Lord at his *second coming* to the earth.

Satan's Purpose for the Gathering

Psalm 2 shows us the motivation of the kings to lead their armies
together to prepare for the return of Christ. But, the scene in Luke 4:5–7
provides us with a glimpse into the spiritual realm, where we see the motivation of Satan to gather the kings and their armies for that great day.

In his temptation of Jesus in Luke 4, Satan claims to have the authority to grant world rule to whomever he wishes. In other words, he
can appoint anyone he chooses to be king of the world. Jesus not only
did not dispute Satan's claim to have this authority, but elsewhere Jesus
calls Satan the ruler of this world.[10] This indicates that Satan's claim
that this world is his kingdom is a legitimate claim.

However, the Bible reveals that Jesus will return to the earth to
establish *his* kingdom upon the earth. At that time, he will wrest this
world from Satan's grip.

This is why Satan will gather the armies together against Christ in
the future. He will seek to war against Christ in order to try to stop him
from claiming this world as *his* kingdom.

As we have seen in Revelation 16, Satan will gather the armies together at the Valley of Megiddo. However, as we have mentioned, this is not where the armies will wage war.

The Place of the Battle

In Joel 3:2, the Lord shows us that the Valley of Megiddo will only be the *initial* gathering place of the armies of the world, for they will head down into the Valley of Jehoshaphat from there. The Valley of Jehoshaphat is another name for the Kidron Valley—the valley that separates the Mount of Olives from the Temple Mount. The gathering described in Joel relates to the gathering in the Valley of Megiddo in that the gathering begins at Megiddo, but then the armies stream to the south down the Kidron Valley.

Though the Valley of Megiddo is a vast plain, it cannot contain the armies of the entire world. But Scripture does not claim that all the armies arrive at or are located in the valley at the same time. It seems that the armies begin to converge on the valley, but while waiting on other armies to arrive, those that have reached that area first will begin to move on down the Valley of Jehoshaphat.

We saw in Revelation 16 that Satan seems to be the one who will gather the kings and their armies to the great battle. However, in Joel 3, God states *he* will bring them together to judge them for what they have done to Israel during the tribulation period (especially the last half). This means that even though Satan believes it is his plan to assemble the armies together, ultimately, it would not happen if it did not fit into God's perfect plan, leading to the establishment of his kingdom. In this spiritual chess match, Satan seeks to checkmate God, but the Lord, who knows beforehand all of Satan's moves, only allows Satan to move pieces in such a way as to draw himself into checkmate by God.

As mentioned, the Valley of Jehoshaphat is the biblical name for the modern-named Kidron Valley that runs between the Mount of Olives and the Temple Mount. That valley cuts between the place where Jesus will return to the earth (the Mount of Olives) and the place where Jesus will ascend to sit on his throne to rule the earth (the Temple Mount).

Zechariah 14:2–4 reveals that Jesus' feet will rest upon the Mount of Olives at his second coming.[11] At his return, Jerusalem will be overrun with Gentile armies, which will ransack houses and ravish women. At that time, half of the city will be taken captive.

As the massive number of troops from these armies pours down into the Kidron Valley, the valley will not be large enough to contain the multitude. As a result, this flood of troops will wash into the city and surrounding region, including the Mount of Olives.

Jesus Prepared for Battle

According to the description presented in Zechariah 14, this massive assembly of troops will not catch Jesus off guard. He will be fully prepared for the battle. For "the Lord will go forth and fight against those nations, as He fights in the day of battle."

Since this announcement is given prior to the statement that, "in that day His feet will stand on the Mount of Olives, which faces Jerusalem on the east," we are led to understand that he will go to the Mount of Olives for the purpose of doing battle. It will not be as if he returns to the Mount of Olives and is then surprised by the armies. Not at all! Instead, he will surprise the armies by his overwhelming and decisive victory over them.

Just as in his triumphal entry prior to his crucifixion, following his return to the earth, Jesus will ride (a white horse instead of a donkey colt) down the Mount of Olives, across the Kidron Valley, and up the Temple Mount from where he will rule. Satan understands that is the route Jesus will take, which is why he will gather the troops in that area. Satan will attempt to keep Jesus from ascending the Temple Mount in order to stop him from beginning his rule.

As we have seen, the gathering of the nations to war will be Satan's way of preparing for the return of Christ. However, before Jesus returns, God will deal with two cities that will have key roles during the last half of the day of the Lord. We will look at those cities—and God's judgment upon them—in the next chapter.

CHAPTER 20
A Tale of Two Cities

In 1985, Saddam Hussein began the arduous task of restoring the ancient city of Babylon.[1] He spent over five hundred million dollars to reconstruct the city and build a modern residence on the ruins of Nebuchadnezzar's palace. It is said that Saddam believed himself to be something of a reincarnated King Nebuchadnezzar. The Iraqi dictator imitated the ancient ruler by having his name inscribed on the bricks used to rebuild the city. He even went so far as to mint coins that emphasized the connection between himself and Nebuchadnezzar. Unfortunately for Saddam, his grand plans for the city of Babylon were interrupted by the US invasion of Iraq. However, despite Saddam's removal from power and subsequent execution, the work to rebuild Babylon has continued.

According to several Web sites, the United Nations Educational, Scientific, and Cultural Organization is pumping millions of dollars into Babylon and several other historical sites in Iraq.[2] With the help of private donors, the UN is hoping to turn Babylon into a thriving center of tourism and commerce. If everything goes according to plan, Babylon will be a cultural center complete with shopping malls, hotels, and maybe even a theme park.[3]

During the tribulation period, two cities will arise to prominence, each of which will have a special relationship to the beast, the world ruler. One of those cities is of such importance to the rule of the beast—and will have such a significant effect on the earth-dwellers of that era—that the book of Revelation refers to it in four chapters—from 16:19 through 19:4.

The Identification of Mystery Babylon

Because that city will have such importance to the beast and to the world as a whole in the tribulation period, it warrants some discussion in this study. We will begin with the identification of that city. But, to identify it, we will need to play detective with the clues found in Revelation 17:3–9.

In those verses, this particular city is portrayed as a woman riding the beast and is identified as "Mystery, Babylon the Great." The word *mystery* in front of her title, Babylon the Great, indicates that Babylon is not her real name.[4] Hence, Babylon is used as a code word.

This is not the only place in the New Testament where Babylon is used as a code word for another city. In 1 Peter 5:13, the apostle Peter uses Babylon to refer to the city from which he wrote the epistle—Rome. At the time of writing both 1 Peter and Revelation, it was not advantageous to use a clear reference to Rome, so a code word was employed—but a code word the first century Christians would have understood. Therefore, the use of Babylon as a code provides us with the first clue of the identification of the city described in Revelation 17 and 18—Rome.

Another clue to her identity is the geographical description provided in 17:9, where we learn there " 'are seven mountains [hills] on which the woman sits.' " The word translated as *mountains* from the original language (Greek) in which Revelation was written can also be translated as *hills*. Understanding that enables us to see this is a city of seven hills. There is one famous city that has historically been known as the city of seven hills. It is Rome.

We are provided with the clearest clue of all to her identity in verse 18 of the same chapter when an angel makes this identification to the apostle John: "And the woman whom you saw is that great city which reigns over the kings of the earth." The clue that helps us to identify this city is the use of the present tense of *reigns*, which tells us this city was *the* preeminent city when the book of Revelation was written.

Though there is disagreement on the dating of when Revelation was written, there is very good evidence both internally (within the book) and externally that Revelation was written in AD 68.[5] But, even if the book was written as late as AD 95 (as some would posit), the city that ruled over the earth at that time was Rome.

Finally, there is one other clear piece of evidence showing us that Rome, and not literal Babylon, is the true identity of this city. That evidence is found in Revelation 18:19, in which this city is described as "that great city, in which all who had ships on the sea became rich by her wealth!" Clearly, she is a port city, one that has access to ships from the sea. That cannot allude to literal Babylon, but it certainly could refer to Rome. Therefore, putting all of these clues together, we can see that the true identity of "Mystery Babylon" is Rome.

The Beast's Connection to Rome

As we have discovered from Revelation 17, the beast will be a man who was a first-century Roman emperor. In fact, he will be one of the first five emperors. This means he was associated with this city when he was a first-century Roman emperor. In fact, if the beast is, say, Augustus Caesar, then he was associated with Rome when the city was at the height of its influence and power.

Why would we suggest Augustus as the possible candidate for the identity of the beast? He was the architect of the Roman Empire, and he was an administrative genius. Since Satan started at the very top by offering the rule of the world to the best possible candidate—Jesus—it seems likely that he would then go to the one he might consider as the next best individual for the job, which could be Augustus. Satan will certainly need a great administrator to rule the entire world for his kingdom, so Augustus may fit that job description.

Now, let us learn more about this city that is important enough to be described by two full chapters of the book of Revelation and to be mentioned in three others.

Rome Will Ride the Beast

Back in verse 3, the woman (Rome) is pictured riding a scarlet beast. This scarlet beast refers to the flagrantly immoral beast of Revelation who will be granted authority by Satan to rule the world the final forty-two months before Jesus returns to the earth.[6]

The picture of the woman riding the beast is a metaphor that communicates the dependence of this city on the beast. Apparently, the rise of this city (in terms of power, wealth, influence, etc.) will be due, in some respect, to the rise of the beast to power. Since Rome was associated with this former emperor, it may use that association to build itself into the most prestigious city on earth.

Rome: A Future Luxurious City

We learn more about this city in the following verses of Revelation. For example, 17:4 gives us this picture: "The woman was arrayed in purple and scarlet, and adorned with gold and precious stones and pearls, having in her hand a golden cup full of abominations and the filthiness of her fornication." Then, in 18:7, we learn this about the city: " 'She glorified herself and lived luxuriously.' "

These descriptions clearly present the city as luxurious. In biblical times, purple and scarlet thread were expensive and were only worn by the wealthy. Furthermore, the addition of gold and precious stones and pearls, as well as the declaration that she lived luxuriously, in this description identify this city as opulent. She will drip with wealth!

Revelation 18 also speaks of the merchandising that will occur in this city, showing us that merchants will become wealthy by doing business with Rome in the future. The picture presented in chapter 18 displays Rome as extremely wealthy and luxurious with merchandise of every kind for sale. The portrayal paints future Rome as a city of exorbitance and abundance in wealth, possessions, consumerism, and play.

The Spiritual Fornication of Rome

Verse 2 of Revelation 17 proclaims that Rome will commit fornication. This refers to godlessness or spiritual unfaithfulness, which is the way the term "fornication" is oftentimes used in the Old Testament.[7] Thus, Rome will lead "peoples, multitudes, and nations" far away from God.

Chapter 18 discloses this information about the city:

> "Babylon . . . has become a dwelling place of de-
> mons, a prison for every foul spirit, and a cage for ev-
> ery unclean and hated bird! For all the nations have
> drunk of the wine of the wrath of her fornication, the
> kings of the earth have committed fornication with
> her, and the merchants of the earth have become rich
> through the abundance of her luxury. . . . The kings of
> the earth who committed fornication and lived luxu-
> riously with her . . . . And the merchants of the earth
> will weep and mourn over her . . ."

Here we learn that this city will be inhabited by demons. Due to ob-
scene godlessness, it will be a haven for all that is unholy. Clearly, Rome
will be more anti-Christian than we can imagine.

Once more the luxuriousness of the city is emphasized, and we see
that world leaders and businessmen will become rich by doing business
with her. Based on that information, we know that the kings and merchants of the earth will, themselves, be godless. In fact, all who do business and experience wealth during this era will have to align themselves
with the godless stance of both the beast and the incredibly influential
city of Rome. This includes the merchants of the earth; for when the
city meets her end, they will weep and mourn over her, as they will realize that since this city made them rich, her death will mean the end of
their opulent lifestyle.

In addition, she will be the city described as "the great harlot who
corrupted the earth with her fornication." This shows that Rome will
be a worldwide influence, leading all of the nations down the path of
extreme godlessness.

But, this future culture will go far beyond godlessness. Take notice
of what the following verses in Revelation tell us about Rome's future
response toward Christians. First of all, in 17:6, the apostle John reveals:
"I saw the woman, drunk with the blood of the saints and with the blood
of the martyrs of Jesus." Then, 18:24: " announces 'And in her was found
the blood of prophets and saints, and of all who were slain on the earth.' "
Finally, in 19:2, we learn that " 'the blood of His servants [was] shed by

her.' " These verses reveal the true character of this city and show us how Satanically-inspired it truly will be, as Rome will persecute Christians, putting many to death.

The Judgment of Rome

However, there is good news in all of this. This godless city, which will severely persecute followers of Jesus, will not escape God's judgment as demonstrated in Revelation 16:18–19. At the very end of the tribulation period, God will use a great earthquake to judge the city.[8]

More information on Rome's judgment is given to us in Revelation 17:16–18, where the ten horns mentioned in these verses refer to ten kings who will serve as rulers of provinces under the authority of the beast.[9] In addition, the ten kings will bring about Rome's desolation by using something that will cause her to burn. In doing so, God will use these kings to fulfill *his* purpose.

But, why would the ten kings destroy the city? The answer may be that it is likely the city will take away profits and power from the regions over which they rule. If so, then it is highly likely they will destroy Rome due to jealousy and greed.

Earlier we noted that God will cause a great earthquake to judge this city. However, it appears that the ten kings will launch a possible nuclear attack in judgment on this city, as indicated by the description "make her desolate and naked, eat her flesh and burn her with fire." So, which is correct? Actually, both statements are correct. Apparently, God will cause a great earthquake to tear the city apart, and he will use the ten kings to bring final desolation on the city to complete his judgment of this ungodly and ruthless city.

The Lesson of God's Sovereignty

In addition to relating that the kings will destroy the city, verses 16–18 also tell us about God's sovereignty. We see his control from his utilization of the ten unbelieving kings to fulfill his purpose of destroying the city. Again, we are reminded that God will be in full control of what will occur in the future tribulation period, in the same way he is in control of what occurs in our lives today.

Therefore, if the perfectly good God of the universe is truly sovereign, then we do not need to be anxious about what will occur in our lives. We can trust he will allow in our lives only what will be utilized by him for ultimate good. We can trust he will take care of us while we encounter difficulties and apparent tragedies. And, we can trust he will judge those who do evil against us.

Rome Consumed

Verses 5–8 of Revelation 18 reveal that at the height of her power and wealth, Rome will believe she is untouchable from God's judgment, as expressed in this statement borne out of arrogance: " 'She says in her heart, "I sit as queen, and am no widow, and will not see sorrow." ' " However, " 'in the measure that she glorified herself and lived luxuriously, in the same measure [God will] give her torment and sorrow.' "

Before the seven-year tribulation period ends, God will have "remembered her iniquities." He will "repay her double according to her works."

This last statement does not mean God will give twice the consequence of judgment as this ungodly city deserves. Instead, it is a way of emphasizing that God will *certainly* provide the judgment she has acquired for herself. She will not escape!

This is demonstrated by the declaration of the angel from heaven in verse 8, which shows that God's judgment will be poured out suddenly and in massive intensity. Rome will experience more than one plague at the same time, on the same day. She will be "utterly burned with fire," meaning this city will be completely consumed by fire. There will be nothing left but the "death and mourning and famine" that will follow such a catastrophic occurrence.

The principle that is true for this city is true for all the ungodly: though it may appear that the ungodly get away with their sin, God will judge. The wicked believe God does not see their wickedness;[10] therefore, no one will judge them. However, Psalm 11:7 announces that "upon the wicked he will rain coals, fire and brimstone and a burning wind; this shall be the portion of their cup." Thus, they will *not* escape!

The Mourning of the Kings of the Earth

We have seen that the ten kings serving directly under the beast will rejoice at the destruction of the city. But, at least two other groups will have different responses to Rome's judgment. For example, the kings of the earth will deeply mourn the city's demise. When they see the smoke of her burning, they will be "standing at a distance for fear of her torment, saying, 'Alas, alas, that great city Babylon, that mighty city! For in one hour your judgment has come'" (Revelation 18:9–10).

How do we know that the kings of the earth are different kings from the ten kings ruling directly under the beast? Their responses to the fate of the city are completely different. While the ten kings will hate the city and bring about her desolation, the kings of the earth will deeply mourn and lament the city's passing. It seems that these kings benefit from this powerful city. Possibly, Rome will enrich these kings in some way economically. Most likely, the city will somehow enable them to retain their rule, which of course these kings will be interested in preserving.

During that future era, only wicked men will rule—those who are against God and his purposes. These kings will have wicked and self-centered desires, such as the desire to remain in power, no matter what the cost might be. It seems logical, then, that they will mourn Rome's demise, not because of some philanthropic reason—some great benefit the city has provided their people—but due to their own self-centered purpose: that of retaining power and wealth.

But, while they mourn the city's ruin, they will stand at a distance for fear of her torment. Why? It is highly likely that the city's judgment is the result of a nuclear attack from the ten kings. If so, then their response from a distance makes sense. The kings of the earth will seek to stay away from the radiation that will result.

Aside from this response by the kings of the earth, "the merchants of the earth will weep and mourn over her, for no one buys their merchandise anymore." Like the kings of the earth, their reaction will be purely self-centered. They will mourn her obliteration because that will mean they will no longer have a market for their goods. And since they are merchants, they make their living selling things; thus, Rome's ruin will mean they no longer have a means to make money.

The Mourning of the Merchants

Another group will also mourn the city's end—those who trade on the sea. Verses 17–19 of Revelation 18 present their response in this way:

"Every shipmaster, all who travel by ship, sailors,
and as many as trade on the sea, stood at a distance
and cried out when they saw the smoke of her burn-

ing, saying, 'What is like this great city?' They threw dust on their heads and cried out, weeping and wailing, and saying, 'Alas, alas, that great city, in which all who had ships on the sea became rich by her wealth! For in one hour she is made desolate.' "

That Rome will be so greatly missed by anyone trading via the sea tells us that she will be the major port city of that day, the center of commerce for the world. Notice also that when all who make their living by the sea mourn this city, they will do so by standing *at a distance*. Like the kings of the earth, these seafarers will also fear the nuclear radiation resulting from the attack upon this city. So, while grieving the loss of all that Rome had meant to them, they dare not get too close to her now!

Literal Babylon

We began this chapter with the title, "A Tale of Two Cities," but up till now, we have not lived up to the billing, for we have only focused on one city, Rome. But, there is another city that will be notable during the last half of the day of the Lord. That city is literal Babylon.

As we have seen, in the book of Revelation, Babylon refers to Rome. However, literal Babylon will also be a significant city in the tribulation period.

The chapters devoted to presenting the greatest amount of information about the role of Rome during the future seven-year era are chapters 17 and 18 of Revelation. Interestingly, these two chapters, which mention Babylon, present many parallels with chapters 50 and 51 of Jeremiah, which also mention Babylon. In fact, there are so many parallels to these chapters in Jeremiah that speak of a *literal* Babylon that some Bible teachers believe Revelation 17 and 18 must refer to literal Babylon. However, we have seen that Revelation 17–18 describe future Rome.

But, Jeremiah chapters 50 and 51 *do* describe literal Babylon. For example, 50:1 makes clear that these two chapters speak of literal Babylon. It does so by announcing that the word of the Lord in these chapters is spoken against Babylon and then clarifying that this Babylon is "the land of the Chaldeans." This phrase can only refer to literal Babylon.

Several of the declarations regarding literal Babylon have not yet been fulfilled. These include Babylon's sudden destruction,[11] its complete destruction,[12] God's people fleeing the city,[13] and Israel and Judah re-united following Babylon's fall.[14] We can only conclude by the lack of fulfillment of God's forecast for Babylon that Jeremiah chapters 50 and 51 will be fulfilled in the future.

The Beast's Two Cities

One deduction that can be made from this is the possibility that not only will Rome be a prominent city during the tribulation period, but Babylon will be, as well. While Rome could be the beast's capital city throughout much of the last half of the day of the Lord, Babylon could be his capital *after* he turns his back on Rome—some time prior to the destruction of the city. It only seems logical that before the beast allows his ten kings to destroy Rome, he will first need to turn *his* back on the city. But, in order for him to do that, he will need to have already chosen and begun to reside in a new capital city—Babylon.

Or, it could be that Babylon is his Middle East capital, while Rome is his Western capital. With two capital cities for this future world ruler, it would mean he has a connection with one of them (Rome) as the former Roman emperor and as the other (Babylon) as the king of the North who arises from Iraq (where, of course, Babylon is located).

If so, then God will judge *both* cities during tribulation period. Then, as we see in Revelation 19:1–2, heaven will declare: "Alleluia! Salvation and glory and honor and power belong to the Lord our God! For true and righteous are His judgments!"

However, before the earth can see the salvation of the Lord, Israel will need to call upon the Lord. In the next chapter, we will see how that happens.

CHAPTER 21
A Cry in the Dark

B y the end of his life, musician Giuseppe Verdi was recognized as a master of dramatic composition. His works astonished the world of music with a power, subtlety, and brilliance that marked the ultimate in Italian grand opera. But, he didn't begin his career with such success.

As a youth, he was denied entrance to the Milan Conservatory because he lacked the necessary training. Although his musical abilities were apparent in childhood, as an innkeeper's son he did not possess the formal education and background required.

Yet, time does strange things. After Verdi's fame had spread worldwide, the school was renamed the "Verdi Conservatory of Music." This turn of events is a reminder that endings are not always like their beginnings.

This is the lesson regarding Israel and her Messiah. When Jesus came to Israel in the first century, he was rejected and put to death by the nation. But fortunately, endings are not always like their beginnings, as Israel will one day soon not only believe in Jesus as her Messiah, but will cry out to him to deliver the nation out of a very dark time.

Gathering to Jerusalem

In chapter 7, we saw that near the end of the tribulation period, Satan will gather together the armies of the nations in order to try to prevent Christ's rule when he returns to the earth. They will gather in the valley of Megiddo (the Jezreel Valley) in northern Israel, but then stream down to the Kidron Valley (the Valley of Jehoshaphat). There they will seek to keep Jesus from successfully traveling from the Mount of Olives—the point at which he will return to the earth—to the Temple Mount, where he will ascend his throne to rule the earth.

However, there will be such a massive amount of soldiers in that mobilization that the Kidron Valley will not be able to hold them all. For example, verses 1 and 2 of Zechariah 12 pull back the curtain of this gathering to show us what will actually occur behind the scenes as a result of the massive influx of troops into that region:

> Thus says the Lord, who stretches out the heavens,
> lays the foundation of the earth, and forms the spirit
> of man within him: "Behold, I will make Jerusalem
> a cup of drunkenness to all the surrounding peoples,
> when they lay siege against Judah and Jerusalem."

Chapters 12–14 of Zechariah function as one unit. The unit presents Israel turning to the Lord in a time of dire need at the very end of the tribulation period crying out to God for deliverance. In addition, it shows God's response to Israel's cry by sending Jesus back to physically save Israel from her enemies.

God's Trap for the Armies of the World

Verses 1 and 2 of Zechariah chapter 12 introduce God as the creator of the heavens, the earth, and of "the spirit of man within him," thus presenting him as the master of mankind and man as the servant at God's beck and call. This focus prepares us for the Lord's announcement in these verses. It implies God's luring of the armies of the nations to Judah, occurring shortly after the kings of the earth and their armies begin to assemble in the Valley of Megiddo. Furthermore, as the creator who possesses all power and sovereignty over his creation, he will indeed fulfill his announcement of judgment upon the nations that come against Jerusalem.

Judah is southern Israel, the area in which Jerusalem, the Mount of Olives, the Kidron Valley, and the Temple Mount are located. There will be such a monumental amount of troops flowing south from the Valley of Megiddo prior to the return of Christ that neither the Kidron Valley nor Jerusalem will be able to contain them all. It will take the entire region of Judah (and probably more) to host that many troops.

Though Satan will gather the armies to "lay siege against Judah and Jerusalem," God will be laying a trap for them, utilizing Jerusalem to be "a cup of drunkenness" for these demonically-led troops. While they are "drinking" up Jerusalem by laying siege against the city, they will become prey for God's judgment—targets to take down as easy as a man in a drunken stupor.

The Lord paints the picture of using Jerusalem as his tool of judgment in this fashion in verses 3 and 4:

> "And it shall happen in that day that I will make Jerusalem a very heavy stone for all peoples; all who would heave it away will surely be cut in pieces, though all nations of the earth are gathered against it. In that day," says the Lord, "I will strike every horse with confusion, and its rider with madness; I will open My eyes on the house of Judah, and will strike every horse of the peoples with blindness."

God reminds us of the seemingly overwhelming odds against Jerusalem in that day by stating that "all of the nations of the earth are gathered against it." But, when the Lord is on the side of his people, no matter how much in the minority they may be, *they* become the overwhelming favorites.

The striking of the horses with confusion and the riders with madness will clearly demonstrate that the defeat of the nations' troops will be due to the Lord's judgment, not by anything Jewish followers of Christ will accomplish. Just as in the conquering of the Canaanites by the Joshua-led Israelites, victory will come by trusting the Lord.

God's Use of the Leaders of Judah to Fight the Armies

However, just as God utilized the Jews under Joshua's leadership to achieve victory over their Canaanite enemies, similarly, he will employ Jews in the future to obtain conquest over their worldwide enemies. The Lord explains this plan in verses 5–9 of Zechariah 12.

God announces he will make the leaders of Judah powerful instruments of his fiery judgment. "They shall devour all the surrounding peoples" as he seeks "to destroy all the nations that come against Jerusalem." Surprisingly, God will use inhabitants of Jerusalem to deliver her from her enemies. To do that, God declares he will enable the leaders of Judah to destroy those coming against the city.

The Lord grants us insight into how he will deliver his holy city by the hands of his people. For example, he declares that those dwelling in Jerusalem at the time of the siege will be imbued with God's strength against their enemies. To demonstrate his power and glory, he will grant even the weaker Jews in Jerusalem the warrior ability of David, who destroyed tens of thousands of armed men.[1] These descendants of David will be given the conquering power of God with the all-powerful angel of the Lord going before them in victory.

As we have mentioned, God will allow the nations to come against Jerusalem in order to judge them. As they invade, they will be stepping into his trap.

God's Purpose for Good for Israel

But, God will also employ the siege to accomplish a good purpose for his people—those Jews who have believed in Christ prior to the siege. The siege will bring upon his people great difficulties in order to prepare them for a greater eternal experience. As is his purpose for trials and sufferings for all believers, God will seek to grow these Jewish believers to prepare them for greater reward in his impending kingdom.

While Zechariah 12:1–9 describes Israel's future physical salvation, verses 10–14 that follow describe what leads up to this deliverance. They reveal God's necessary preparation for the nation of Israel to bring his kingdom to the earth.

In Scripture that is well-known to many Christians, God promises in verse 10 what he will do for Israel at that time and how Israel will respond, as a result.

194

"And I will pour on the house of David and on the inhabitants of Jerusalem the Spirit[2] of grace and supplication; then they will look on Me whom they pierced. Yes, they will mourn for Him as one mourns for his only son, and grieve for Him as one grieves for a firstborn."

The word in this verse translated from the original Hebrew writing as *Spirit* could also be translated as *spirit*. This would change the meaning from the Holy Spirit to "an attitude or principle that inspires action." It seems that the first part of verse 10, in which God will pour out the spirit of grace and supplication, is *not* speaking of receiving the indwelling Holy Spirit when one believes in Christ for eternal life.[3] This, instead, describes God granting motivation to turn to him for help.

Notice on whom God will pour out this *spirit* at that time. He will pour it out on Jews ("the house of David")—specifically, the inhabitants of Jerusalem.

Keep in mind that faithful Jewish believers in Christ who reside in Jerusalem during the first half of the tribulation period (under the ministry of God's two prophets) will flee Jerusalem into the surrounding wilderness at the very middle of the tribulation period—that is, when the abomination of desolation occurs. Other Jewish believers in Christ who choose to stay put in Jerusalem and Judea will be hunted down and killed. This means that Jerusalem will be "cleansed" of all Christians before we arrive at the time when God pours out "the spirit of grace and supplication." This also means that Jews who are still residing in Jerusalem near the end of the tribulation period before the occurrence of Zechariah 12:10 will not have received eternal life prior to this.

However, verse 10 provides evidence that these Jews in and around Jerusalem when the invasion of the armies of the nations occurs *will* believe in Christ just prior to his return.

The statement, "they will look on Me whom they pierced," also appears in John 19:34 and 37, which present occurrences while Jesus is on the cross. Here is what those verses say: "But one of the soldiers pierced His side with a spear, and immediately blood and water came out. . . . And again another Scripture says, 'They shall look on Him whom they pierced.' "

While both verses in John 19 contribute to our understanding of Zechariah 12:10, verse 37 actually quotes from it. Putting the two verses together with the context of the death of Christ on our behalf, we see what the Jews portrayed in Zechariah 12 will understand. They will come to the realization that the Messiah—Jesus—died at the hands of their ancestors. This is essentially what the apostle Peter announced in Acts 2 to first-century Jews who were from Jerusalem, beginning in verse 14, where he identifies his audience, and—extending beyond verse 36—he levels a convicting charge in this way: "Men of Judea and all who dwell in Jerusalem . . . this Jesus, whom you crucified, [is] both Lord and Christ. "

Therefore, the Jews in Judea described in Zechariah 12 will come to believe in Jesus Christ for eternal life at that point. They will then direct supplication to God.

Israel's Call for Christ

"Supplication" is a humble prayer to God. The two things supplication implies in this context are: 1) these Jews are brought to humility before God, and 2) they cry out to God for his help. No doubt, the primary motivating factor moving them to cry out to the Lord for his help is that Jerusalem is being ravished by the Gentile armies at that point.

The very end of verse 10 announces that the Jews of that day in and around Jerusalem " 'will mourn for Him as one mourns for his only son, and grieve for Him as one grieves for a firstborn.' " Since a firstborn son has always been highly treasured in Israel, this shows an intense grieving for the one they have pierced. But, it would make no sense for them to mourn in this way if they did not believe they put to death the Messiah (the Christ). This is another indicator that they will believe in Jesus for eternal life.

In addition, "only son" and "firstborn" also point to Jesus Christ. He is "the only begotten Son of God" (John 3:16) and "the firstborn from the dead" (Colossians 1:18) and will be "the firstborn among many brethren" (Romans 8:29) in the future kingdom. This is further indication—their looking to this one and their mourning of him—of their faith in him for eternal life.

Revelation 1:7 merges Zechariah 12:10 with Daniel 7:13–14 in predicting Jesus' return in this way: "Behold, He is coming with clouds, and every eye will see Him, and they also who pierced Him." This merging combines the revelation of these Jews in the future looking upon him whom they have pierced with the scene in Daniel in which Jesus receives his kingdom. In addition, this merge shows us when these Jews will believe in Jesus: it will be just before, and at the time of, his return to the earth to physically deliver them. Therefore, the scene in Zechariah 12 will be played out at the *very end* of the day of the Lord.

The Mourning of Jews for the Crucified One

The passage in Zechariah 12 continues in verses 11–14 with the sustained theme of mourning the pierced one by these Jews. For example: "In that day there shall be a great mourning in Jerusalem, like the mourning at Hadad Rimmon in the plain of Megiddo."

It seems that Hadad Rimmon refers to the slaying of godly King Josiah in the plain of Megiddo by Pharaoh Necho.[5] When he was killed, the hope of the nation seemed to be gone prior to its fall at the hands of Babylon. The dirges written by the prophet Jeremiah mourning the death of Josiah symbolize the grieving experienced by those from Judah, particularly the godly. The mourning in that future day for the perfectly godly one who is coming as king will rival ancient Jews' grieving for the godly King Josiah.

As described in verses 11–14, the mourning will display sorrow that will be public and private, national and individual, personal and family. As Charles Feinberg points out:

> The mourning will extend from the highest to the lowest of the land. The mention of the house of David shows the kings to be guilty; the house of Nathan, prophets guilty; the house of Levi, the priests guilty; and the house of Shimei, the ordinary Levites (Numbers 3:21) guilty.[6]

The Repentance of Israel

This very intense and sincere mourning in Zechariah will lead these Jews to repentance. We know that because of the teaching on repentance by the apostle Paul in 2 Corinthians 7:10: "For godly sorrow produces repentance leading to salvation, not to be regretted; but the sorrow of the world produces death." This salvation mentioned by Paul does not refer to the gift of eternal life, but refers to God's *deliverance*[7] of his people from being spiritually defeated by present struggles and into the experience of victory. That is what Israel will experience when the nation repents by turning to the Lord in the future.

This same message was presented by the apostle Peter in Acts 3:19–21. The potential results presented in these verses are "times of refreshing and the times of restoration of all things." Both of these phrases refer to the arrival of the future kingdom of God upon the earth. The kingdom will come when God sends "Jesus Christ whom heaven must receive" until that time.

So, the promise is the coming of the kingdom when Israel upholds its part by its response to the Lord. At first, it seems like Israel needs to meet two conditions—they must repent and be converted. However, *be converted* is a poor translation of a Greek word that means to turn back, or turn to.[8] In this case, it means to turn to the Lord, which is, essentially, what repentance means.

Thus, Peter announced this: when Israel turns to the Lord, Jesus will return to the earth to establish the kingdom of God upon the earth. God is waiting for the repentance of Israel in order to bring his kingdom to the earth, which will come about in his perfect timing.

God is even now preparing the stage for the events leading up to the return of Christ. In the next chapter, we will see that when he returns, it will be for deliverance and for judgment.

CHAPTER 22
The Incredible Rescue

In his commentary on the book of Daniel, Donald Campbell cites an interview between Billy Graham and the Konrad Adenauer, then chancellor of Germany, in which Mr. Adenauer asked Mr. Graham a series of questions:

"Do you believe Jesus Christ rose from the dead?"

Graham: "Yes, sir, I do."

"Do you believe he ascended and is in heaven now?"

"Yes, sir, I do."

"Some say Jesus Christ will return and reign on this earth. Do you believe that?"

"Yes, sir, I do."

After a brief pause, Mr. Adenauer said, "So do I. If he doesn't, there is no hope for this world!"[1]

There is no greater demonstration of the truth of Chancellor Adenauer's declaration than the tribulation period. But, the good news is that Jesus guarantees that he will return to this earth to establish his kingdom.

Immediately After the Tribulation . . .

During the final week leading up to his crucifixion, Jesus led his disciples up to the Mount of Olives, where they asked him, "What will be the sign of your coming, and of the end of the age?" In answer to this question, Jesus gave his famous discourse on events that will occur during the final seven years leading up to his return to the earth.

He then describes his return to the earth in Matthew 24:29–31, announcing it will take place following "the tribulation of those days," a phrase that refers to the persecution Jewish believers will experience during the second half of the tribulation period. At the very end, cataclysmic events will occur, such as the "darkening of the sun and moon" and "the shaking of the heavens," which will include "stars falling from heaven."

Jesus describes scenes from two Old Testament passages connected with his return to the earth. The first of those—"the Son of Man appearing in heaven"—is found in Daniel 7:13–14. There we find that following "his coming with the clouds of heaven," Jesus will receive the kingdom to rule over the earth.

The second scene mentioned in Matthew 24:29–31 comes from the passage we examined in the last chapter, Zechariah 12, and is referenced by this phrase: "all the tribes of the [land of Israel] will mourn." This also describes Jesus' return to the earth, not only by the context of Zechariah 12, but also by the emphasis by Jesus that he will return immediately after the tribulation at the end of the day of the Lord.

In That Day . . .

After believing in Jesus Christ, the Jews of Jerusalem will mourn, indicating their repentance at having participated in the crucifixion of the Christ. Therefore, in relation to the time of the return of Christ, they will mourn just before Jesus returns to the earth.

After describing the mourning and repentance in chapter 12, Zechariah then summarizes that day in this way in 13:1–2:

> "In that day a fountain shall be opened for the
> house of David and for the inhabitants of Jerusalem,
> for sin and for uncleanness. It shall be in that day,"
> says the Lord of hosts, "that I will cut off the names
> of the idols from the land, and they shall no longer be

remembered. I will also cause the [false] prophets and the unclean spirit to depart from the land."

This pictures God's grace poured out on the Jews in Jerusalem when he cleanses them from sin. At this point, the Lord will cleanse the land, leaving righteousness to reign. Of course, this also indicates they will have believed in Jesus as the Christ by then.

Incredible Persecution . . . Great Potential Reward

Zechariah 13:1–2 gives an overview of the end of the tribulation period and the initiation of the kingdom following the return of Christ to the earth. But, several verses later, we receive a picture of what the last half of the tribulation period will be like for Israel. Note verses 8–9:

> "And it shall come to pass in all the land," says the Lord, "That two-thirds in it shall be cut off and die, but one- third shall be left in it: I will bring the one-third through the fire, will refine them as silver is refined, and test them as gold is tested. They will call on My name, and I will answer them. I will say, 'This is My people', and each one will say, 'The Lord is my God.' "

It is shocking to think that, during the last half of the tribulation period, two-thirds of all Jews living in the land of Israel will die! The awful carnage of Jews will be like reliving the Holocaust. For Jews in the land who do not die during the tribulation period, it will be a very difficult time, as pictured by the metaphor of refining silver and gold through fire.

The apostle Peter seems to pick up on this very metaphor as he writes to first-century Christian readers who were enduring suffering brought on by persecution. Note 1 Peter 1:6, 7, 9:

> In this you greatly rejoice, though now for a little while, if need be, you have been grieved by various trials, that the genuineness of your faith, being much more precious than gold that perishes, though it is tested by fire, may be found to praise, honor, and glory at the revelation of Jesus Christ, . . . receiving the end of your faith—the salvation of your souls [lives].

The Greek word translated as *souls* in the last word in this passage can also be translated as *lives*.[2] "Salvation" in 1 Peter actually refers to future kingdom reward—specifically, rule with Christ in the kingdom.[3] "The salvation of your lives," then, refers to Christians experiencing life to the fullest degree forever due to obedience to Christ.

Peter is sharing with us in these verses that believers in Christ should rejoice in the midst of trials and suffering, knowing that God is using their suffering to grow them spiritually. As a result of growing his people through suffering now, God is preparing them for possible kingdom rule with the Lord.

Therefore, God will use the suffering of persecution in the lives of believing Jews in the latter half of the day of the Lord in the same way. He will use the suffering they will experience to *refine* them for the kingdom—to prepare them for great, eternal reward.

Israel's Response . . . Calling on the Lord

According Zechariah 13:9, those Jews will respond in the midst of their "refining process" by calling upon the Lord. The context tells us they will call upon the Messiah for deliverance, and Jesus will answer their prayer by returning to the earth to deliver them from their enemies.

Once before, Jews in Jerusalem called for help when they cried out "Hosanna!" ("Help us, please, Lord!") at the triumphant entry of Jesus into Jerusalem upon a donkey colt. That crowd believed Jesus to be the Messiah, and they thought he was coming into Jerusalem to liberate them politically from the rule of the Romans. However, at that time, the cry represented a minority of Jews and did not represent the Jewish leadership as a whole, while the future cry of the Jews in Jerusalem will represent the majority of those left alive at the time.

This prayer of Jews in Israel at the end of the day of the Lord comes at the very end of Zechariah 13. Chapter 14 shows the answer to that prayer. But, before the answer is revealed, God uses the first two verses to review what the situation in Jerusalem will be at that time:

> Behold, the day of the Lord is coming, and your
> spoil will be divided in your midst. For I will gather all
> the nations to battle against Jerusalem; the city shall
> be taken, the houses rifled, and the women ravished.
> Half of the city shall go into captivity, but the rem-
> nant of the people shall not be cut off from the city.

Israel's Need of Deliverance

According to these verses, Jerusalem will be in need of deliverance at that time because it will be overrun by the armies of the nations. It will be in captivity, with soldiers breaking into houses and stealing from them, mistreating (i.e., raping) women, etc. But, the remnant will "not be cut off from the city."

The "remnant" refers to those Jews who are faithful—who have not only believed in Christ for eternal life, but who faithfully follow him as disciples. This remnant is the group of Jews left alive after two-thirds of all those living in Israel die.

Though the city is overtaken and ravaged, the faithful will not be "cut off." That is, they will not be overcome and killed.[4] God will allow them to remain in order to cry out for the Messiah to return and deliver his people.

The Answer to Israel's Call for Help

The answer to this cry for help by these Jews is revealed in Zechariah 14:3–4a: "Then the Lord will go forth and fight against those nations, as He fights in the day of battle. And in that day His feet will stand on the Mount of Olives, which faces Jerusalem on the east."

He will answer by returning to the earth to physically deliver the Jews from their enemies. And when he returns, he will come as a warrior, to "fight against those nations, as He fights in the day of battle."

We are also informed *where* he will return to battle his enemies—to the Mount of Olives. It is from the Mount of Olives that he ascended,[5] and it will be to the Mount of Olives that he will return. And, as we have noted, Satan knows that, which is why he will assemble the nations to that area to do battle in preparation of Jesus' return.

The Way of Escape

The last half of verse 4, along with verse 5, present the way of escape for the remnant:

> And the Mount of Olives shall be split in two,
> from east to west, making a very large valley; half of
> the mountain shall move toward the north and half of
> it toward the south. Then you shall flee through My
> mountain valley, for the mountain valley shall reach

to Azal. Yes, you shall flee as you fled from the earthquake in the days of Uzziah king of Judah.[6] Thus the
Lord my God will come, and all the saints with You.

When Christ returns, the Lord will supernaturally provide for the
escape of the remnant by creating a powerful earthquake to split the
Mount of Olives in two. The Jews of Jerusalem will then escape their
enemies via the massive valley produced by the quake.

When the Saints Come Marching In

When He does come back, He will not return alone. All the saints
will come with him.

"All the saints" represent every person who has believed in Christ
for eternal life from the time of Adam onward. They are those believers
who have either died or who have joined Christ in the air at the time of
the rapture of the church. Jude quotes "Enoch, the seventh from Adam,"
who prophesied about this accompaniment in this way: "Behold, the
Lord comes with ten thousands of His saints" This means that each of us
who has believed in Christ for eternal life will be with him at his return
to deliver Israel at that time.

The King's Judgment against His Enemies

Following His return, Zechariah the prophet makes this announcement in 14:9: "And the Lord shall be King over all the earth." Jerusalem
is singled out two verses later, as it is described in this way: "The people
shall dwell in it; and no longer shall there be utter destruction, but Jerusalem shall be safely inhabited." Jesus will successfully save Jerusalem,
which will be at peace from her enemies from then on.

In presenting the return of Christ to deliver the Jews and Jerusalem
from their enemies, Zechariah seems to skip over Jesus' judgment leveled upon the nations. He mentions his return, the deliverance of the
Jews, the announcement of Jesus as king over the earth, and the salvation of Jerusalem. But, there is no mention of Christ's victory over, or
judgment upon, Satan's armies—that is, until verses 12–15.

Following the picture of deliverance in verse 11, Zechariah does a
slight "rerun" to show us how God will judge those who have fought
against Jerusalem. This is the picture painted in verse 12: "And this shall
be the plague with which the Lord will strike all the people who fought

against Jerusalem: their flesh shall dissolve while they stand on their feet, their eyes shall dissolve in their sockets, and their tongues shall dissolve in their mouths."[7]

The judgment of God upon all the people who fought against Jerusalem is pictured by the same verb, *dissolve*, used three times—once for the body as a whole ("their flesh") and once each for a different body part ("eyes" and "tongues"). Though this kind of decay and putrefaction would naturally occur over time with corpses, this judgment will occur with swift suddenness while these are still alive. It will occur while they stand upon their feet.

As this judgment is being poured out, this will be the scene:

It shall come to pass in that day that a great panic from the Lord will be among them. Everyone will seize the hand of his neighbor, and raise his hand against his neighbor's hand; Judah also will fight at Jerusalem. And the wealth of all the surrounding nations shall be gathered together: Gold, silver, and apparel in great abundance. Such also shall be the plague on the horse and the mule, on the camel and the donkey, and on all the cattle that will be in those camps. So shall this plague be.

One might think Jesus would be the lone battler against the armies of the nations. But, surprisingly, the Jews will participate in battling for the deliverance of Jerusalem, as we see in this statement: "Judah also will fight at Jerusalem." Not only will Jesus do battle, but so will the surviving Jews in southern Israel.

Judgment will not only come in a physical way upon those of the nations who ravished Jerusalem, but God's judgment will also be displayed in other ways, as he gathers their wealth from them and brings the same physical plague upon their animals. Thus, the Lord will bring complete destruction upon the enemies of God's people (believing Jews) and of his beloved city, Jerusalem.

The Coming of the Warrior

God provides us with another picture of the return of Jesus to judge his enemies in Revelation chapter 19, beginning with verse 11: "Now

I saw heaven opened, and behold, a white horse. And He who sat on him was called Faithful and True, and in righteousness He judges and makes war."

Because Jesus is "Faithful and True," he will *definitely* return to establish his kingdom. When he does, he will be looking toward the judgment of his enemies at his return. This is why Jesus is depicted wearing "a robe dipped in blood," representing, in this context, the blood of his enemies that he will shed in judgment at his return.

In this description in Revelation 19, Jesus is not only presented as a fierce warrior coming in judgment of his enemies, but also as the king of all rulers. He is presented as the one who will rule with an iron fist, keeping perfect control and order in his kingdom and eliminating all who resist him.

The Winepress of God

Moreover, Jesus is presented as "treading the winepress of the fierceness and wrath of Almighty God," a figure that stems from Isaiah 63:1–6 and refers to Jesus' fierce judgment upon his enemies. "The winepress" is a simile for judgment. As the juice of grapes being trampled splatters the clothing of the one working in the winepress, so the trampling of his enemies in judgment will be such that their blood will splatter his garments.

In Revelation 14:20, also in the context of the return of Christ in judgment,[8] we are presented with this similar picture: "And the winepress was trampled outside the city [Jerusalem], and blood came out of the winepress, up to the horses' bridles, for one thousand six hundred furlongs [approximately 180 miles]." Here, God gives us a very graphic picture of the judgment that will occur at the return of Christ—blood flowing for one hundred and eighty miles up to the horses' bridles—a presentation of unimaginable slaughter!

A Picture of Slaughter

The picture of slaughter continues as we return to the presentation of the return of Jesus in Revelation 19:17–19, where an invitation is given to carrion-eating birds to feast upon a massive amount of corpses. As in Revelation 14:20, this too portrays an almost unbelievable slaughter!

Because this battle is so incredibly important, it is also portrayed in the Old Testament, particularly in Ezekiel 39:4. The Lord gives a warning to the armies of those nations. He warns that they will suffer massive casualties, with their corpses being fed to the birds of prey. Sound familiar? Both the amount of casualties and the resulting feeding from the corpses by the birds of prey remind us of what we saw in Revelation 19 at the return of Christ.

Weapons and Bodies

Following the defeat of all who will come against Israel at the return of Christ, Ezekiel 39 drives home an important point by presenting the destruction of the weaponry and the burying of the bodies. Verses 9–13 reveal that there will be such slaughter of those who gather to war against Jesus at his return that, amazingly, Israel will be burying their bodies for seven months afterward! In addition, the Israelites will be destroying their weapons for seven years! These numbers tell us there will be an incredible number of troops and weaponry from the armies of the nations that will gather against Christ for his return! Moreover, against such incredible odds, the Jews will deal the nations an overwhelming defeat!

The Judgment of the Beast and False Prophet

In returning to Revelation 19, verses 20 and 21 reveal that God's two fervent enemies, the beast and the false prophet, will be captured and cast alive into the lake of fire! In addition, 100 percent of the troops assembled against Israel and Christ at his return will be killed. There will be no survivors from the millions who will gather together to wage war against him!

But, the return of Christ to the earth is not just about the Lord's complete judgment of the armies gathered against Jesus at his return; his return is all about preparing for the establishment of God's kingdom upon the earth. His judgment of his enemies is just part of that preparation.

Lessons from the Return of Christ

There are some important lessons we can glean regarding the return of Christ. First, we see that God will vindicate his people. Since the Lord will be victorious over his enemies, his people are on the winning side, in the ultimate sense. Believers who have been persecuted by unbelievers will be raised up over their enemies at the return of Christ.

Second, God will judge the enemies of his people; he will right wrongdoing. We can bank on that. Our sense of justice will be completely fulfilled from that point on—forever!

Third, the Lord will curse those who curse Israel.[9] Historically, God has eventually judged all who have opposed and persecuted the Jews. A perusal of the Old Testament, for example, will demonstrate the veracity of this statement. From Amalek to Assyria to Babylon, God has judged those nations that have come against Israel. A case could also be presented that this pattern has continued to the present day.

It will be no different in the future. He will judge the beast and his false prophet who persecute the Jews during the tribulation period. And the Lord will judge the nations who gather against Jerusalem.

Fourth, God will fulfill his promises. For example, when Israel turns to the Lord by crying out to Jesus for deliverance, Jesus will, in fact, return—to deliver Israel and to establish God's kingdom upon the earth, just as he has promised. We can definitely depend on God to fulfill every one of his promises.

Finally, God will answer prayer for the peace of Jerusalem. He shows the importance of praying for Jerusalem in places such as Psalm 122:6 and Isaiah 62:18. God not only promises he will answer that prayer, but he also guarantees blessing for believers who will pray in that way.

Wrap-Up

As we have seen, when the majority of Jews cry out for the return of Jesus to deliver them, Jesus will return in deliverance and judgment. His return to the earth will be seven years to the day following the rapture of the church. Based upon the clear and detailed revelation of God, we can see that the world will not end in 2012. However, could the world as we know it change in 2012? Could we be that close to the rapture and the inception of the seven-year tribulation period? We will examine that question in the epilogue.

EPILOGUE
How Soon?

Can We Know If We Are Near?

Though we have seen that the world will not end in 2012, could it be that the rapture and the inception of the seven-year tribulation period could occur as soon as 2012? And if so, can we know if we might be that close to those prophetic events?

Some Christians do not believe we can know if the rapture and the day of the Lord are near. After all, Jesus seemed to indicate that when he made this proclamation about the timing of the rapture in Mark 13:32: "But of that day and hour no one knows, not even the angels in heaven, nor the Son, but only the Father."

Note that in this verse, Jesus revealed that even *he* did not know when the rapture would take place. However, some things have changed since that announcement. For example, Jesus is now at the right hand of God,[1] "with authorities and powers having been made subject to Him."[2] Instead of playing the role of the meek lamb of God, he currently fulfills a very different role, one as high priest interceding on our behalf. As our high priest, he has intimate knowledge of the specific struggles of all believers.[3] While serving on the earth in the role he then carried out, his knowledge was limited. His exaltation into heaven brought him expanded knowledge to go with his new, exalted role. In fact, it is hard to believe Jesus does not *now* know when he will come in the air for us, since it seems unlikely that the Father has not revealed his plan to his Son since his exaltation.

So, what does this mean in relation to Mark 13:32? What Jesus proclaimed in that verse *was* true when he proclaimed it, but things have changed with his new role. Thus, the statement in Mark 13:32 represented what *was* true with Jesus, but does not represent his current understanding.[4]

If any part of Mark 13:32 has changed in its relationship to what is currently true, then its entirety may also be relegated to a past application that may no longer be the situation today. This would mean that believers could gain a clearer understanding of the timing of the day of the Lord as we draw closer to it. In other words, Christians living near the end of the church age who have their eyes wide open to what God is doing in the world through the fulfillment of his prophetic word could know that they are very close to the occurrence of the rapture and the beginning of the day of the Lord. In fact, the apostle Paul announced this possibility to Christian readers in 1 Thessalonians 5:4 when he wrote this: "But you, brethren, are not in darkness, so that this Day should overtake you as a thief."

This Day refers to the day of the Lord.[5] While he announced two verses earlier that, to the world, "the day of the Lord so comes as a thief in the night," he clearly stated in verse 4 that it should not overtake believers in this way. What did he mean by that? He meant that non-Christians will be caught by surprise by this period of time, but Christians should see it coming.

Of course, as we have seen, Christians living on this side of the tribulation period will be removed from the world on the day it begins. But, the emphasis indicated by the analogy of a thief in the night is upon the element of surprise. Therefore, Christians who are spiritually alert should not be surprised by the timing of the day of the Lord (and, as well, the rapture of the church). The implication is that those believers who are living just prior to that era should foresee its approach.

If that is true, then might we be close to the rapture of the church and the beginning of the Day of the Lord? And if so, how close?

The Return of the Jews to Israel

At the end of the nineteenth century, God began to fulfill Ezekiel 37, which predicts that God would bring Jews into the land of Israel in order to prepare for the salvation of Israel. Israel's *spiritual* salvation will take place within the seven-year tribulation period prior to the return of Christ, while Israel's *physical* salvation will occur at the return of Jesus to the earth. Thus, the fulfillment of Jews immigrating into the land of Israel would indicate the nearness of the day of the Lord. So, how close is that fulfillment?

Prior to Israel becoming a state in 1948, the Jewish population grew to 600,000 in five great waves of immigration. More than 3 million more have followed, and Israel's Jewish population now stands at 5.5 million. "Of the world's population of just over 13 million Jews, Israel's is the biggest portion, having surpassed America's in 2006."[6]

In referring to the immense number of immigrants to Israel in comparison to the smaller number of citizens, Sergio DellaPergola, a prominent demographer at the Jewish People Policy Planning Institute, a Jerusalem think tank, announced: "There is no place in the world where the number of immigrants is five times the number of the people who were there. It is unprecedented."[7]

However, since the occurrence of that great influx, the immigration into Israel has achieved a slowdown. In fact, according to DellaPergola, "Israel is nearing zero growth from immigration."[8] This may indicate that Israel is nearing the number of Jews God has appointed to be in the land when the prophetic era begins. If so, the day of the Lord may be right around the corner.

Israel's Possession of Jerusalem

Another important indicator of the nearness of the day of the Lord is Israel's possession of Jerusalem. When God put Jerusalem back into the hands of Israel in 1967, it fulfilled Jesus' prophecy of Luke 21:24, where he announced that the Jewish capital would be under Gentile control "until the times of the Gentiles are fulfilled." Since the times of the Gentiles refers to God's focus upon Gentiles for salvation, Israel's current possession of Jerusalem signals that God has begun to turn his attention toward Israel for salvation. Since that salvation will occur during the day of the Lord, that seven-year period cannot be far away.[9]

Three Jewish Groups Prepare for the Messiah

In addition, Jewish groups have come together in Israel to prepare for the coming of the Messiah. For example, the Temple Mount and Land of Israel Faithful Movement in Jerusalem, a movement that is seeking to rebuild the temple to prepare for the coming of the Messiah, has already hand-hewed the cornerstone for the temple.[10] Also, The Temple Institute has already created what is needed for temple service, such as the utensils used in temple service and the garments of the high priest.[11] As noted, the temple will be rebuilt in Jerusalem within the first half of the day of the Lord in fulfillment of Scripture.[12]

Moreover, in October of 2004, the Sanhedrin was reestablished. "The Sanhedrin is the name given in the *mishna* to the council of seventy-one Jewish sages who constituted the supreme court and legislative body in Judea during the Roman period. . . . The Jewish Sanhedrin is a governmental body that resembles aspects of both the U.S. Senate and the Supreme Court."[13] A major role of the ancient Sanhedrin was to legislate and judge the observance of the Mosaic law.[14] Since the tribulation period will begin with the reestablishment of a strong focus on the Mosaic law in the land of Israel, might the reestablishment of the Sanhedrin be a movement of God preparing for the soon arrival of the day of the Lord? The timing of this, along with the recent formation of the two Jewish groups cited above, seems to be beyond a coincidence. It is as if God is preparing the Jews in Israel for salvation in all possible ways.

The Focus on Rebuilding the Temple

Recently, the focus on rebuilding the temple in Jerusalem has heightened significantly. This is compelling, since the temple will be rebuilt on the Temple Mount as a result of the peace treaty between ten nations and Israel. According to Daniel 9:27, "sacrifice and offering" are part of the treaty (for when the treaty is broken, sacrifice and offering cease), and since Jews cannot provide sacrifice and offering without a temple, rebuilding the temple will be part of the treaty. And, we know that the temple will definitely be rebuilt by the middle of the seven-year tribulation period.[15] In fact, it will likely be rebuilt well before that three-and-a-half-year mark.[16]

But, seeing how the Temple Mount is so Arab-sensitive, and because the Dome of the Rock and the al-Aqsa Mosque reside there, how will it be possible to rebuild the Jewish temple there? An article entitled "Trouble in the Holy Land"[17] reveals a highly influential Muslim scholar and best-selling author (with sixty-seven million copies of his books in circulation!) named Adnan Oktar (who uses the pen name of Harun Yahya) who is working with the reestablished Jewish Sanhedrin to try to accomplish this very thing! According to Oktar, the temple of Solomon "will be rebuilt and all believers will worship there in tranquility."[18]

A recent survey of Jews in Israel found that 64 percent of them want the temple to be rebuilt,[19] which is a staggering figure, since it seems that not long ago, Israel was primarily a secular state. The tide is changing, preparing for the rebuilding of the temple in the near future.

The Focus on Peace and Security

We have also seen that since September 11, 2001, the world has begun to seriously focus on peace and security. One year following the attack upon the United States on 9/11, President Bush used the phrase "peace and security" three times in his address to the United Nations General Assembly on September 12, 2002. In his first public address after being elected president, Barack Obama used the same phrase, "peace and security," when he announced: "To those who seek *peace and security*: We support you." Also, in an address to the UN General Assembly Interfaith Conference on November 12, 2008, former Prime Minister, and current Ministry of Foreign Affairs, of Israel, Shimon Peres addressed the need for peace and security in the Middle East and called for help from the UN to achieve it. On June 4, 2009, the Israeli Foreign Ministry Department published this official response to President Obama's Cairo speech: "We share President Obama's hope that the American effort heralds the beginning of a new era that will bring about an end to the conflict and lead to Arab recognition of Israel as the homeland of the Jewish people, living in *peace and security* in the Middle East."[20]

"Peace and security" will be the proclamation of the world just prior to the rapture of the church.[21] There seems to have been an increased emphasis on peace and security by world leaders even within the past year.[22] Could it be that we are close to entering into that brief period of time that will immediately precede the day of Lord? Time will tell.

The Focus on a Middle East Peace Treaty

Another indicator of the closeness of the tribulation period is the strong focus by the world on achieving a Middle East peace treaty with Israel.[23] In pushing for this peace treaty, Jordan's King Abdullah II recently claimed: "In Arab and Muslim minds, the most emotional aspect is the Palestinian cause and that of Jerusalem. And from there leads all the other problems."[24] The king continued by stating that "the core issue, the major grievance in the Arab and Muslim" is the issue between Israel and the Palestinians. Therefore, according to King Abdullah, with an accomplished peace treaty being effected between Israel and the Palestinians, "the core issue, the major grievance in the Arab and Muslim world [would be] solved." In fact, when asked the best way for the US to persuade Iran to retreat from its nuclear program and the best way to solve threats from terroristic groups such as al-Qaeda, King Abdullah II responded, "Solving the Israeli-Palestinian problem." In other words, from the perspective of a Muslim leader of an Arab nation, every terroristic problem would be solved with a peace treaty between Israel and the Palestinians, and according to the king, this treaty *must* be done within the next eighteen months.[25]

Recently, there has been a shift from a focus on a two-party peace plan between Israel and the Palestinians to a regional peace plan with Israel.[26] It has become increasingly apparent that in order to accomplish a true Middle East peace treaty with guaranteed terms, other nations would need to guarantee the terms of the treaty, which falls more in line with the treaty predicted in the book of Daniel, where *ten* nations will ratify the treaty with Israel. Ironically, Iran is being used by God to move the peace process in a more biblical direction.

Iran's race toward nuclear capability has made its Arab neighbors very nervous, and along with the apparent possibility of the Obama administration allowing Iran to achieve that goal, these Arab countries are pulling for Israel to attack the Persian country.[27] This strong Arab support of Israel—which is a first—could create the kind of good will that may allow for five of these countries to be guarantors of a treaty with Israel.[28]

Israeli Prime Minister Benyamin Netanyahu has recently been working with Egypt, Saudi Arabia, and Jordan regarding the Iranian issue, but for what purpose? Likely, these meetings were used to gain support on both sides—support from the Arab countries for Israel's attack upon Iran and, if Israel were to put a crippling blow upon Iran, support from the Arabs for a regional peace plan. These three countries may be three of the co-signers of a future treaty with Israel, while the US Middle East envoy George Mitchell declared that the peace plan would also include Syria and Lebanon. Of course, it remains to be seen which ten nations will guarantee the terms of the peace treaty with Israel. However, if all of these countries will be ratifiers of the peace treaty, then we are looking at the five nations from the Eastern half of the old Roman Empire, which may signal that the signing of the treaty may be near.

If Israel were to attack and successfully set back Iran's march toward nuclear weaponry, this could pave the way for the peace treaty with Israel. After all, something will need to occur to Iran to halt its goal of destroying the peace process in the Middle East.[29] A crippling attack upon Iran could also potentially cause an overthrow of its tenuous, radical government. If a government coup were to occur in Iran, it could pave the way for the king of the North to conquer that country, as per Daniel 8. In addition, it would place a decimating blow upon terror groups in the Middle East being funded and supported by Iran, which could cause the world to begin to cry out, "Peace and security." This would also move Israel and Arab nations to focus singularly upon a Middle East peace treaty once the Iranian problem is out of the way.

Preparation for the King of the North

One more factor that could indicate the nearness of the day of the Lord is the removal of Saddam Hussein as president of Iraq, a necessary preparation to pave the way for the rise of the king of the North. Since Hussein's removal, persecution from Muslims against the Assyrian population—the group from which the king of the North will arise—has become rampant.[30] In fact, since his removal, half of all Assyrians in the country have fled.[31] Under Hussein, the Assyrians were protected, enjoying life as the educated class (the doctors, attorneys, teachers, etc.). However, once he was removed from office, Assyrians—who consider themselves Christians—have been severely persecuted by the Muslim majority and have fled for their lives.[32] At this rate of flight from the country, it will not be long until there are no Assyrians left in Iraq. There is no sign that the persecution of Assyrians will let up any time soon, so something will need to occur soon to fulfill prophecy regarding the king of the North.

One possibility could be legislation to protect the Assyrians. However, that does not seem likely. In fact, on September 24, 2008, the Iraqi

Parliament took an adversarial approach to the Assyrians by eliminating article 50 of the Provincial Election Law, which had been adopted on July 22, 2008. That article guaranteed quotas (a specific number of seats) in the governorate's regional councils for the minorities, including the Assyrian Christians.[33] Though Iraqi Prime Minister Nouri al-Maliki promised security for everyone, the murders and mass exit of Assyrians have continued at an alarming rate.[34]

Since government intervention on behalf of Assyrians will probably not occur, the survival of the Assyrians seems to depend on their self-defense, which has already begun to take shape. According to a recent UPI article,[35] a number of Iraqi Assyrians have formed militias in northern Iraq[36] for self-preservation. However, for these militias to be effective against the intense and organized attacks of fanatical Muslims, they will need to rally around an effective and charismatic leader to arise soon—and they will, forming the beginning of the military machine that will conquer the Middle East.

The severe persecution of the Assyrians will likely provide significant motivation for the king of the North to arise from within that group in order to defend them from extinction in Iraq. Since the persecution from the radical Muslim element will undoubtedly not let up, this Assyrian leader will need to aggressively conquer those who seek the elimination of his people. Because this king will begin his rise to power following the rapture of the church, the removal of Saddam Hussein, along with persecution and flight of the Assyrians, seem to indicate the nearness of the day of the Lord.

The Ineffectiveness of the Church

Possibly one of the most effective arguments for the soon approach of the rapture and the inception of the day of the Lord is the ineffectiveness of the church to reach a growing world population with the gospel of Christ. It appears that the gap is quickly widening between the amount of people receiving eternal life and the number of individuals dying and entering into eternity separated from God.

Since Jesus gave the church the responsibility of reaching the nations for Christ,[37] it would seem that this growing gap is due to ineffectiveness on the part of the church. It could be argued that this ineffectiveness is a result of the church's increasing lukewarmness[38] and complacency, as well as its movement away from the clear and biblical gospel.[39] Since God desires all men to be saved,[40] how long can he sit by and watch a growing number of people on their way to hell? Knowing God's heart from the pages of Scripture, it seems that it cannot be long before he takes the church out of the world in order to initiate a more effective outreach to the world. When he does, he will begin again with the two prophets of Revelation 11, who will clearly and effectively proclaim the biblical gospel of Christ to Israel, who will, in turn, take the gospel to the nations.[41] This cannot be far away.

Our Location in Church History

Another indicator that we may be close to the rapture of the church is an argument based on where we may be in church history. This argument begins with the seven churches of Revelation.

There are scholars who believe that these churches represent both historical (first-century) churches as well as historical eras of the universal church.[42] In other words, these seven churches represent seven ages of the church age.[43] According to these same scholars, we are currently in the age of Laodicea, the final stage of the church age.

Church	Characterized by	Representation	Approx. Representative Dates[44]
Ephesus	Zeal[45]	Apostolic Church	AD 33-100 [67 yrs.]
Smyrna	Persecution[46]	Persecuted Church	AD 100-311 [211 yrs.]
Pergamos	Compromising[47]	State Church	AD 311-590 [279 yrs.]
Thyatira	Corruption[48]	Papal (Pagan) Church	AD 590-1517 [927 yrs.]
Sardis	Deadness	Reformed Church	AD 1517-1730 [213 yrs.]
Philadelphia	Faithfulness[49]	Missionary Church	AD 1730-1900 [170 yrs.]
Laodicea	Lukewarm[50]	Apostate Church	AD 1900-Rapture [110+yrs.]

Furthermore, if we go by the pattern of the approximate representative periods shown in the chart above, the age of Laodicea should be close to completion. We arrive at this understanding based on the pattern of their chronological lengths. These eras increase in time, beginning at sixty-seven years and climbing to a peak of nine hundred twenty-seven years during the era in the middle of these representative ages. These periods of time then descend to the final era, which is already one hundred ten years in length.

The Financial Crisis and a One-world Currency

Another indicator that we may be near to the day of the Lord is the current worldwide economic crisis. As a result of the crisis, many Israelis living abroad are now returning to Israel.[51] The Old Testament shows that God will bring Jews back into the land to prepare for the salvation of Israel in the seven-year day of the Lord.[52] Of course, the climbing number of expatriate Jews returning to Israel is part of God's plan for them. God could be using the financial crisis to bring Jews back into the land who will be open to the gospel preached by God's two prophets in Jerusalem.

In connection with the financial crisis, there has surfaced a discussion of going to a one-world currency. Russia, China, and the European Union are all in favor of this proposal, and US treasury secretary, Tim Geithner, has also given his tacit approval.[53] This could be very significant in light of Revelation 13:16–18, which shows that at the very midpoint of the day of the Lord, the beast will issue an edict that no one will be able to buy or sell anything without taking his mark and committing to worshipping him as God. In order for him to be able to give that decree, there will already need to be in place the ability to control the world's economy. To do that, it seems there must be a one-world economic system with a world bank (which currently exists) and a one-world currency. Serious talk of the one-world currency has been motivated by the financial crisis in order to help countries that are in financial trouble. Could we already be on the verge of making this currency a reality, thus preparing for the midpoint of the tribulation period? If so, we could be very near to the day of the Lord.

More Than Forty Years

Finally, Israel has been in possession of Jerusalem for over forty years now in fulfillment of a prediction by Jesus. In Luke 21:24, he announced that Jerusalem would be under Gentile control "until the times of the Gentiles are fulfilled." The times of the Gentiles refer to God's focus upon the Gentiles for salvation. This means that since 1967, God has been turning his focus toward Israel for salvation. Since the tribulation period is when Israel will experience salvation, it appears that era is soon approaching. In fact, it has already been more than forty years since the fulfillment of Luke 21:24. Forty years constitute a biblical generation, and forty is a significant biblical number. This may indicate that God has graciously given us a few extra years to prepare for the return of Christ. It may also signal that the initiation of the day of the Lord and the occurrence of the rapture of the church could be very near.

In early 1992, The Jerusalem Report ran an article entitled, "Waiting for the Rebbe."[54] Here is the content of that article:

> The slogan "Prepare for the coming of the Messiah" accompanied by a rising red sun, has appeared on a hundred billboards across Israel. Paid for by the Chabad organization of the Lubavitch Hasidim,[55] it will also soon appear on neon signs mounted on hundreds of private cards. A million pamphlets explaining why Chabad believes the Messiah's arrival is imminent are being distributed.
>
> News that the Lubavitcher Rebbe, Menachem Mendel Scheerson, has given the go-ahead to his followers to build him a house in Israel has electrified Chabad.
>
> For Chabad Hasidim, the possibility of Scheerson's arrival here is a key sign indicating that the Messiah's appearance is imminent. "The rebbe has repeatedly said that when he comes to Israel, it will be together with the Messiah," says Chabad spokesman Rabbi Menachem Brod. . . . Near the site of the intended house is a sign proclaiming, "The Time of Your Redemption Has Come."

Some in Israel are beginning to look for their Messiah. Could this indicate that the time of her redemption has come? Based on this anticipation by God's chosen people, along with the other indicators presented in this epilogue, the commencement of the seven-year day of the Lord, initiated by the rapture of the church, may be nearer than we think. May the Lord find us ready when he comes.

Glossary

2012 – The year in which a growing number of people, based on the Maya long calendar, believe the world "as we know it" may end.

2012 Phenomenon – The growing interest in the possibility that the world as we know it may end.

144,000 – The Jewish evangelists, twelve thousand from each Jewish tribe, who believe in Jesus Christ for eternal life at the beginning of the tribulation period and who fan out into the world to reach the nations with the gospel throughout the rest of that seven-year period.

Abomination of desolation – Spoken of by the prophet Daniel and Jesus in reference to the event at the midpoint of the tribulation period in which the beast of Revelation enters the temple in Jerusalem to abominate it, setting himself up as God. This event signals the imminent desolating activity of the beast in which he seeks to destroy believing Jews. Jesus announced that Jews who believe in Jesus during the first half of the seven-year tribulation period are to flee for their lives when they see this occur.

Abyss – The place of the dead, also the bottomless pit. It is the place from which the beast of Revelation will arise to inhabit the body of the king of the North.

Alignment of the Planets – A theory propounded by advocates of the 2012 phenomenon that, right on cue with the Maya calendar, the sun will be in the center of our galaxy with all the planets lining up behind it on December 21 of 2012, which, they believe, will create increased instability in the inner core of the earth, possibly causing cataclysmic phenomena such as hurricanes, earthquakes, volcanic eruptions, massive tidal waves, and tsunamis.

Angel – A celestial being with rank and power; a spirit that ministers; God's agents and messengers.

Anointing – The crowning of a new king; to make holy or sacred; to appoint for a purpose.

Antichrist – The false prophet in the book of Revelation; the "beast from the land"; the second beast. He will be the Jewish world religious leader (not ruler) who will be able to work miracles to deceive people and will cause the world inhabitants to worship the first beast, the world ruler.

Armageddon – Literally, the "hills of Meggido." The armies of the earth will gather in the plain in this region for preparation to bring war against Christ when he returns to the earth. (The war against Christ will not take place in this area; instead it will occur east of Jerusalem.)

Assyrian, the – The king of the North, empowered by Satan, who will arise from Iraq and conquer the Middle East and northern Africa. He will appear to be slain in Jerusalem and rise from the dead as the beast. (His body will be inhabited by the spirit of one of the first five Roman emperors, at which point he will become the beast.)

Beast – The man who assumes rule of the entire world after killing the two future prophets of God, and who will be worshipped as God by the world's inhabitants for the last three and a half years before the return of Christ. He once existed on the earth as one of the first five Roman emperors and will come from the place of the dead (the abyss) to inhabit the body of the king of the North at the midpoint of the tribulation period.

Believer – One who has received eternal life by believing in Jesus Christ for it.

Blasphemy - Speaking against God and his work.

Book of Life – The book of God in which are recorded the names of all who belong to God's eternal kingdom.

Bowl Judgments – The judgments of God that will be poured out upon the earth during the last half of the tribulation period.

Brethren – All who belong to the family of God by faith in Jesus Christ.

Christ – The Greek term for Messiah, "the Anointed One." According to the gospel of John, this term refers to the giver of eternal life. In addition, the Christ is the one who will deliver Israel from her enemies at his return to the earth and who will establish and rule over God's kingdom upon the earth.

Christian – One who has believed in Jesus Christ for eternal life; brethren; saints; believers.

Church – The universal group of all who have believed in Jesus Christ for eternal life during the time beginning at Pentecost in AD 33 and concluding at the rapture of the church.

Covenant – An oath or promise from God.

Crucifixion – The horrific Roman form of punishment by death by being nailed to a cross; the death Jesus died to pay for all of the sins of humanity forever.

Day of the Lord – Refers to the future age in which God will pour out judgments upon the earth, beginning seven years before the return of Jesus Christ to the earth to establish God's kingdom. This term almost always refers in the Bible to the seven-year period leading up to the return of Christ to the earth; however, Peter indicates in 2 Peter 3:10 that there is a sense in which it extends through the first thousand years of Jesus' rule upon the earth. (In that case, it would portray the ultimate judgment of God upon the earth—the total annihilation of the world.)

Demon – An evil spirit; a by-product of fallen angels taking the form of men and having sexual relations with women at a particular point in human history prior to the flood of Noah's day (mentioned in Genesis 6:1–6; see also 2 Peter 2:4–5 and Jude verse 6). God judged them by drowning them in the flood, and from that time onward, they have been disembodied spirits. (During the time of Jesus and the apostles in the first century, these spirits sought to possess the bodies of people.)

Disciple – One who has believed in Jesus Christ for eternal life and who, in addition, obediently follows him and his teaching.

Dragon, the – A metaphor of Satan used in the book of Revelation.

Eternal Life – Life with God forever, given as a free gift by Jesus Christ to anyone and everyone who believes him for it and which, once received, can never be lost.

Eternal State – The eternal aspect of the kingdom of God that begins following God's destruction of the universe and creation of a new one without the existence of sin.

Evangelize – To present the good news of eternal life received as a free gift by believing Jesus for it.

Fornication, Spiritual – Refers to following the world's idolatrous system and departing from God's principles.

Geomagnetic Reversal of the Earth – The alternation of the earth's magnetic polarity. According to proponents of the 2012 phenomenon, the earth's internal magnetic field reverses, on average, about every 300,000 to 1 million years and will once again in 2012, creating potentially catastrophic results to the earth.

Gentile – As a noun, referring to a person who is not a Jew; as an adjective, referring to that which belongs to a Gentile or Gentiles.

Glorified Body – The glorious, powerful, sinless, and immortal body a believer will receive when raised from the dead, which will preserve one's identity.

God's Word – The Bible; God's communication to mankind (such as through prophets).

Gospel – A translation of Greek and Hebrew words that literally mean "good news." It can refer to various "good news" subjects such as the message of God's provision for eternal life (i.e., the crucifixion and resurrection of Jesus); the message of the offer of, and reception of, eternal life (offered by Jesus and received only by believing Jesus for it); and God's future kingdom upon the earth.

Haughtiness of Men – Arrogance toward God; independence from God.

Heaven – While God exists everywhere at the same time (called omnipresence), heaven is the spiritual dimension of the locale of the special presence of God and his angelic beings. The term heaven is also used of the sky. (Note that in 2 Corinthians 12:2–3, the apostle Paul refers to three heavens—the third being paradise, the spiritual dimension of the special presence of God—while theologians believe the other two refer to the atmosphere and to what we call outer space.)

Hell – The abode of the wicked; hades (Greek), sheol (Hebrew); state of punishment where unbelievers will experience torment and mental anguish, the center of the earth. (However, before the ascension of Christ, sheol and hades both referred to the general place of the dead.)

Holy City, the – Jerusalem, the capital of Israel and, in the future, the capital of God's kingdom upon the earth.

Hope – Referring to any of God's future promises; certain expectation of God's guarantee.

Hypocrite – One who professes beliefs that he is not willing to uphold.

Imminent – Threatening to occur immediately.

Iniquity – Sin.

Israelite – A descendent of Israel (Jacob); a Hebrew; a Jew.

Jew – A descendent of Israel (Jacob); one of the chosen people of God.

Judah – One of the twelve Jewish tribes that formed a kingdom; descendents of Jacob and Leah; the tribe from which the Messiah came.

Judea – A province in southern Israel in which Jerusalem is located.

Judgment – Divine retribution; the act whereby Jesus, as judge, assesses the thoughts, intents, hearts and works of men.

Judgment Seat of Christ – The assessment by Jesus, occurring immediately before the inauguration of God's kingdom, of the lives of Christians to determine their eternal experience (reward or lack thereof) in God's kingdom.

224

GLOSSARY

King of the North – The Assyrian who will arise from Iraq and conquer the Middle East and northern Africa by Satan's help, during the first half of the tribulation period. At the midpoint of that seven-year time frame, he will appear to be slain and rise from the dead, at which point the spirit of one of the first five Roman emperors will inhabit his body, and he will become the beast of Revelation—the ruler of the world.

Lamb, the – Referring to Jesus Christ as the sacrificial provision of God in perfect payment for all of our sins.

Little Horn – A metaphor for the king of the North at the point when he has a little authority (prior to conquering the Middle East).

Lucifer – A name meaning "bearer of light" or "morning star" and which refers to the splendor and brilliance of the greatest of angels before he rebelled against God and became known as the Devil and Satan.

Mark of the Beast – Something placed on the forehead or right hand of individuals within the last half of the tribulation period that commits them to worship the beast as God and which provides for them to buy and sell things.

Maya Long Count Calendar – The 5,125-year calendar that will come to an end on December 21, 2012, marking the day that a growing number of people believe could be the last day for this world as we know it.

Messiah – The anointed one; the Christ; the expected king of God's kingdom and deliverer of the Jews; Jesus Christ.

Millennial Kingdom – The first thousand years of God's kingdom upon the earth following Jesus' return to the earth.

Ministry – Service for the sake of Christ.

Muslim – One who follows the religion of Islam, a follower of Allah.

New Testament – The twenty-seven books of the Bible given by inspiration of God (to either apostles or those associated with apostles) in the first century following the death and resurrection of Jesus Christ. These books make up the document for the new covenant, which was initiated by the blood (death) of Christ.

Old Testament – The thirty-nine books of the Bible given by inspiration of God to prophets prior to the first advent of Jesus Christ. These books provide God's directions for life under the old covenant.

Pagan World System – The universal government based on worship of false gods; idolatry.

Parable – A story told by Jesus to teach his disciples a key truth.

Peace and Security – Mentioned by the apostle Paul in 1 Thessalonians 5:3, it refers to a brief period of time in which the world will believe it has finally achieved security and world peace.

Pharisee – A Jewish religious leader noted for strict obedience of Old Testament law, though Jesus blasted Pharisees for being hypocrites (see Matthew 23).

Planet X – A planet some believe has been cited and tracked by NASA and which is believed to pass so near the earth in 2012 that it could cause catastrophic results.

Polar Reversal of the Earth – The belief by proponents of the 2012 phenomenon that the North Pole and the South Pole of the earth will switch places, causing potentially catastrophic results to the earth.

Pontius Pilate – A procurator (governor) who allowed Jesus to be put to death by crucifixion.

Prophecy, Bible – God's declaration of events to come.

Prophet – A spokesman who proclaims a message given to him by direct communication from God.

Rapture of the Church – The rapid seizing of believers from the earth by Jesus when he comes in the air for them. This event will occur seven years before his return to the earth and on the same day of the initiation of the day of the Lord.

Redemption of Man – The purchase of man's salvation by Christ's death on the cross in payment for man's debt of sin.

Repent – To move back from being wayward from God into fellowship with him.

Resurrection – Rising from death to life with a glorified body.

Return of Christ – The event in which Jesus will return to the earth to deliver Israel from her enemies and establish God's kingdom upon the earth.

Revelation, Book of – The Apocalypse; the final book of the New Testament; the New Testament book known for providing detailed information regarding the future seven-year tribulation period, the return of Christ to the earth, his thousand-year rule on the earth, the judgment of unbelievers, and the eternal state.

Reward – The fruit of one's labor or works; a greater kingdom experience given by Jesus for faithfulness to him.

Righteousness – Holiness, purity; being right with God; the work of Christ.

GLOSSARY

Roman Empire, Old – An autocratic form of government established by Rome, which included large territorial holdings in Europe, around the Mediterranean, and including much of the Middle East and northern Africa at the height of its holdings. The term is used to describe the Roman state and its boundaries during and after the time of the first emperor, Augustus (the Roman ruler when Jesus was born), lasting nearly five centuries.

Sabbath – The seventh day of the week, and the one day of each week God called for Israel, under the law, to rest and to worship him.

Salvation – Deliverance. It is used in the Bible for various forms of deliverance, including deliverance from sin by Jesus' death on the cross, deliverance of Christians from the outpouring of God's judgment upon the earth via the rapture of the church, and deliverance of believing Israel from her enemies by Jesus at his return.

Satan – The Devil; the great accuser and hater of man; the chief of fallen angels; the Dragon; the prince of this world; the one who will give authority to the beast to rule the world; the one who will seek to eliminate believing Jews from the earth; and the one who will gather the armies of the earth to try to stop Jesus from taking his rightful rule over the earth at his return.

Scribe – A scholar of Jewish law and tradition who copied Jewish law and taught it to the people.

Seal Judgments – A series of judgments poured out by God upon the earth throughout the seven-year tribulation period.

Seal – To establish; to confirm, authenticate.

Second Coming – See Return of Christ.

Sin – Anything that falls short of God's perfect standards either in commission or omission. Disobedience to God; any violation of God's will; wickedness in action or thought.

Son of Man – An Old Testament term used of the Messiah and referring to his rule over the earth in the future, which Jesus applied to himself.

Temple, the – Any of the three successive houses of worship in Jerusalem in use by the Jews in biblical times, the first built by Solomon, the second by Zerubbabel, and the third by Herod. A fourth will be built as a result of a provision of the seven-year treaty with Israel. (The day on which this treaty goes into effect will also be the first day of the day of the Lord.)

Temple Mount – The elevated area in east Jerusalem where the temple was built and where it will be rebuilt as a result of a provision of the seven-year treaty with Israel.

Testimony – Proclamation of faith in Jesus Christ.

Thief-in-the-Night – A metaphor used in the New Testament to portray being caught off guard by the rapture of the church and the initiation of the day of the Lord. The shared use of that phrase by both events indicates the two will occur contemporaneously.

Transgression – Sin; violation of God's will.

Tribes, the Twelve – Referring to those descending from the twelve sons of one ancestor, Jacob (Israel); a reference to Jews in Israel.

Tribulation Period – The seven-year period that will be a fulfillment of the seventieth week of Daniel (Daniel 9:24–27) during which God will bring Israel to salvation and pour out his judgments upon the earth, bringing a multitude of Gentiles to believe in Jesus for eternal life as well. This period will begin on the first day the seven-year treaty between Israel and ten nations begins.

Trumpet Judgments – A series of judgments God will pour out upon the earth during the first half of the tribulation period.

Vision – A vivid spiritual appearance to an individual chosen by God through which God communicates his truth.

Witness – One who testifies to God's truth, which has been communicated directly to the witness, accompanied by miraculous power to demonstrate the veracity of the witness.

Woe – A curse from God; heavy calamity.

Wrath of God – Temporal punishment of sin (never equated with hell or the torment of eternal separation from God).

Selected Bibliography

ARTICLES

Bell, Jr., Albert A. "The Date of John's Apocalypse: The Evidence of Some Roman Historians Reconsidered." *New Testament Studies 25.*

Hodges, Zane. "The Rapture in 1 Thessalonians 5:1–11." *Walvoord: A Tribute,* ed. by Donald K. Campbell, 67–80. Chicago: Moody Press, 1982.

Hodges, Zane C. "The First Horseman of the Apocalypse." *Bibliotheca Sacra.* October 1962: 324–334.

Yamauchi, Edwin M. "Cultural Aspects of Marriage in the Ancient World." *Bibliotheca Sacra.* July–September 1978: 241–52.

BOOKS

Archer, Jr., Gleason L. *The Expositor's Bible Commentary: Daniel and the Minor Prophets, Volume 7.* ed. Gabelein, Frank E. Grand Rapids, MI: Zondervan Publishing House, 1985.

Bauer, Walter, Arndt, William F. and Gingrich, F. Wilbur. A *Greek-English Lexicon of the New Testament and Other Early Christian Literature.* Chicago: The University of Chicago Press, 1980.

Brown, Francis, Driver, S.R. and Briggs, Charles A. A *Hebrew and English Lexicon of the Old Testament.* Oxford: Clarendon Press, 1980.

Bruce, F. F. *The New Testament Documents: Are They Reliable?* Downers Grove, IL: Inter-Varsity Press, 1964.

Campbell, Donald K. Daniel: *Decoder of Dreams.* Wheaton, IL: Victor Books, 1977.

Campbell, Donald K. Daniel: *Decoder of Dreams.* Wheaton, IL: Victor Books, 1981.

Cohen, Gary G. and Kirban, Salem. *Revelation Visualized.* Chattanooga, TN: AMG Publishers, 1981.

Culver, Robert. *Daniel and the Latter Days.* Chicago: Moody Press, 1977.

Culver, Robert. *The Histories and Prophecies of Daniel.* Winona Lake, IN: BMH Books, 1980.

Davids, Peter H. *The First Epistle of Peter.* Grand Rapids, MI: William B. Eerdmans Publishing Company, 1990.

Dyer, Charles H. *The Rise of Babylon*. Wheaton, IL: Tyndale Publishing House, 1991.

Eck, Werner. *The Age of Augustus*. Translated by Deborah Lucas Schneider; new material by Sarolta A. Takacs, Oxford: Blackwell Publishing, 2003.

Epp, Theodore H. *Practical Studies in Revelation, Volumes I & II*. Lincoln, NE: Back to the Bible, 1969.

Geisler, Norman L., ed. *Inerrancy*. Grand Rapids, MI: Zondervan Publishing House, 1980.

Geisler, Norman L. and Mix, William E. *A General Introduction to the Bible*. Chicago: Moody Press, 1968.

Gaebelein, Arno C. *The Gospel of Matthew, An Exposition*. 2 vols. in 1. Neptune, N.J.: Loizeaux Brothers, 1910.

Glickman, S. Craig. *Knowing Christ*. Chicago: Moody Press, 1980.

Hirsch, E. D. Jr.. *Validity in Interpretation*. New Haven, CT: Yale University Press, 1967.

Hitchcock, Mark. *Cashless: Bible Prophecy, Economic Chaos, & the Future Financial Order*. Eugene, OR: Harvest House Publishers, 2009.

Hodges, Zane. *Power to Make War: The Career of the Assyrian Who Will Rule the World*. Dallas, TX: Redencion Viva, 1995.

Hodges, Zane C. *Jesus: God's Prophet*. Dallas, TX: Kerugma, Inc.

Hodges, Zane C. *Power to Make War*. Dallas, TX: Redencion Viva, 1995.

Hoehner, Harold W. *Chronological Aspects of the Life of Christ*. Grand Rapids, MI: Zondervan Publishing House, 1977.

Hort, F.J.A. *The First Epistle of Peter*. London: Macmillan, 1898; rept. in *Expository and Exegetical Studies*. Minneapolis: Klock and Klock, 1980.

Jeremias, Joachim. *The Parables of Jesus*. Translated by S. H. Hooke, London: SCM, 1963.

Johnson, Elliott E. *Expository Hermeneutics: An Introduction*. Grand Rapids, MI. Zondervan   Publishing House, 1990.

Joseph, Lawrence. *Apocalypse 2012: A Scientific Investigation Into Civilization's End*. New York: Broadway Books, 2007.

Keil, C.F. *Volume IX: Biblical Commentary on the Book of Daniel*, ed. C. F. Keil, and F. Delitzsch *Commentary on the Old Testament in Ten Volumes*. Grand Rapids, MI: William B. Eerdmans Publishing Company, 1980.

SELECTED BIBLIOGRAPHY

Keil, C.F. *Volume X: Minor Prophets, II*: 404, ed. C. F. Keil, and F. Delitzsch, *Commentary on the Old Testament in Ten Volumes*. Grand Rapids, MI: William B. Eerdmans Publishing Company, 1980.

LaHaye, Tim. *Revelation Unveiled*. Grand Rapids, MI: Zondervan Publishing House, 1999.

Lang, G. H. *The Revelation of Jesus Christ*. Miami Springs, FL: Conley & Schoettle Publishing Co., Inc., 1985.

Lang, G. H. *The Revelation of Jesus Christ: Selected Studies*. Miami Springs, FL: Conley & Schoettle Publishing Co., Inc., 1985.

Luck, G. Coleman. *Daniel*. Chicago: Moody Press, 1958.

McDowell, Josh. *Evidence that Demands a Verdict: Vol. 1*. Campus Crusade for Christ, Inc. 1972.

Moulton, James Hope and Milligan, George. *The Vocabulary of the Greek Testament: Illustrated from the Papyri and Other Non-Literary Sources*. Grand Rapids, MI: Wm. B. Eerdmans Publishing Company, 1980.

Mounce, Robert. *The Book of Revelation, The International Commentary on the New Testament*, edited by F. F. Bruce. Grand Rapids, MI: William B. Eerdmans Publishing Co., 1977.

Pentecost, J. Dwight. *Things to Come*. Grand Rapids, MI: Zondervan publishing House, 1980.

Plummer, Alfred. *An Exegetical Commentary on the Gospel According to S. Matthew*. Grand Rapids: Wm. B. Eerdmans Publishing Co., 1953.

Robinson, John A. T. *Redating the New Testament*. Philadelphia, PA: The Westminster Press, 1976.

Ryrie, Charles Caldwell. *Revelation*. Chicago: Moody Press, 1968.

Shelley, Bruce. *Church History in Plain Language*. Waco, TX: Word Books, 1982.

Smith, J.B. *A Revelation of Jesus Christ*. Scottdale, PA: Herald Press, 1961.

Tan, Paul Lee. *Encyclopedia of 7,000 Illustrations: Signs of the Times*. Rockville, MD: Assurance Publishers, 1988.

Trench, Richard C. *Notes on the Parables of Our Lord*. New York: Appleton, 1851.

Turretin, Francis. *The Doctrine of Scripture*. Edited and translated by John W. Beardslee III. Grand Rapids, MI. Baker Book House, 1981.

Unger, Merrill F. *Unger's Bible Dictionary*. Chicago: Moody Press, 1966.

Walvoord, John. *Daniel: The Key to Prophetic Revelation*. Chicago: Moody Press, 1981.

Walvoord, John F. *Daniel: The Key to Prophetic Revelation*. Chicago: Moody Press, 1971.

Walvoord, John F. *The Revelation of Jesus Christ*. Chicago: Moody Press, 1966.

Wood, Leon. *A Commentary on Daniel*. Grand Rapids, MI: Zondervan Publishing House, 1973.

Zuck, Roy B. *Basic Bible Interpretation*. Wheaton, IL: Victor Books, 1991.

WEB SITES

"American politicians and the White House flooded with calls for 'Operation Assyrian Province,' Jan. 18, 2007." www.aina.org/habash.htm and www.assist-news.net

"Bulletin of the Atomic Scientists."www.thebulletin.org/content/doomsday-clockoverview.html (June 3, 2008).

"Economists for Peace and Security." (http://www.epsusa.org/. (May 12, 2009).

"Emerging Threats: Iraqi Christians Forming Ad Hoc Militias." UPI. http://www.upi.com/Emerging_Threats/2008/10/29/Iraqi_Christians_forming ad hoc militias/UPI-77471225314406/#top (October 31, 2008).

"Is the Era of Mass Immigration to Israel Over?" *Jesus Lives*. http://www.jesus-lives.co.za/2008/09/12/is-the-era-of-mass-immigration-to-israel-over/ (October 16, 2008).

"Israel's reaction to President Barack Obama's speech in Cairo." *Israel Ministry of Foreign Affairs*. http://www.mfa.gov.il/MFA/Government/Communiques/2009/Israel_reaction_President_Obama_speech_Cairo_4-Jun-2009.htm (June 5, 2009).

"Jordan: Israel Faces War If It Does not Agree to Arab Terms." Arutz Seva. http://www.israelnationalnews.com/. (May 2, 2009).

"Nibiru." http://en.wikipedia.org/wiki/Nibiru_collision.

"Pole Shift." http://en.wikipedia.org/wiki/Polar_Shift.

"The Re-established Jewish Sanhedrin." *The Sanhedrin*. http://www.thesanhedrin.org/en/index.php/The_Re-established_Jewish_Sanhedrin (February 26, 2009).

"Trouble in the Holy Land", http://www.wnd.com/index.php?fa=PAGE.view&pageId=105938, (August 5, 2009).

SELECTED BIBLIOGRAPHY

"Security Council presidential statement reiterates urgent need for renewed efforts to achieve comprehensive peace in Middle East." *Relief Web.* http://www.reliefweb.int/rw/rwb.nsf/db900SID/ASHU-7RY3XR?OpenDocument (May 12, 2009).

"Spirit." http://dictionary.reference.com/browse/spirit (June 6, 2007).

"Survey: 64% Want Temple Rebuilt," http://www.ynetnews.com/Ext/Comp/ArticleLayout/CdaArticlePrintPreview/1,2506,L-3754367,00.html (August 1, 2009).

"U.S. Envoy Talks Middle East Peace with Syria's Assad." *Silobreaker.* http://www.silobreaker.com/mitchell-says-no-mideast-peace-at-lebanon-expense-16_2262382370436939801 (June 29, 2009).

"US-MIDEAST: Regional Players Key to Salvaging Peace Process." *Global Intelligence News.* http://globalintel.net/wp/2008/12/04/us-mideast-regional-players-key-to-salvaging-peace-process/ (June 29, 2009).

"U.S. Trying to Push for Peace between Israel, Syria." *English Peoples Daily Online.* http://english.people.com.cn/90001/90777/90854/6676972.html (June 13, 2009)

Council for Peace and Security Association of National Security Experts in Israel. (http://www.peace-security-council.org/. (May 12, 2009).

Peace and Security. http://www.un.org/en/peace/ (May 12, 2009).

Peace and Security Initiative. http://www.peaceandsecurityinitiative.org/ (May 12, 2009).

Research Guide to International Law on the Internet. http://www2.spfo.unibo.it/spolfo/PEACE.htm. (May 12, 2009)

Temple Mount & Eretz Yisrael Faithful Movement – Jerusalem. http://www.templemountfaithful.org/ (February 26, 2009).

The Temple Institute. http://www.templeinstitute.org/main.htm. (February 26, 2009).

http://churchofcriticalthinking.org/planetx.html.

http://eastonsbibledictionary.com/smyrna.htm (March 6, 2009).

http://www.2012endofdays.org/general/why-2012.php.

http://www.scivee.tv/node/6179.

Anderson, Scott J. "Barack Obama: A Meteoric Rise." *CNN Polotics.com.* http://www.cnn.com/2008/POLITICS/08/18/revealed.obama.profile/index.html (January 15, 2009).

Barzanji, Yahya. "Iraqi Archbishop Decries Christian Slayings." *The Associated Press*. http://www.philly.com/philly/wires/ap/news/nation_world/20090427_ap_iraqiarchbishopdecrieschristianslayings.html (April 28, 2009).

Benjamin, Robert. "UN Pouring Millions into Rebuilding Babylon." *End Times Prophecy News*. www.rb59.com/prophecy-news/2006/04/un-pouring-millions-into-rebuilding.html (August 7, 2008).

Brouwer, Christine "Will the World End in 2012?" http://abcnews.go.com/International/story?id=5301284&page=1 (July 3, 2008).

Chester, Tom. "No Tenth Planet Yet from IRAS." http://spider.ipac.caltech.edu/staff/tchester/iras/no_tenth_planet_yet.html (February 26, 200).

Corsi, Jerome. "U.S. Backs Global Alternative to Dollar." *World Net Daily*. http://www.worldnetdaily.com/index.php?fa=PAGE.view&pageId=92207 (April 20, 2009).

Dina Kraft, Dina. "Economic Crisis Prompting Israeli Expats to Return Home." *JTA The Globle News Service of the Jewish People*. http://jta.org/news/article/2009/04/27/1004696/economic-crisis-prompting-israelis-expats-to-return-home (April 28, 2009).

Finley, Michael "The Correlation Question," http://members.shaw.ca/mjfinley/corr.html (November 2003).

Gedalyahu,Tzvi Ben. "Jordan: Israel Faces War If It Does not Agree to Arab Terms." http://www.israelnationalnews.com/ (May 2, 2009).

Gentlemen, Jeffery. "Unesco intends to put the magic back in Babylon." *The New York Times*. www.iht.com/articles/2006/04/13/news/babylon.php (August 7, 2008).

Geryl, Patrick. "Pole Shift and Pole Reversal." http://survive2012.com/index.php/geryl-pole-shift.html.

Gollust, David. "Clinton Promises New US Proposals for Mideast Peace." *VOA News*. http://www.voanews.com/english/archive/2009-05/2009-05-27-voa50.cfm?CFID=244606798&CFTOKEN=54798652&jsessionid=8830f5a2f41513f8e5933230593996949685 (June 29, 2009).

Glick, Caroline. "Netanyahu's Peace Plan." *The Jerusalem Post*. http://www.jpost.com/servlet/Satellite?cid=1242212438938&pagename=JPost%2FJPArticle%2FShowFull (June 19, 2009).

Glick, Caroline B. "Opportunity is knocking at Israel's door." *Jewish World Review*. http://www.JewishWorldReview.com (May 12, 2009.)

Glick, Caroline B. "What Israel's Arab Neighbors Grasp that the Obama Administration Won't." *Jewish World Review*. http://www.jewishworldreview.com/0409/glick042709.php3 (April 28, 2009).

234

SELECTED BIBLIOGRAPHY

Jenkins, John Major. http://alignment2012.com/.

Kenney, Brooke. "Who Is The 2012 Group? And What's The Big Deal About 2012, Anyway?" http://brookenney.com/2012Group.htm.

Kruszelnicki, Karl S. "Mayan Apocalypse, 2012," http://www.abc.net.au/science/articles/2008/04/15/2217547.htm?site=science/greatmomentsinscience&topic=space (April 15, 2008).

Luttermoser, Donald. "Planetary Alignments: Fact or Fiction?" http://www.etsu.edu/physics/etsuobs/starprty/22099dgl/planalign.htm (March 18, 2006).

Malmström, Vincent H. "The Astronomical Insignificance of Maya Date 13.0.0.0." http://www.dartmouth.edu/~izapa/M-32.pdf.

McBride, Edward. "Baghdad's grand projects in the age of Saddam Hussein." *Metropolismag.* www.metropolismag.com/html/content_0699/ju99monu.htm (August 7, 2008).

MacDonald, G. Jeffrey "Does Maya calendar predict 2012 apocalypse?" http://www.usatoday.com/tech/science/2007-03-27-maya-2012_n.htm (March 27, 2007).

Morrison, David. "Nibiru and Doomsday 2012: Questions and Answers." http://astrobiology.nasa.gov/ask-an-astrobiologist/intro/nibiru-and-doomsday-2012-questions-and-answers (June 1, 2009).

O'Neill, Ian. "2012: No Geomagnetic Reversal." http://www.universetoday.com/2008/10/03/2012-no-geomagnetic-reversal/ (October 3, 2008).

O'Neill, Ian "2012: No Planet X." http://www.universetoday.com/2008/05/25/2012-no-planet-x/ (May 25, 2008).

Plait, Philip. "Harmonic Con(game)vergence." http://www.badastronomy.com/bad/misc/planets.html (December 28, 2008).

Schaff, Philip. *History of the Christian Church.* http://www.ccel.org/s/schaff/history/About.htm (March 5, 2009.)

Schaff, Philip. "History of the Christian Church, Volume II : Ante-Nicene Christianity, A.D 100–325." *Christian Classics Ethereal Library.* http://www.ccel.org/ccel/schaff/hcc2.v.iv.xv.html (March 6, 2009).

Schoenberg, Shira. "The Sanhedrin." *Jewish Virtual Library.* http://www.jewishvirtuallibrary.org/jsource/Judaism/Sanhedrin.html (February 26, 2009).

Sitler, Robert K. "The 2012 Phenomenon: New Age Appropriation of an Ancient Mayan Calendar," *http://caliber.ucpress.net/doi/abs/10.1525/nr.2006.9.3.024* (January 23, 2006).

Webster, David. "The Uses and Abuses of the Ancient Maya." Prepared for *The Emergence of the Modern World* Conference, Otzenhausen, Germany. http://www.anthro.psu.edu/faculty_staff/docs/Webster_GermanyMaya.pdf.

Wensierski, Peter and Zand, Bernhard. "Christians on the Run in Iraq." *Spiegel Online International.* http://www.spiegel.de/international/world/0,1518,587345,00.html (October 31, 2008).

Wikipedia, the free encyclopedia. "Babylon." http://en.wikipedia.org/wiki/Babylon (August 7, 2008).

Williams, Rosa "No Fear of 2012: Part 1." http://hoth.ccssc.org/blogs/blog5.php/2009/01/26/no-fear-of-2012-part-1 (January 26, 2009).

Williams, Rosa. http://hoth.ccssc.org/blogs/blog5.php/2009/01/27/no-fear-of-2012-part-2 (January 27, 2009).

Xuequan, Mu. "Russian FM calls for efforts to resume peace process in Middle East." *China View.* http://news.xinhuanet.com/english/2009-05/12/content_11355977.htm (May 12, 2009).

End Notes

CHAPTER 1

1. Christine Brouwer, "Will the World End in 2012?", http://abcnews.go.com/International/story?id=5301284&page=1, accessed August 16, 2009.
2. Ibid.
3. Michael Finley, "The Correlation Question," http://members.shaw.ca/mjfinley/corr.html, accessed October 6, 2009.
4. Vincent H. Malmström, "The Astronomical Insignificance of Maya Date 13.0.0.0", http://www.dartmouth.edu/~izapa/M-32.pdf, accessed October 6, 2009.
5. David Webster, "The Uses and Abuses of the Ancient Maya," Prepared for The Emergence of the Modern World Conference, Otzenhausen, Germany, http://www.anthro.psu.edu/faculty_staff/docs/Webster_GermanyMaya.pdf, accessed October 6, 2009.
6. Robert K. Sitler (2006). "The 2012 Phenomenon: New Age Appropriation of an Ancient Mayan Calendar," http://caliber.ucpress.net/doi/abs/10.1525/nr.2006.9.3.024, accessed October 6, 2009.
7. G. Jeffrey MacDonald, "Does Maya calendar predict 2012 apocalypse?", posted March 27, 2007 at http://www.usatoday.com/tech/science/2007-03-27-maya-2012_n.htm, accessed October 6, 2009.
8. John Major Jenkins, http://alignment2012.com/, accessed October 7, 2009.
9. Malmström, Op cit.
10. Ibid. Dr. Malmström reasons that due to the timing of when the calendar calculation took place, the one responsible for it must have been an Olmec priest because "the timing of his calculation pre-dates by fully four centuries any known calendrical glyphs from the area of Maya settlement."
11. Ibid.
12. Karl S. Kruszelnicki, "Mayan Apocalypse, 2012," http://www.abc.net.au/science/articles/2008/04/15/2217547.htm?site=science/greatmomentsinscience&topic=space, accessed October 7, 2009.
13. http://www.2012endofdays.org/general/why-2012.php, accessed October 7, 2009.
14. MacDonald, op. cit.
15. Brooke Kenney, "Who Is the 2012 Group? And What's the Big Deal About 2012, Anyway?" http://brookenney.com/2012Group.htm, accessed October 6, 2009.

16. Ibid.

17. To some this may sound like the young girl plucking pedals from a daisy one by one, repeating, "He loves me; he loves me not . . ."

18. Ian O'Neill, "2012: No Geomagnetic Reversal," posted October 3, 2008 at http://www.universetoday.com/2008/10/03/2012-no-geomagnetic-reversal/, accessed October 6, 2009.

19. An example can be seen in Patrick Geryl's post, "Pole Shift and Pole Reversal," at http://survive2012.com/index.php/geryl-pole-shift.html, accessed September 1, 2009.

20. O'Neill, Ibid.

21. See the video at http://www.scivee.tv/node/6179, accessed October 7, 2009.

22. See http://en.wikipedia.org/wiki/Polar_Shift, accessed October 7, 2009.

23. Patrick Geryl, "Pole Shift & Pole Reversal in 2012," http://survive2012.com/index.php/geryl-pole-shift.html, accessed October 7, 2009.

24. O'Neill, op cit.

25. Op cit, http://abcnews.go.com/International/story?id=5301284&page=1.

26. "Does Maya calendar predict 2012 apocalypse?", posted March 27, 2007 at http://www.usatoday.com/tech/science/2007-03-27-maya-2012_n.htm accessed October 6, 2009. Joseph forecasts widespread catastrophe in his book, Apocalypse 2012: A Scientific Investigation Into Civilization's End. (New York: Broadway Books, 2007).

27. Dr. Rosa Williams, "No Fear of 2012: Part 1" at http://hoth.ccssc.org/blogs/blog5.php/2009/01/26/no-fear-of-2012-part-1, accessed October 6, 2009.

28. Op cit.

29. Dr. Rosa Williams, http://hoth.ccssc.org/blogs/blog5.php/2009/01/27/no-fear-of-2012-part-2, accessed October 7, 2009.

30. Dr. Donald Luttermoser, "Planetary Alignments: Fact or Fiction?", http://www.etsu.edu/physics/etsuobs/starprty/22099dgl/planalign.htm, accessed October 7, 2009.

31. Philip Plait, "Harmonic Con(game)vergence," http://www.badastronomy.com/bad/misc/planets.html, accessed October 7, 2009.

32. MacDonald, op. cit.

33. A typical presentation of this theory can be found at http://churchofcriticalthinking.org/planetx.html, accessed October 7, 2009.

34. See http://en.wikipedia.org/wiki/Nibiru_collision, accessed October 7, 2009.

35. David Morrison, "Nibiru and Doomsday 2012: Questions and Answers." http://astrobiology.nasa.gov/ask-an-astrobiologist/intro/nibiru-and-doomsday-2012-questions-and-answers, accessed October 7, 2009.

36. See http://en.wikipedia.org/wiki/Nibiru_collision, accessed October 7, 2009.

END NOTES

37. Morrison, op. cit.
38. Ibid.
39. See the excellent discussion of this at: Tom Chester, "No Tenth Planet Yet from IRAS," http://spider.ipac.caltech.edu/staff/tchester/iras/no_tenth_planet_yet.html, accessed October 7, 2009.
40. Ian O'Neill, "2012: No Planet X," http://www.universetoday.com/2008/05/25/2012-no-planet-x/, accessed October 7, 2009.

CHAPTER 2

1. *Bulletin of the Atomic Scientists*, www.thebulletin.org/content/doomsday-clockoverview.html, accessed June 3, 2008.
2. The approach in this book is based on the understanding that the Bible is the inspired word of God and is to be interpreted as any other great literature—with the literal, historical, grammatical hermeneutic. For a defense of this approach, see F.F. Bruce, *The New Testament Documents: Are They Reliable?* (Downers Grove, IL: Inter-Varsity Press, 1964); Norman L. Geisler, Editor, Inerrancy (Grand Rapids, MI: Zondervan Publishing House, 1980); Norman L. Geisler and William E. Mix, *A General Introduction to the Bible* (Chicago: Moody Press, 1968); E.D. Hirsch, Jr., *Validity in Interpretation* (New Haven, CT: Yale University Press, 1967); Elliott E. Johnson, *Expository Hermeneutics: an Introduction* (Grand Rapids, MI: Zondervan Publishing House, 1990); Josh McDowell, *Evidence that Demands a Verdict: Vol. 1* (Campus Crusade for Christ, Inc, 1972); Francis Turretin, *The Doctrine of Scripture*, edited and translated by John W. Beardslee III (Grand Rapids, MI: Baker Book House, 1981); Roy B. Zuck, *Basic Bible Interpretation* (Wheaton, IL: Victor Books, 1991).
3. This phrase was also used by Jesus in the same way—just prior to his ascension into heaven. The apostles had just posed this question to Jesus: "Lord, will You at this time restore the kingdom to Israel?" (Acts 1:6). The question dealt with when God would fulfill his promise of delivering Israel from her enemies (such as Rome), at which time the Messiah would rule the earth from Jerusalem. In response, Jesus announced this: "It is not for you to know times or seasons which the Father has put in His own authority." Since the apostles' question dealt with the fulfillment of God's future kingdom upon the earth, Jesus' use of the *times and the seasons* in his reply indicates that particular phrase refers to a future period of time.

   This term may have originated with Daniel 2:21 with Daniel's statement that God changes the *times and the seasons*. (The Septuagint version of Daniel 2:21 uses the same Greek words for times and seasons (χρονος, καιρος) as are used in Acts 1:7 and in 1 Thessalonians 5:1.) If so, when used in the New Testament, it may stress God's control over

239

the future. That provides a very comforting thought for a seven-year period whose description seems anything but comforting (although Paul reminds us in 1 Thessalonians 4:13–18 and 5:1–11 that Jesus will deliver all current believers in Christ from that foreboding era).

4. Isaiah 2:12, 17, 19
5. Amos 5:18–19
6. Zephaniah 1:14–18
7. The subject is presented as *they*. This separates that group of people from the readers who are identified in chapter one as believers in Jesus Christ. The contrast between the two parties is presented in verses 1–3 (of 1 Thessalonians 5): "*You* have no need that I should write to *you*. For *you* yourselves know . . . . For when *they* say . . . sudden destruction comes upon *them*, . . . And they shall not escape" (emphasis added). This contrast clearly shows that *they* in that passage are unbelievers.
8. It is likely that this peace and security will be connected with an announcement of the treaty with Israel in which ten nations will guarantee the terms of the treaty. This will be the treaty (*covenant*) presented in Daniel 9:27—but more on that in chapter 5.
9. This is presented in John 3:16, where we catch a glimpse of the immense love God has for the unbelieving world, a love so great he offered up his own Son for it.

CHAPTER 3

1. Of course, this is not because Paul is against expressing sorrow over death. After all, Jesus himself expressed sorrow at the death of a friend (John 11:35). Rather, he wants his readers to be comforted regarding the fate of their departed, believing loved ones.

   Those who have no hope refer to unbelievers—those who do not have *assurance* of possessing eternal life, for, in the Bible, *hope* is synonymous with *assurance*. That is because the Bible uses the word *hope* differently than we might use it in our everyday vernacular.

   For example, we might say something like, "I *hope* it doesn't rain today, because I need to mow the lawn." (Or, "I *hope* it does rain today, because I need to mow the lawn.") In using the word in that way, we are defining *hope* as an *uncertain* expectation. However, according to the Bible, *hope* is a *certain* expectation; it is God's promise regarding the future. Therefore, *hope* in the Bible is *assurance* for those who believe God's word.

   An area in which Christians have *hope* is in Christ's return; they can have the *assurance* that Jesus will return for them because his return is guaranteed by Scripture. In addition, they have the *hope* they will receive glorified bodies that will never experience suffering or corruption;

this is because the Bible promises this is what will occur. A Christian's *hope* regarding these truths is a *guaranteed certainty* that they will occur. *Hope*, in the biblical sense, then, does not have the meaning of, "I *hope* they will happen." Instead, Christians *know* those events will occur; they have *assurance* of what God has promised.

God wants us to *know* what will occur for deceased believers in Christ. This is the reason Paul has for communicating this passage (1 Thessalonians 4:13–18) to us.

2. *The church* refers to all who have become believers in Christ from the time of Pentecost (see Acts 2) until Jesus comes in the air for believers.

3. Though the word *rapture* does not appear in the Bible, the concept certainly does, as we see in this chapter. The lack of appearance of the word does not mean it is not a biblical concept. After all, the word *trinity*, or *triune*, does not appear in the Bible, but that does not mean, of course, that God is not a trinity, or is not a triune God.

4. In discussing the death of Christians, in 2 Corinthians 5:1–8, the apostle Paul proclaims in verse 8 that "to be absent from the body is to be present with the Lord." And in writing about whether he would remain alive or die—in Philippians 1:21–26—he revealed that when a Christian *departs* (dies), he goes to be with Christ (verse 23). Not only does a Christian remain completely conscious at death, but, in fact, at that point, he enters into an experience in which he is far more alive than at any time of his existence (cf. 2 Corinthians 5:4).

5. *The last trumpet* refers to the second trumpet sound. The first is for the *dead in Christ* to receive their glorified (resurrected) bodies. Then, *the last trumpet* will sound for those believers alive at that time to receive their glorified bodies. Among other things, the trumpet, in biblical times, was blown to announce anticipated events of great joy. The *rapture of the church* is such an event for believers alive today.

6. Here is how the outline of the book fleshes out phrase by phrase: I. The *manner of entry* expresses the basic content of 2:1–12 and refers to Paul and Silas' approach toward the Thessalonians; II. "How you turned to God from idols" is presented in 2:13–3:13 and refers to the reception of the Thessalonians to the gospel of Jesus Christ; III. Serving "the living and true God" is the theme of 4:1–12, detailing Paul's exhortation to his readers to live their lives in holiness; IV. Waiting "for His Son from heaven" is a reference to 4:13–18, describing the *rapture of the church*; V. "Jesus who delivers us from the wrath to come," (which can be translated "who will deliver us from the coming wrath," since it is referring to a future deliverance) is the overview of 5:1–11 about the day of the Lord. (The author is indebted to Zane Hodges for this outline, which first appeared in Zane Hodges, "The Rapture in 1 Thessalonians 5:1–11,"

in *Walvoord: A Tribute*, ed. by Donald K. Campbell (Chicago: Moody Press, 1982), pp. 67–80.)

7. Compare Matthew 24:36–44, Luke 12:35–40, and Revelation 16:15 with 1 Thessalonians 5:2–4 and 2 Peter 3:10.

8. *The Son of Man* is an expression borrowed from Daniel 7:13–14, where it refers to the Messiah as the future ruler of the earth. Jesus applied that same meaning in this passage in Matthew 24.

9. The Bible does not say that Jesus and believers return to heaven following the rapture. In fact, the Bible seems to indicate that they do not return to heaven. First of all, there is no statement that Jesus and believers return to heaven.

   Secondly, Jesus uses the same word (*parousia*, Greek, παρουσια) in Matthew 24, to portray *both* the rapture of the church (verses 37 and 39) and his return to the earth (verse 27), indicating one trip toward the earth, not two. The use of this word in verses 37 and 39 show that Jesus' coming begins unexpectedly (with the rapture)—without a sign—but it concludes with a sign at the end of the tribulation period (see verses 29–31), seven years later. It is the same coming (or trip from heaven to earth), though the return spans a seven-year period. (For an excellent presentation of this view, see Zane C. Hodges, *Jesus: God's Prophet* (Dallas, TX: Kerugma, Inc.), pp. 15–32.)

10. The standard Greek lexicon defines the Greek word used in this passage for *coming* (παρουσια) as "presence." Then, it follows that definition with this one: "coming, advent as the first stage in presence." (Walter Bauer, William F. Arndt, and F. Wilbur Gingrich, A Greek-English Lexicon of the New Testament and Other Early Christian Literature (Chicago: The University of Chicago Press, 1980), s.v. "ω   ," p. 629.) This perfectly describes Jesus' coming as presented in Matthew 24; it presents Jesus' presence in stages, with stage one being the rapture, followed by a seven-year hiatus, and ending with the final stage of Jesus' return to the earth.

11. The reason his coming to the earth (verse 30) is mentioned prior to his coming in the air (verse 37) is the way Jesus is answering the questions his disciples ask in verse 3. Verses 4–31 answer the second question ("What will be the sign of Your coming?") with the answer that *he* is the sign (note verse 30, "then the sign of the Son of Man will appear"). In verse 36, Jesus goes back to answer the first question ("When will these things be?") by stating, "But of that day and hour, no one knows." This answer shows he is speaking of the initiation of all that he has described in verses 4–35 (the day of the Lord), which is initiated by the rapture of the church.

   The "delay" in this trip from heaven to earth might be illustrated, for example, by a flight from Dallas, Texas, to Charlotte, North Carolina, routed through Atlanta, Georgia. Suppose the individual taking this trip decided to spend a couple of days in Atlanta to visit a friend, then boarded a plane and continued on toward Charlotte. Though there would be a layover in Atlanta, this would still be seen as one trip, not two separate trips. In the same vein, Jesus' coming to the earth from heaven is part of the same "trip" with a seven-year layover in the sky.

12. It may appear to some that the flood did not begin until seven days after Noah entered the ark (cf. Gen. 7:7–10); however, the flood actually came seven days after God gave Noah the command to gather the animals and provision into the ark. It could have taken Noah seven days to organize everything into the ark. If so, then Noah and his family may not have entered the ark until just prior to the coming of the flood. Certainly, Jesus links the two events (entering the ark and the coming of the flood) to the same day.

13. Walter Bauer, William F. Arndt, F. Wilbur Gingrich, and Frederick Danker, *A Greek-English Lexicon of the New Testament and Other Early Christian Literature* (Chicago: The University of Chicago Press, 1980), s.v. $\pi\alpha\rho\alpha\lambda\alpha\mu\beta\alpha\nu\omega$, p. 619.

14. For the use of *airo* in Matthew 24:39, Bauer, Arndt, Gingrich, and Danker provide this definition: "take away, remove with no suggestion of lifting up," which indicates a very different meaning than the use of *paralambano*. Ibid, s.v.   , p. 24.

15. Jesus may use the illustration of a thief for two reasons: 1) it emphasizes the point he makes in verses 42 and 44—just as a homeowner does not know when a thief might come, we don't know when Jesus will come for us; and 2) if we are not watching for Jesus' coming, the thief of unpreparedness could steal away from us the opportunity to rule with Christ—given to those who finish faithfully. (Note that Jesus makes this point to believers in Revelation 3:11: "Hold fast what you have, that no one may take your crown.")

16. This fact is clarified even more in Mark's recording of Jesus' pronouncement in 13:32: "But of that day and hour no one knows, neither the angels in heaven, nor the Son, but only the Father."

Though Jesus remained fully divine at his first advent to the earth, he laid aside certain attributes he always had as God, which included omniscience (being all-knowing). Thus, when Jesus stated that even he did not know when the rapture would occur (Mark 13:32), it was due to him laying aside his omniscience before coming to earth the first time. (As Philippians 2:5–7 indicates, though Jesus was equal to God [and, in fact, *is* God—cf. John 1:1; Rom. 9:5; 1 Tim. 2:5; Heb. 1:8; 2 Peter 1:1; 1 John 5:20], he laid aside [literally, emptied himself ($\varepsilon\kappa\varepsilon\nu\omega\sigma\varepsilon$ $\mu o\rho\phi\eta\nu$) of] some of the attributes of deity.) As such, he laid aside the three omni's—omniscience [all-knowing], omnipotence [all-powerful, as he worked miraculous signs by the power of the Holy Spirit—cf. Matt. 12:28], and omnipresence [existing everywhere at the same time]. However, it would seem that Jesus *now* knows when he will come in the air. If so, then his statement in Mark 13:32 was for the time he was upon the earth and does not necessarily indicate that no one will know ahead of time regarding the occurrence of the rapture.

In addition, Jesus encourages his followers in Matthew 24:32–33 to "learn this parable from the fig tree: When its branch has already become tender and puts forth leaves, you know that summer is near. So you also, when you see all these things, know that it is near—at the doors!" Though this statement specifically applies to those who believe in Christ during the tribulation period, the principle seems to apply to all of his followers: be alert to his soon appearing by watching the signs (i.e., world events—particularly in regard to Israel) of your time.

17. For more indicators that we may be chronologically close to the occurrence of the rapture, see the epilogue of this book, entitled, "How Soon?"

18. Basically, every ministry a believer has is an opportunity to serve others in some way. However, though verses 45–47 have application for every Christian, verse 45 is specifically aimed at the apostles. After all, the one pictured in the parable has significant authority over all other believers (a *ruler* over Jesus' *household*) and is responsible for teaching them his word (*giving them* [spiritual] *food*) when they are ready to take it in (*in due season*).

19. This refers to nourishing fellow believers in Christ by teaching (feeding) them God's Word. This same passage is present in Luke 12 where Jesus presents it in response to Peter's question, "Lord, do You speak this parable only to us, or to all people?" which indicates he had the apostles in mind first and foremost; however, verse 48 also applies well beyond them.

20. While the faithful servant in verses 45 and 46 takes care of (serves) his fellow servants, the servant portrayed in verses 48 and 49 mistreats his fellow servants. In the New Testament, serving one another (our fellow believers) is an extremely important measure of faithfulness to Christ.

21. See Hebrews 10:24–25 where Christians are exhorted to "not forsake the assembling together" with fellow believers.

22. For example, one view that encourages the thinking Jesus will delay his coming is the one that teaches the rapture will not occur until the end of the tribulation period. In that view, there is a delay of *at least* seven years!

23. The judgment seat of Christ is where all believers will appear to have their lives assessed in regard to faithfulness or lack of faithfulness, resulting in reward or lack of reward in God's kingdom. *Weeping and gnashing*

of teeth does not have to depict hell. Instead, it refers to sorrow or great regret, which will be the case of any believer, one day, who did not live for Christ.

24. An example of a rebuke by Jesus at the judgment seat of Christ is presented in parabolic form in Matthew 25:26.

25. If verses 48–51 portrayed an unbeliever who is living like an unbeliever, then he would not be a hypocrite. Instead, he would be living consistently according to his true identity.

CHAPTER 4

1. See Daniel 9:2.

2. See Jeremiah 25:9–12. According to 2 Chronicles 36:21, Judah would be in captivity one year for every Sabbath year she violated. God's law regarding the Sabbath year called for Israel to farm the land for six years, but, on every seventh year, the land was not to be farmed; it was to rest. (*sabbath* means *rest*.) This would call for great faith on Israel's part, for the Jews would need to trust God for his provision during this seventh year. However, Judah (southern Israel) did not have that kind of faith at that time. So, for 490 years—seventy Sabbath years—Judah continuously farmed the land. As a result, God announced he would force a rest for the land by taking ten thousand of Judah's best workers (young men) and by taking control of southern Israel! Judah would be disciplined by being taken into captivity one year for every Sabbath year she violated—seventy! (This shows the mercy and graciousness of God, for he could have disciplined Judah for every *year* the Jews were in disobedience, which would have been 490 years in captivity!)

3. As we will see, the context of Daniel 9:24–27 demonstrates that the prophecies specified could only fit within the time frame if the *weeks* mentioned are properly understood as seven-year periods. In addition, Daniel's original readers were familiar with the concept of *weeks of years*; after all, Daniel and his people were in captivity when he recorded this passage due to the failure of the Jews to keep the law of Sabbath rests (in which they were to allow the land to lie fallow every seven years, providing a Sabbath rest for the land just as they were to observe a Sabbath rest every week of days—cf. Lev. 25; Deut. 15). In fact, they were banished to exile in Babylon for seventy years—one year for every sabbatical year they violated (see 2 Chron. 36:21). This means that their violation of this part of God's law covered *seventy weeks of years*, or a total of 490 years—the exact amount of time covered by the prophecy of Daniel 9:24–27!

Also, we will see that one *week* of the seventy weeks of prophecy in Daniel 9 has yet to be fulfilled. When we compare the book of Daniel with the book of Revelation, we can see that this final *week* presents the fulfillment in Revelation as a period of seven years. (Compare, for example, Daniel 7:25 and 12:7 with Revelation 11:3 and 12:14; also compare with Revelation 11:2 and 13:5.)

4. Jerusalem was the location of the temple that existed in Daniel's day, and is the city in which two future temples will be built. (One will be erected during the first half of the future tribulation period, and one will be built at the beginning of the millennial reign of Christ.) The temple was the hub of all Jewish religious activity, including the offering of gifts and sacrifices to God.

5. See Acts 3:19–21.

6. This is how this Hebrew verb is used in Daniel 6:18, for example. It is also used this way in Job 9:7 and 37:7.

7. See Revelation 2:27; 12:5; 19:15.

8. See Isaiah 32:15–16; 42:3–4; Jeremiah 23:5.

9. See 2 Peter 3:10 and Revelation 21:1.

10. 2 Peter 3:13

11. We can particularly see that in Romans 5:11.

12. Jeremiah 23:5–6 depicts the millennial kingdom, the first thousand years of Jesus' rule upon the earth. Following that era, God will destroy the present universe (including, of course, the earth) and will create *new heavens and a new earth in which righteousness reigns* (2 Peter 3:13; see also verses 9–12 and Revelation 21:1). Thus, once Jesus brings righteousness to the earth—by his return—it will be *everlasting*.

13. For references to this temple, see Isa. 66:20–21; Jer. 33:15–18; Ezek. 20:40–41; 37:26; 40:1–46:24; and Zech. 14:16–17.

14. Nehemiah 2:1–5

15. For an excellent discussion of the dates in this lesson, see Harold W. Hoehner, *Chronological Aspects of the Life of Christ* (Grand Rapids, MI: Zondervan Publishing House, 1977), pp. 115–139.

16. The transliterated Hebrew word is *Meshiach*.

17. The transliteration of this word is *Christos*.

18. The Hebrew word (krt) translated "cut off" is used of putting to death of people in general (Genesis 9:11; 41:36), of enemies (Isaiah 11:13; Micah 5:8), and of the wicked (Psalm 37:9, 22, 28, 34, 38; Proverbs 2:22; Hosea 8:4; and Nahum 2:1).

19. Ibid, p. 138.

20. Because a Jewish calendar year is 360 days, rather than 365 days of a solar year, the time period from March 4, 444 BC to AD March 30, 33 is 173,880 days, which equals 483 prophetic years to the very day!

21. God not only *knows* everything that will occur, but he also *determines* events to accomplish his perfect plan which is laid out in his Word, the Bible.

22. See Eph. 3:14, 20.

END NOTES

CHAPTER 5

1. Paul Lee Tan, *Encyclopedia of 7,000 Illustrations: Signs of the Times* (Rockville, MD: Assurance Publishers, 1988), p. 1481.
2. See Isaiah 8:7–8; 59:19; and Jeremiah 46:7–8 where the concept of *flood* or *overflowing* (river) refers to invading armies with large amounts of troops. (This is probably the idea in Daniel 11:22 as well.)
3. The reason Jews have not been able to offer up sacrifices to God since AD 70 is the temple (*the sanctuary*) was destroyed in AD 70. Thus, the temple will need to be rebuilt to fulfill some of the conditions of the treaty mentioned in verse 27.
4. Passages such as Matthew 24:15; 2 Thessalonians 2:4; and Revelation 11:1–2, as well as Daniel 9:27 show that the temple will be rebuilt sometime before the middle of the day of the Lord (the seven-year tribulation period).
5. Both the extent of time between losing the city and regaining it, as well as the way Israel obtained Jerusalem from that war, signaled a true miracle from God!
6. The Hebrew word for *people* is a collective noun that takes singular verbs. A separate word *he* is not written here in Hebrew, but is translated in English because of the singular verb. But, if the singular verb refers to *people*, then it should be translated as *they* in English. This also seems more likely in view of the rest of verse 27.
7. Though no identification is made of *many* in this passage, the angel Gabriel shows it refers to Israel by announcing that the *seventy sevens* refer to Daniel's people (the Jews) and their capital city, Jerusalem. Robert Culver points out that this Hebrew word for *many* "is used in Isaiah 52:14 of the Jewish nation that rejected Christ at His first coming, and in Isaiah 53:12 of the same Jewish nation of the sins He bore"—Robert Culver, *Daniel and the Latter Days* (Chicago: Moody Press, 1977), p. 162.
8. The Greek (the language in which the New Testament was originally recorded) word for *hills* is the same as that for *mountains*. If one were comparing these to something else, they might be more akin to the Black Hills of South Dakota than to the Rocky Mountains of Colorado.
9. See Romans 11:26 and Revelation 7:9–14.
10. See Zechariah 13:8–14:4; Romans 8:17; James 1:2–4; 1 Peter 1:6–7; 4:12–13.
11. See Romans 8:17.
12. See Zechariah 13:8–14:4.
13. Note the apostle Peter's promise in that regard in Acts 3:19–21.
14. See Matthew 24:21. The context indicates great persecution upon believing Jews in the last half of the day of the Lord.

CHAPTER 6

1. Philip Yancey, *The Bible Jesus Read* (Grand Rapids, MI: Zondervan Publishing House, 1999), p. 180.

2. For example, see Revelation 7:9–17.

3. Sackcloth was the garment of mourning and repentance (see Jonah 3:5–10, for example, and compare with Luke 11:32.) Note, also, Jesus' admonition in Matthew 11:21: "Woe to you, Chorazin! Woe to you, Bethsaida! For if the mighty works which were done in you had been done in Tyre and Sidon, they would have repented long ago in sackcloth and ashes." The command to *repent* appears in the book of Revelation ten times, demonstrating its emphasis for both believers and unbelievers. But, the ministry of these two witnesses is for the purpose of calling Israel to repentance. (Israel will first repent, then will believe in Jesus for eternal life. See Acts 3:19–21. [Though repentance is not a necessary requirement for anyone to receive eternal life, the nation of Israel, portrayed in the Old Testament as a strong-willed son of God, will need to repent in order to be prepared to receive the free gift of eternal life by believing in Jesus Christ for it.])

4. See Revelation 10:1; 11:1.

5. It was John who recorded the book of Revelation.

6. It has more allusions to the Hebrew Scriptures (the Old Testament) than any other New Testament book.

7. The three and a half days in which their bodies lie on the street provide a preview and a warning of the three and a half years to follow in which Jewish believers will be persecuted and killed.

8. See Rev. 13:4.

9. Daniel's seventieth week is the final seven years of the prophesied 490 years of God working with Israel to bring the nation to righteousness and to bring his kingdom to the earth.

10. This verse also shows that their ministry was predicted in Zechariah 4 (see, especially, verses 2, 3, 11–14).

11. See, for example, Matthew 23:34–35 and Luke 11:49–51.

12. This is not to say that the prophets of Revelation 11 will actually be Moses and Elijah returned. In fact, when Jesus stated in Matthew 11 that John the Baptist would have fulfilled the role of Elijah if Israel would have been open to his ministry of repentance (verse 14), he was saying that there will be one coming in the future in the "spirit and power of Elijah" (Luke 1:7) who will fulfill the role of Elijah, but he will not literally be Elijah. One of these two prophets will embody the "spirit and power of Elijah," while the other will embody the "spirit and power" of Moses—but they will not be the same individuals who graced the pages of the Old Testament.

13. See 2 Kings 1:12.
14. As mentioned earlier, this will be the time frame of "the days of their prophecy."
15. See James 5:17.
16. See 8:13; 9:12.
17. We will learn much more about these judgments in chapter 17, including what they are and why God will bring them upon the earth.
18. Zane Hodges provides a plausible suggestion as to why those who are stung by these insects are unable to commit suicide when he writes that "perhaps . . . the sting causes physical incapacity"—Zane Hodges, *Power to Make War: The Career of the Assyrian Who Will Rule the World* (Dallas, TX: Redencion Viva, 1995), 89.
19. Because of judgments such as these in the Old Testament, there are some critics of the Bible who believe the Bible speaks of two different gods—a god of the Old Testament who is angry and judgmental and a god of the New Testament who is a god of love. However, the presentation of God we have seen from the book of Revelation shows that view of those critics to be wrong. Those future judgments, presented in the New Testament, show God presented consistently with the way he is portrayed in the Old Testament. Yet, they present him to be longsuffering in love toward mankind, in seeking to bring people to him, just as he is presented as longsuffering in love in the Old Testament (particularly toward Israel).

CHAPTER 7

1. Note that in our last chapter we pointed out that a third of the trees and all grass will burn up, a third of the sea will turn to blood, a third of the creatures in the sea will die, and a third of mankind will die.
2. Remember that all believers are taken into the air at the initiation of the day of the Lord via the rapture of the church.
3. Scripture indicates that God is drawing Jews back to the land in order to be saved (See Ezekiel 37). Also, the 144,000 are from the twelve tribes of Israel, which indicates they are likely from Israel. In addition, they will believe in Christ at the beginning of the seven-year tribulation period, and the gospel will begin in Jerusalem at that time and will not go out to the rest of the world until later. Thus, all of the indicators show the 144,000 are from the land of Israel, and it is in Israel where they become disciples of Jesus.
4. That is, it is not literal (is not literally describing individuals who have never had sexual intercourse) but representative of faithfulness.
5. Since the book of Revelation has more allusions to the Old Testament than any other New Testament book, then we should look in the Old

Testament for help to understand terms in Revelation. It would only make sense, then, that the meaning of *virgins* in Revelation 14—for a perfect representation of Israel (twelve thousand from each of the twelve tribes of Israel)—would be the same as that used of Israel in the Old Testament.

6. For a defense of the identity of the harlot as Rome, see chapter 21.

7. Though the angel who has "the everlasting gospel" in Revelation 14:6 calls for people to "fear God" and "worship Him" because "the hour of His judgment has come" (referring to the return of Christ to deal with his enemies) in verse 7, the message of verse 7 is *not* the content of the gospel. As has always been the case throughout history, and also during the tribulation period, the gospel will not be proclaimed by an angel, but by people. The picture of the vision of verses 6 and 7 is the angel bringing the gospel from heaven to the earth to be proclaimed by the 144,000. The angel simply calls for all men to fear God.

8. We have seen that their ministry will occur throughout the first 1,260 days of the day of the Lord. (See Rev. 11:3, 6 for this time period.) We have also seen that the trumpet judgments will be poured out during the ministry of the two prophets.

9. They will particularly be taught from the New Testament, since being Jewish, they will probably have an understanding of the Hebrew (Old Testament) Scriptures.

10. See Matthew 28:19–20 to see that baptizing and teaching all that Christ commanded are both aspects of making disciples.

11. This is pictured by the woman in Revelation 12:6, 14, who represents Israel.

12. See Matthew 24:21.

CHAPTER 8

1. This was a much faster ascent than the rapid rise of Barack Obama, described by a CNN article as "one of the most rapid—and unexpected—ascents in American political history" (http://www.cnn.com/2008/POLITICS/08/18/revealed.obama.profile/index.html, accessed January 15, 2009). Obama's career as a politician began in 1996, when he was elected unopposed to the Illinois state senate. Eight years later, he was elected to the US Senate, and four years after that, he was elected president of the United States.

2. Note that Daniel explains that God puts kings in power and removes their power (Daniel 2:21). In addition, Jesus explains Pontius Pilate's authority in this way: "You could have no power at all against Me unless it had been given you from above" (John 19:11). See also declarations such as John 3:27 and 1 Corinthians 4:7 that show that everything anyone has—including any authority—is due to God granting it.

END NOTES

3. Daniel 2:21
4. 1 Thessalonians 5:3
5. See Rev. 11:5.
6. See Luke 16:19–31.
7. See Daniel 11:2–4. Also see 8:20–22.
8. 2 Thessalonians 2:8
9. See Matthew 24:29–31.
10. Specifically, the Lord will dwell in Israel's capital, Jerusalem, via the presence of the Messiah (see Jeremiah 3:17; Zechariah 8:2–3.).
11. See Micah 5:2–5a.
12. Micah 5:4–5a describe Jesus' future rule upon the earth; then 5:5b–6 shows what will happen immediately *prior* to Jesus' rule upon the earth.
13. See Hodges, op cit, p. 24.
14. If we compare Daniel 2 with Daniel 7, we can see that the fourth kingdom mentioned in Daniel 7 refers to the Roman Empire, which is represented by *ten horns*. (Biblically, a *horn* can be a metaphor for authority or rule.) According to verse 8 in Daniel 7, a little horn representing the king of the North arises from *among them*, indicating he is of the territory that once belonged to the Roman Empire.
15. See www.aina.org/habash.htm and www.assistnews.net ["American politicians and the White House flooded with calls for 'Operation Assyrian Province'", Jan. 18, 2007] for examples.
16. Jordan is referred in Daniel 11:41 as Edom, Moab, and the prominent people of Ammon.
17. The idea of conquering is portrayed by the following phrases in Daniel 11:40: "'shall enter the countries, overwhelm them, and pass through."
18. Cf. Matt. 24:15 and 2 Thess. 2:3–4.
19. *The sanctuary shall be cleansed* refers to Christ's return, at which point he will not only rescue Israel, but the temple as well.
20. As we saw in an earlier lesson, this act of the man of sin is also known as the abomination of desolation (see Matt. 24:15; Dan. 12:11), at which point he abominates the temple.
21. This is based on a Jewish calendar of 360 days per year.

CHAPTER 9

1. S. Craig Glickman, *Knowing Christ* (Chicago: Moody Press, 1980), p. 37.
2. This is the Jewish temple that will be rebuilt in Jerusalem.
3. See Daniel 8:19 where *indignation* is a translation of the same Hebrew word that is translated as *wrath* in 11:36. The context of chapter 8 seems to argue that this indignation will be from *the little horn* (the same figure as the king of the North in chapter 11) and will be experienced by Israel.

4. See Rom. 8:17.

5. In fact, it may be that Egypt, for example, will see how unstoppable he is, which prompts the preemptive attack against him. Egypt may believe the only hope it has of bringing him under control will be to try to catch him off guard with a first strike.

6. John Walvoord, *Daniel: The Key to Prophetic Revelation* (Chicago: Moody Press, 1981), 274. This would fit the Jewish orientation of Daniel. See Walvoord's work for more evidence for the basis of this view.

7. Assyrians are generally either Eastern Orthodox or Chaldean Catholic.

8. Of course, it is not a contradiction, since the Bible does not contradict itself.

9. See the last chapter.

10. As Zane Hodges points out: " 'Strongholds' were a familiar part of the Greek culture spread by Alexander the Great. In ancient Greece, the word *acropolis* referred to a walled stronghold built on a hill inside a city. Temples and shrines were often located within the fortified area. The Acropolis of Athens, with its main temples, is the best known example of this." Then, in commenting on Daniel 11:38, he writes: "We should probably conclude that at this time Satan will have many religious 'strongholds.' That is, the King of the North will honor him at temples and shrines situated in high, well-protected locations." (Op cit, p. 14)

11. As pointed out earlier, the king begins his rise to power 220 days following the start of the tribulation period, and he will become king of the world on the 1,260th day of the tribulation period. On a Jewish calendar, he will therefore ascend to king of the world in 2.8 years!

12. See Genesis 1:28; Psalm 8:6–8; Hebrews 2:5–8.

13. See John 12:31; 14:30; 16:11, where Jesus bestows this title upon Satan.

CHAPTER 10

1. The promotion of Lucifer worship will be a part of worshipping Satan.

2. This prophecy has not been fulfilled, which means it *will* be fulfilled in the future.

3. Hebrew is the original language in which this passage, like most of the Old Testament, was written.

4. *Sheol* is used here—as it is used elsewhere in the Old Testament—as the place of the dead. Its New Testament counterpart is *the abyss*, as in Romans 10:7 where *the abyss* is also presented as the place of the dead.

5. See Acts 3:19–21; Zech. 12–14.

6. It seems that the king will arrive in Jerusalem at the midpoint of the day of the Lord. Further discussion on the events to follow will corroborate that time frame.

7. Zane Hodges offers this explanation: The topography of Jerusalem to the north of the ancient walls offers an obviously suitable location for the king's royal tents. This would be in the upper Kidron Valley to the northeast of the Temple Mount. The slopes of the Mount of Olives would be to the southeast of the king's encampment (*Power to Make War*, p. 24).

8. The Kidron Valley divides the Mount of Olives, where Jesus will return to the earth (cf. Zech. 14:4), and the Temple Mount, where Jesus will ascend to rule his kingdom. Satan will move the king—along with the armies of the earth—to attempt to cut off Jesus so he cannot ascend the Temple Mount to begin his kingdom rule. More will be said about that in chapter 18.

9. Note that according to Daniel 7, this treaty will be broken at the midpoint, or three and a half years following its commencement.

10. Cf. 2 Thess. 2:8; Rev. 19:11–20.

CHAPTER 11

1. The lone exception at this point of time is Israel.

2. This is the meaning of the use of *sea* in Daniel 7 from which Revelation 13 draws much of its imagery. Note especially verse 2 of Daniel 7, where the sea is called *the Great Sea*, a clear reference to the Mediterranean Sea (see Numbers 34:6–7 and Joshua 15:47). For examples of this understanding, see Gleason L. Archer, Jr., *The Expositor's Bible Commentary: Daniel and the Minor Prophets, Volume 7*, ed. Frank E. Gabelein (Grand Rapids, MI: Zondervan Publishing House, 1985), p. 85; Robert Culver, *The Histories and Prophecies of Daniel*, Winona Lake, IN: BMH Books, 1980), p. 106; G. Coleman Luck, *Daniel* (Chicago: Moody Press, 1958), p. 84; and Leon Wood, *A Commentary on Daniel* (Grand Rapids, MI: Zondervan Publishing House, 1973), p. 180. The amillennialist interpretation of Daniel 7:3, of seeing the sea not as a literal sea but as a spiritual metaphor is represented by C.F. Keil when he states that the sea represents "the whole heathen world" (see C.F. Keil, *Biblical Commentary on the Book of Daniel in Commentary on the Old Testament, Volume IX*, ed. C.F. Keil and F. Delitzsch (Grand Rapids, MI: William B. Eerdmans Publishing Company, 1980), pp. 222–223.) (For an excellent discussion of the interpretation of prophecy, see J. Dwight Pentecost, *Things to Come* (Grand Rapids, MI: Zondervan Publishing House, 1980), pp. 1–64.)

3. The beast will begin as the king of the North, whose area of rule is east of the Mediterranean Sea. He will later become the beast who, as we will discover, once ruled from Rome, which is west of the Mediterranean Sea. In addition, the area the beast once ruled, the Roman Empire,

was both east and west of the Sea. Therefore, his identity is linked with the Mediterranean Sea, which is a logical metaphor for his return to ascendency.

4. The present tense *reigns* means that it was *the great city* that held power over the kings of the earth when the book of Revelation was written in the first century, which clearly was the city of Rome.

5. Though some Bibles translate the Greek word in that verse as *mountains*, it is also the word for *hills*.

6. The Greek word translated here as *the bottomless pit* is translated as *the abyss* in Romans 10:7, where we learn it is the place of the dead (where Jesus went when he died). *Before* the ascension of Christ into heaven, *all* who died went to *the abyss*, or hades—though believers were separated from unbelievers by a large gulf (see Luke 16:19–31). *After* the ascension of Christ, only unbelievers went into the abyss following death.

7. For an excellent defense of dating Revelation at AD 68 or 69, see John A. T. Robinson, *Redating the New Testament*, pp. 221–253. Also, see Albert A. Bell, Jr., "The Date of John's Apocalypse: The Evidence of Some Roman Historians Reconsidered," *New Testament Studies* 25, pp. 92–102.

   In addition, note the mention of seven Roman kings in Rev. 17:9–10, five of which had already died by the time Revelation was written. If this, in fact, refers to the first five Roman emperors, which it most likely does (see footnote #141 on this), then the apostle John was writing during the reign of Servius Sulpicius Galba, who ruled AD 68–69, following the death of Nero (in the spring of 68).

8. The connection between these kings and the city is readily apparent. The *seven heads* refer to both the hills upon which the city sits (verse 9) and the seven kings mentioned in verse 10. Though *the kings* seem to be connected with the beast and *the hills* to the city, there is a definite connection with all the parties (the beast, the city, the hills, and the kings) presented. One aspect of the connection is portrayed by the city riding the beast, while another is seen by the use of the same metaphor—*heads*—to refer to both hills and kings. The apostle John could easily have separated the kings from the city by the use of a different metaphor for the kings than he used for the hills upon which the city sits. However, he did not—and there is only one explanation why he did not: he wanted the reader to see the connection of both the hills and the kings to this city, as well as to the beast.

9. These seven kings must have been somewhat significant to be mentioned in this prophetic context in this way. In the apostle John's day, the only set of seven kings who were truly significant ones were Roman emperors. And the only set of seven Roman emperors that might be set

apart from the others is the first seven. The first seven fit the dating of Revelation at AD 68, as we will later see.

10. If he were not coming back from the dead, one would have to wonder in what sense he would—in the future—experience destruction. As Robert Mounce explains: "At the time of writing, the beast has not yet ascended from the abyss (19:8). He is an eighth in the sense that he is distinct from the seven" (Robert Mounce, *The Book of Revelation*, The International Commentary on the New Testament, edited by F. F. Bruce, Grand Rapids, MI: William B. Eerdmans Publishing Co., 1977, p. 316). G. H. Lang commented that "one of these seven is to be the eighth of this series of monarchs and the final head of the Gentile world ruler: the final ruler because he shall war against the Lamb at His coming, be overthrown, and be cast direct into perdition (19:19–21)" (G. H. Lang, *The Revelation of Jesus Christ: Selected Studies* (Miami Springs, FL: Conley & Schoettle Publishing Co., Inc., 1985, p. 269).

11. The lion is also presented as a symbol of Babylon by one of Daniel's contemporary prophets—Jeremiah (see Jeremiah 4:7; 49:19; 50:17, 44). We can also see in comparing the order of the symbols for empires that they symbolize the same empires in Daniel chapter 7 as in Daniel chapter 2. Thus, as Daniel 2:38 announces, Babylon is the first kingdom mentioned. For further discussion on this, as well as on the other animals symbolized here, see Leon Wood, *A Commentary on Daniel* (Grand Rapids, MI: Zondervan Publishing House, 1973), pp. 181–185; also see John F. Walvoord, *Daniel: The Key to Prophetic Revelation* (Chicago: Moody Press, 1971), pp. 153–159.

12. Historically, the Medo-Persian Empire succeeded the Babylonian kingdom. Moreover, Daniel 8 (especially verse 20) reveals this as the dual empire of the Medes and the Persians. (Though the animal for this empire in chapter 8 is pictured as a ram, the similarity of one part of this kingdom "raised up" over the other [compare 7:5 with 8:3] show this to be the same kingdom as portrayed in Daniel 7.)

13. Greece historically followed Medo-Persia and is identified as such in Daniel 8:21.

14. The others in the list of the first five Roman emperors were basically either misfits or insane.

15. Upon his death, Augustus was declared a god by the senate, to be worshipped by the Romans. (See Werner Eck, translated by Deborah Lucas Schneider; new material by Sarolta A. Takacs, The Age of Augustus (Oxford: Blackwell Publishing, 2003), p. 124.) This indicates the stature of Augustus among those over whom he ruled, but might this also have been a foreshadowing pointing to the identity of the beast?

In addition, when Augustus came into power in the first century, he immediately began to assail the specific problems causing the deplorable conditions and effectively ushered in a new age for the Roman world. It seems the beast will enter into his rule under similar conditions (but even worse) and will begin to rule with the promise of bringing in a new age for the world. These similarities may also point to the revivification of Augustus.

16. The same word for *live* is used of Jesus in the book of Revelation representing his resurrection from the dead. For example, in 1:18 Jesus describes himself as "He who lives, and was dead, and behold, I am alive forevermore." And, with a use of that word in the past tense—just as it is used of one of the heads who was slain—Jesus, in 2:8, describes himself as one "who was dead and came to life [lived]." Thus, the picture of the one "who was wounded by the sword and lived" is that of one who will apparently be killed and rise from the dead.

17. The name Lucifer is found in Isaiah 14:12 and means "light bearer."

18. The apostles back up this point in their prayer to the Lord: "For truly against Your holy Servant Jesus, whom You anointed, both Herod and Pontius Pilate, with the Gentiles and the people of Israel, were gathered together to do whatever Your hand and Your purpose determined to be done" (Acts 4:27–28). God has always been in full control of whomever obtains authority, including granting authority to evil men to crucify his Son.

CHAPTER 12

1. Cited in Donald K. Campbell, *Daniel: Decoder of Dreams* (Wheaton, IL: Victor Books, 1977), pp. 131–132.

2. Though this describes something that has not yet happened, the past tense is used. The explanation for the phenomenon is that what is described in the book of Revelation is what the apostle John has seen in a vision given by God. So, what John records is what has already transpired in his vision; thus, the material oftentimes appears in the past tense, though the events have not yet occurred in reality.

3. In Revelation 2:8, Jesus describes himself as the one "who was dead, and came to life." The Greek word translated as *came to life* is the same Greek word in the very same Greek tense (*ezasen* [εζησεν]) which is translated as *lived* in describing what occurs to the beast in Revelation 13:14 following the reception of his deadly wound. In other words, that Greek word presents Jesus' resurrection and so, when used of the beast, it seemingly pictures the same experience of him.

4. He will be one of the first five Roman Emperors. See Revelation 17:8–11 and the explanation of this passage in the previous chapter.

5. See Revelation 11:6, 10.

6. This will occur the very evening of the 1,260th day of their ministry (Rev. 11:3, 7).
7. See Exodus 30:10; Leviticus 16:3–34.
8. Cf. Lev. 9:7; 16:6.
9. The mention of the Sabbath is one clue Israel will observe the Law, but also the stress on temple sacrifices during the first three and a half years of the tribulation period indicates this as well. (The stress on temple sacrifices is shown by the cessation of *sacrifice and offering* by the breaking of the treaty with Israel in Daniel 9:27 and by the mention of the temple in Matt. 24:15 and 2 Thess. 2:3–4.) Under the Law, travel on the Sabbath is severely limited.
10. This is the meaning of Jesus' statement in Matthew 24:21.
11. The birth of the child by the woman represents the Messiah as a *"child"* of Israel—that is, a Jew.
12. For Jesus' current session at the right hand of God, see Hebrews 1:3; 8:1; 10:12; 12:2.
13. For example, see Job 38:7.
14. We will learn in our next chapter that this war in heaven will occur at the midpoint of the tribulation period.
15. See Matthew 24:15–20; Mark 13:14–18; and Luke 17:31–37.

CHAPTER 13

1. According to Revelation 12:10, Satan accuses Christians before our God day and night. This indicates that he currently spends most of his time in heaven.
2. See Jude 1:9. *Archangel* means that Michael possesses the highest rank of all the angels.
3. *Sons of God* is a reference to angels (see the use of this term in Job 38:7 when the *sons of God* sang while he created the earth)—both fallen angels (such as Satan) and unfallen ones (such as Michael).
4. Some see that as the meaning of Isaiah 14:12 (" 'How you are fallen from heaven, O Lucifer, son of the morning! How you are cut down to the ground, you who weakened the nations!' ") and of Ezekiel 28:17 (" 'Your heart was lifted up because of your beauty . . . I cast you to the ground . . .' ") However, oftentimes prophetic statements state a future occurrence as if it had already occurred. In comparing these statements from Isaiah 14 and Ezekiel 28 with Job 1 and 2, along with Revelation 12, we can see that they portray Satan's future humiliation and judgment as if they had already taken place.
5. Though a number of Bible versions read *Armageddon*, the majority of Greek manuscripts on this verse read *Megiddo*.
6. Zechariah 14:2.

7. See Zechariah 13:9; 14:3–4; and Acts 3:19–21.
8. See Exodus 4:22.
9. Since Israel is a *son* of God (or as a *backsliding daughter* in Jer. 31:21–22), the nation is a picture of a believer in Christ (cf. John 1:12; Gal. 4:7; 1 John 5:1.), but one who has drifted far from God (such as the prodigal son of Luke 15). Like a believer in Christ, Israel has an eternal relationship with God (cf. Jer. 31:35–37.); but, like any good father, God desires a *close* relationship—fellowship—with his child.
10. This is not the same as receiving eternal life, which is received only as a free gift by believing in Jesus Christ for it (see John 3:16–18; 6:47; 11:25–26.). The gospel of John, which is written to show unbelievers how to receive eternal life (see the purpose statement in John 20:31), presents the only condition for receiving eternal life: believing in Jesus for it. In addition, repentance is never mentioned—not even once—in the gospel of John, which shows that repentance is not a necessary requirement for receiving eternal life.
11. The need for individual Jews is the reception of eternal life, while the need for the nation is the need for *fellowship* with God.
12. The word *flood* in this verse can also be translated as *river*. Some Old Testament passages can help us to discover the meaning of verse 15. For example, Isaiah 8:7–8 presents *river* in this metaphoric sense: "Now therefore, behold, the Lord brings up over them the waters of the river, strong and mighty—the king of Assyria and all his glory; he will go up over all his channels and go over all his banks. He will pass through Judah, he will overflow and pass over." The word *river* is used in these verses to represent a *flood* of troops. We see the same usage in Isaiah 59:19: "When the enemy comes in like a *flood*, the Spirit of the Lord will lift up a standard against him." While Isaiah 8 mentions the army of Assyria, chapter 59 simply presents *the enemy* in a generic form. Jeremiah 46:7–8, however, uses the same metaphor to describe the flood of troops from another enemy, Egypt: " 'Who is this coming up like a *flood*, whose waters move like the rivers? Egypt rises up like a *flood*, and its waters move like the *rivers*; and he says, 'I will go up and cover the earth, I will destroy the city and its inhabitants." ' " (emphasis added to the above Scriptures.)

    All three of these Old Testament passages use the metaphor *flood* or *river* to represent an army of troops coming against Israel. This is the meaning in Revelation 12:15.
13. *The city* is Jerusalem, for not only is it *the city* of this context—beginning in chapter 11—but it is *the* city of Israel, which is clearly the focus of chapter 12.

END NOTES

CHAPTER 14

1. Of course, he will experience even greater vindication at his return to defeat his enemies and to establish God's kingdom upon the earth. But, Jesus will not truly experience universal vindication until the great white throne judgment (cf. Rev. 20:11–15), when every knee will bow before him and recognize him as Lord (cf. Phil. 2:10–11).

2. As indicated earlier, it is the Jewish calendar that is used in Revelation to mark time.

3. *The beast* that kills them refers to a man who, on the day he commits this terrible act, becomes the ruler of the world (see Revelation 13). He is called a beast because his power and authority are an amalgamation of three other animals presented in Daniel 7 and Rev. 13:2, which represent three other powerful empires—besides the Roman Empire.

4. In AD 70, God used the Roman army, under the command of Titus, to bring severe discipline to Jerusalem by destroying the city and the Jewish temple.

5. The reason God will give these two prophets such authority to bring plagues upon the earth for three and a half years is due to his love for the world. He will seek to use those plagues to cause people to turn to him for help, opening their hearts to the gospel. It will work as many will believe in Christ as we see in Revelation 7:9–14.

6. An illustration of this perception is found in 1 Kings 20 when, in verse 23, the servants of the king of Syria made this announcement regarding the "gods" of the Israelites: "Their gods are gods of the hills. Therefore they were stronger than we; but if we fight against them in the plain, surely we will be stronger than they." If this illustrates what will occur, as described in Revelation 11, then those who had been celebrating the defeat of God's prophets will give God glory as merely the God of heaven, while continuing to worship the god of the earth—the beast.

CHAPTER 15

1. *The saints* in this context specifically refer to Jewish believers in Christ.

2. See Romans 8:29, which is located in the context of suffering (beginning with verses 17b and 18 and continuing through the end of the chapter)—specifically, suffering from persecution (see verses 33–39).

3. Though Jesus died in the first century, he is "the Lamb slain from the foundation of the world" in that his death was planned by God before the world began. And, because God is timeless (outside of time and not dictated by time in any way) and unchanging, this act of Jesus' death was already accomplished in the mind of God from all eternity past.

4. See Revelation 20:10.

5. See John 3:18.

6. See John 3:16–18; 5:24.
7. See John 5:24; 6:47.
8. If everlasting life could be lost, then it could not be viewed in any sense of the word as *everlasting*.
9. See John 1:12; 3:3, 7.
10. See John 11:25–26.
11. See John 10:28–29.
12. See John 3:16–18; 5:24; 6:35–40, 47; 10:28–29; 11:25–26.
13. Jesus indicates there will be unfaithful believers in the tribulation period. For example, take note of Matthew 24:11–14, in which he indicates that the love of many believers will *grow cold*," indicating that those having a fervent love of God and of fellow believers will become spiritually tepid. However, those who do so will die; they will not make it to the end of the tribulation period. (This is the meaning of Matthew 24:13, " 'he who endures to the end will be saved,' " where nine verses [verse 22] later we learn that Jesus is using *saved* in the context as physical preservation. This means that only faithful believers will survive the day of the Lord.) In the context of instructing believers living during the tribulation period in Luke 17:30–33 (" 'the day when the Son of Man is revealed,' " verse 30, refers to the last half of the tribulation period—the three-and-a-half-year era during which the beast will rule), Jesus warns of the real possibility of believers living for themselves (" 'whoever seeks to save his life' "), and, as a result, losing their lives.

    Due to the tremendous pressure to take the mark of the beast during the latter half of the tribulation period, undoubtedly, spiritually indifferent believers will be tempted to take the mark. However, not only will God take the lives of unfaithful believers before the end of the tribulation period, He will necessarily and mercifully do so before they can take the mark of the beast. This is the only way to explain that no believer will take the mark.
14. *Horns* in the Bible are often metaphors for strength and authority. Thus, "his strength (his 'horns') will lie perhaps in his reputation as a gracious and gentle figure—a tower of personal rectitude and holiness"—Zane C. Hodges, Power to Make War (Dallas, TX: Redencion Viva, 1995), 59.
15. As Zane Hodges writes: "The sea is a biblical symbol for great masses of Gentile humanity (Isaiah 60:5; Jeremiah 6:22, 23; Ezekiel 26:3; Rev. 17:15). So, one could take *the earth* (Greek γη = earth or land) as a reference to Israel. In fact, the phrase can even be translated *out of the land*, making a reference to Israel very reasonable" (*Ibid*, p. 58).
16. There is no known Gentile prophet in the Bible.
17. See Matt. 24:4, 11, 24; Mark 13:5, 22.

18. Since this miraculous act will imitate a great Jewish prophet, it seems that this also indicates this false prophet will be Jewish.

CHAPTER 16

1. The Greek word for *mark* (χαραγμα) is used only eight times in the entire New Testament. Seven of those eight uses are found in the book of Revelation, where the word is always used for the *mark* of *the beast.*

2. In English, the word *and* usually connotes something like, "in addition to." However, in both Hebrew and Greek, the original languages of the Bible, *and* can simply be a connector joining two phrases or clauses that refer to the same idea or thought. That is what seems to be the case each time the apostle John mentions these two acts in the book of Revelation, because the two acts appear together so many times in Revelation. The usage of the word *and* is employed in the connection of those two actions in the same way it is sometimes used in Greek, the original language of the book of Revelation, and in Hebrew, the language of the Old Testament, upon which the entirety of the book of Revelation is based.

3. Note the present tense of the display of God's wrath, for example, in Romans 1:18. Also see Revelation 16:2 for a display of temporal judgment on those who take the mark of the beast.

4. Note, for example, Rev. 16:2.

5. See John 5:24; 6:47.

6. See Proverbs 10:27; Ecclesiastes 7:17; Ezekiel 18; James 5:19–20; 1 John 5:16.

7. We can see this displayed in Exodus 15:6 and Psalm 138:7, among other passages.

8. See Exodus 28:36–38.

9. See Revelation 7:3.

10. Op cit, p. 92.

11. Ibid, p. 92.

12. Ibid, p. 92.

CHAPTER 17

1. See Zechariah 14:3–4.

2. For further information on this background, see Joachim Jeremias, *The Parables of Jesus*, translated by S. H. Hooke (London: SCM, 1963), pp. 173–174; Richard C. Trench, *Notes on the Parables of Our Lord* (New York: Appleton, 1851), pp. 200–201; Edwin M. Yamauchi, "Cultural Aspects of Marriage in the Ancient World," *Bibliotheca Sacra* 135:539 (July-September 1978), pp. 241–52.

3. This unit begins at the start of Matthew 24 and concludes at the end of chapter 25. Granted, 24:36–44 deals with the rapture of the church, while

verses 45–51 provide exhortation to Christians living prior to the rapture. It is because of this that some see the connection of the parable of the ten virgins, which is the very next passage, to 24:36–51 in such a way as to interpret it as applying to Christians in the present age. [See Arno C. Gaebelein, *The Gospel of Matthew, An Exposition.* 2 vols. in 1. (Neptune, N.J.: Loizeaux Brothers, 1910), 2:225–236; Alfred Plummer, *An Exegetical Commentary on the Gospel According to S. Matthew* (Grand Rapids: Wm. B. Eerdmans Publishing Co., 1953), p. 343.] However, the introductory then (hote) beginning the parable shows it to chronologically follow 24:36–51, as this is the pattern of usage of this word in the book of Matthew. (See, for examples, its usage within the Mount Olivet Discourse to mark the next chronological happening: 24:9, 15, 30; 25:1, 34, 37, 41, 44, 45.) Based on this use of *then*, 25:1–13 portrays the period of time following the rapture of the church, which is the tribulation period.

4. See Revelation 14:1–5.

5. While the New King James Version (from which most of Scripture citations come) translates this word as *rumors*, its Greek original can be translated as *reports*. That translation seems to lend itself to a more accurate understanding. Jesus is not saying there will be merely *rumors* of wars; He is saying there *will* be wars, of which Jewish believers will hear *reports*.

6. Since the day of the Lord is portrayed in the Old Testament as night falling upon the world (a time of great darkness—cf. Isaiah 13:9–10; Joel 2:1–2; Zephaniah 1:14–15), we can understand why Jesus would picture its midpoint as midnight or, literally, the middle of the night.

7. The connection with verse 13 shows that the description of verse 12 is also about believers in Christ. But, the description itself demonstrates Jesus has believers in mind.

8. See, for examples, John 14:21, 23; and 15:10.

9. See, for example, 15:12.

CHAPTER 18

1. This outline is from Zane C. Hodges, "The First Horseman of the Apocalypse," *Bibliotheca Sacra* (October 1962), p. 329.

2. The seventh seal (Revelation 8:1) emphasizes dramatic expectation, most likely revealing the arrival of the climactic event of the return of Christ to establish his kingdom.

3. This is implied in Revelation 6 by men hiding themselves from the appearance of *the Lamb* of God. In Matthew 24, it is shown by two clues. First, the appearing of the Son of Man presents his return, as the term *Son of Man* is taken from Daniel 7:13–14, picturing the establishment of his rule upon the earth. Second, the phrase, "all the tribes of the earth [land] will mourn," stems from Zechariah 12, which is part of a unit

(chapters 12–14) that presents Jesus' return to the earth to deliver Israel from her enemies and to establish his kingdom.

4. See chapter 25 for a presentation on the judgment seat of Christ and its timing.

5. The identity of the city mentioned in Revelation chapters 17–19 seems to be Rome, as indicated by the following: 1) The description of the city as Mystery Babylon indicates that this does not refer to literal Babylon; 2) the city is described as resting on seven hills (or *mountains*, the same Greek word for *hills*), and Rome has historically been known as "the city of seven hills"; and 3) the present tense of *reigns* in 17:18 portrays *the great city* that held power over the kings of the earth when the book of Revelation was written in the first century, which, clearly, was the city of Rome.

6. The endings of two of the three series of judgments also include great hail.

7. Op cit, Hodges, "The First Horseman of the Apocalypse," pp. 324–334.

8. Even those premillennialists who disagree with Zane Hodges's identification of the rider of the horse in Revelation 6:2 agree that the seal judgments begin at the start of the tribulation period.

9. The sixth seal takes place at the end of the tribulation period.

10. See Revelation 13:5.

11. A number of things point to this as the climax of the book, including: 1) the pointing to this event in the introduction of the book (cf. 1:5, 7; also see the mention of the sword coming out of his mouth in 1:16—which is the instrument of judgment he uses upon his enemies at his return [19:21]; 2) each of the major sections of the book anticipates his return; and 3) in the longest section of Revelation (4:1–22:5), the book portrays each of the three series of judgments leading up to his return.

12. Revelation 13:4

13. The connection between the judgments via Moses and the plagues by the hands of the two prophets of God in the first half of the tribulation period is presented by this description of the two: "They have power over waters to turn them to blood, and to strike the earth with all plagues, as often as they desire" (Revelation 11:6). There is no question that just as the first half of verse 6 links them with the prophet Elijah's conquering of the prophets of Baal, the last half of verse 6 connects them with the prophet Moses' conquering of Pharaoh and the gods of Egypt.

14. Genesis 32:28

15. Merrill F. Unger, "Israel," *Unger's Bible Dictionary* (Chicago: Moody Press, 1966), p. 541.

16. Note verse 12, where he addresses the crowd as "men of Israel."

17. Matthew 3:11

18. See Luke 3:11–14.
19. See Exodus 4:22.
20. This is demonstrated by the absence of the mention of repentance in the gospel of John. The reason this is significant is the purpose statement of the book (found in 20:31) announces that the gospel of John was written to show readers how to receive eternal life (by believing in Jesus Christ for it). Thus, if the book was written to show how to receive eternal life, and repentance is never mentioned (neither the word *repent* or *repentance* is mentioned even once), this means that repentance is not necessary for receiving eternal life.
21. See Acts 19:4.
22. See Exodus 10:2.
23. Compare Exodus 5:2 with 8:19.

CHAPTER 19

1. Satan will give the gathering plenty of time to occur so that the armies are in place and ready to do battle at the return of Christ. It may take several months for all of the armies to fully arrive.
2. See John 12:31; 14:30; 16:11; 2 Corinthians 4:4; and 1 John 5:19.
3. See Luke 4:10–11.
4. Cf. 1 Timothy 3:6.
5. Cf. Isaiah 14:12–14.
6. Revelation chapters 15 and 16
7. See the last chapter for a discussion on this timing.
8. See *The Greek New Testament According to the Majority Text* (Nashville, TN: Thomas Nelson Publishers, 1985), p. 774. This text is built on the reading of the Byzantine manuscripts, which represents the majority of Greek manuscripts.
9. Nazareth is Jesus' boyhood home. Since Nazareth sits upon a large hill overlooking the Valley of Megiddo, it means that every day, while growing up, Jesus viewed the area where future armies would gather against him.
10. See John 12:31; 14:30; and 16:11.
11. Interestingly, this is the area from which he ascended (see Acts 1:9–12).

CHAPTER 20

1. See, for example, Charles H. Dyer, *The Rise of Babylon* (Wheaton, IL: Tyndale Publishing House, 1991), pp. 13–23, plus pictures between pp. 128 and 129, for validation of Saddam Hussein's effort to rebuild Babylon.
2. These include www.iht.com/articles/2006/04/13/news/babylon.php; www.metropolismag.com/html/content_0699/ju99monu.htm; www.rb59.com/prophecy-news/2006/04/un-pouring-millions-into-rebuilding.html; and http://en.wikipedia.org/wiki/Babylon, all accessed on August 7, 2008.

END NOTES

3. Mark Hitchcock states that the United States State Department is contributing $700,000 toward this project via the US embassy in Baghdad. See Mark Hitchcock, *Cashless: Bible Prophecy, Economic Chaos, & the Future Financial Order* (Eugene, OR: Harvest House Publishers, 2009), p. 153.
4. The comma following the word *mystery* seems to indicate that it is not the name *Babylon* that is the mystery, but entire description of this city. However, we need to keep in mind that punctuation did not arrive with the original autographs of God's Word; it was added much later by men. Thus, the comma that is present could just as easily have been absent, in which case, it is the name *Babylon* that is identified as the mystery.
5. For an excellent defense of dating the book at AD 68–70, see John A. T. Robinson, *Redating the New Testament*, pp. 221–253. Also, see Albert A. Bell, Jr., "The Date of John's Apocalypse: The Evidence of Some Roman Historians Reconsidered," *New Testament Studies* 25, pp. 92–102.
6. Scarlet is identified as "flagrantly immoral" (http://dictionary.reference. com/browse/scarlet) as in Isaiah 1:18 where God describes the sins of Israel as being scarlet. The flagrant character of the beast is identified within the same verse as being full of names of blasphemy.
7. See passages such as Leviticus 19:29; 20:5; Numbers 15:39; 2 Chronicles 21:11, 13; Psalm 73:27.
8. See the last chapter on the tribulation judgments to see that the *thunderings*, *lightnings*, and *earthquake* occur just prior to the return of Christ to the earth.
9. See Daniel 7:24; 17:12–13.
10. See Psalm 73:11–12.
11. Jeremiah 51:8.
12. Jeremiah 50:13, 26, 39–40; 51:29
13. Jeremiah 50:8; 51:6, 45
14. Jeremiah 50:4–5, 20; 51:50

CHAPTER 21
1. Cf. 1 Samuel 18:7–8; 21:11; 29:5.
2. Http://dictionary.reference.com/browse/spirit, accessed on June 6, 2007.
3. An example of receiving the Holy Spirit upon believing in Christ for eternal life is what is mentioned in John 7:37–39.
4. Jesus presents this unfortunate reality in more than one place in the Gospels. For example, immediately following his Old Testament illustration of Lot fleeing for his life in Luke 17:28–29, he announces it will be the same situation " 'in the day when the Son of Man is revealed' " (verse 30), which is the final "day," or half of the tribulation period—

the one leading up to the return of Christ to the earth. Jesus then warns Jewish believers to flee for their lives when that "day" begins (verse 31), not turning back, keeping in mind what happened to Lot's wife, who did turn back (verse 32). Of course, Lot's wife lost her life because she did not heed the Lord's warning about saving her life, which leads Jesus to warn that those who seek to save their lives—by remaining where they are in order to hang onto their jobs, possessions, etc.—will lose their lives (verse 33). Based on what he has warned in verses 28–33, then, his description in verses 34–36 is a notification that believers in Christ who stay behind, rather than seeking to escape, will be rounded up by the troops of the beast.

Jesus also presented this truth elsewhere, as recorded in Matthew 10:21–23; 24:10; Mark 13:12; and Luke 21:16.

5. See 2 Chronicles 35:20–27.
6. Feinberg, *op. cit.*, p. 181.
7. This is a proper translation of the Greek word from which *salvation* is translated. (The Greek word is σωτηρια [or *soteria* as transliterated into English].)
8. The word translated here by the phrase *be converted* is *epistrepho* (επιστρεφω), which would more accurately be translated as *turn*, or *turn to*.

CHAPTER 22

1. Donald K. Campbell, *Daniel: Decoder of Dreams* (Wheaton, IL: Victor Books, 1981), p. 89.
2. Walter Bauer, F.W. Gingrich, and Frederick Danker, "ψυχη", *A Greek-English Lexicon of the New Testament and Other Early Christian Literature* (Chicago: The University of Chicago Press, 1979), p. 893.
3. On the word translated as *receiving* (κομιζω) in this verse, F.J.A. Hort stated that it "often in all Greek and in all New Testament means not simply to receive but to receive back, . . . or to get what has come to be one's own by earning" (F.J.A. Hort, *The First Epistle of Peter* (London: Macmillan, 1898); rept. in *Expository and Exegetical Studies* (Minneapolis: Klock and Klock, 1980), p. 47.) In addition, Moulton and Milligan support this view by citing as the definition for this word: "recovering a debt, getting it paid"—James Hope Moulton and George Milligan, "κομιζω," *The Vocabulary of the Greek Testament: Illustrated from the Papyri and Other Non-Literary Sources* (Grand Rapids, MI: Wm. B. Eerdmans Publishing Company, 1980), p. 354. Peter Davids shows his agreement when he states that "the verb for 'receiving' is frequently used for obtaining a prize or reward (2 Cor. 5:10; Eph. 6:8; Heb. 11:13; cf. 1 Peter 5:4). Here the prize or consummation toward which their faith is

directed, that is, 'the salvation of [their] souls' "—Peter H. Davids, *The First Epistle of Peter* (Grand Rapids, MI: William B. Eerdmans Publishing Company, 1990), p. 59.

Moreover, the phrase, *the end of your faith,* as referring to when one will receive back in payment (as a reward) *the salvation of your souls* [*lives*] shows that this refers to future reward received after one's life has ended. (For this meaning of the end ($\tau \varepsilon \lambda o \varsigma$), cf. Romans 6:21–22; 1 Timothy 1:5.) For the Christian (the audience to whom Peter addressed his epistle—cf. 1 Peter 1:2), this can only refer to receiving kingdom reward at the judgment seat of Christ for having lived one's life faithfully to Christ.

4. The Hebrew word translated as *cut off* (trk) in this passage refers to being killed. (See Francis Brown, S. R. Driver, and Charles A. Briggs, "*trk*," A Hebrew and English Lexicon of the Old Testament (Oxford: Clarendon Press, 1980), p. 502.

5. See Acts 1:9–12.

6. C.F. Keil comments that "the comparison of the flight to the flight from the earthquake in the time of king Uzziah, to which reference is made in Amos 1:1, is intended to express not merely the swiftness and universality of the flight, but also the cause of the flight, namely, that they do not merely fly from the enemy, but also for fear of the earthquake which will attend the coming of the Lord"—C.F. Keil, Volume X: Minor Prophets, II: 404, in C.F. Keil and F. Delitzsch in *Commentary on the Old Testament in Ten Volumes* (Grand Rapids, MI: William B. Eerdmans Publishing Company, 1980).

7. Keil claims that the eyes will rot because they "spied out the nakedness of the city of God," while the tongues of these enemies will rot because they "blasphemed God and His people (cf. Isa. xxxvii. 6)" (*op. cit.*, 410).

8. To see the return of Christ in this context, note verse 14 which depicts the Son of Man coming on a cloud, which is also pictured in Daniel 7:13–14 and in Matthew 24:29–31, referring to the return of Jesus to the earth. The judgment of his enemies in this passage is pictured by the Son of Man thrusting his sickle to the earth (verses 15–19), as well as the figure of the winepress in verse 20.

9. See Genesis 12:3.

EPILOGUE

1. See Mark 16:19; Acts 2:33; 7:55, 56.
2. 1 Peter 3:22
3. See Hebrews 4:14–15.

4. This is the case with a number of biblical statements, such as the command for man and woman to not eat of the tree of the knowledge of good and evil, a command we are not under today; God's people being placed under the law (see Romans 6:14); etc.
5. See verse 2 in 1 Thessalonians 5.
6. "Is the Era of Mass Immigration to Israel Over?", http://www.jesuslives.co.za/2008/09/12/is-the-era-of-mass-immigration-to-israel-over/, accessed October 16, 2008.
7. Ibid.
8. Ibid.
9. Israel's possession of Jerusalem is also necessary for the rebuilding of the temple, which will occur during the first half of the day of the Lord as per the treaty of Daniel 9:27.
10. http://www.templemountfaithful.org/, accessed February 26, 2009.
11. http://www.templeinstitute.org/main.htm, accessed February 26, 2009.
12. As discussed, an integral part of the treaty that will initiate the seven-year tribulation period is the provision for sacrifices and offerings (cf. Daniel 9:27), which cannot be accomplished without the temple. The temple will be built and be operational before the midpoint of the day of the Lord when the beast will enter into its holy of holies and defile it (cf. Matthew 24:15; 2 Thessalonians 2:3–4).
13. http://www.thesanhedrin.org/en/index.php/The_Re-established_Jewish_Sanhedrin, accessed February 26, 2009.
14. http://www.jewishvirtuallibrary.org/jsource/Judaism/Sanhedrin.html, accessed February 26, 2009.
15. See 2 Thessalonians 2:3–4 and Matthew 24:15.
16. In fact, in one recent article, an expert claimed that the temple can be rebuilt in less than a year. (See "Trouble in the Holy Land", World Net Daily, http://www.wnd.com/index.php?fa=PAGE.view&pageId=105938, August, 5, 2009, accessed August 6, 2009.)
17. Ibid.
18. Ibid.
19. See "Survey: 64% Want Temple Rebuilt," http://www.ynetnews.com/Ext/Comp/ArticleLayout/CdaArticlePrintPreview/1,2506,L-3754367,00.html, accessed August 1, 2009.
20. See http://www.mfa.gov.il/MFA/Government/Communiques/2009/Israel_reaction_President_Obama_speech_Cairo_4-Jun-2009.htm, accessed June 5, 2009.
21. See 1 Thessalonians 5:3.
22. For example, the United Nations has a Web site devoted to peace and security. In fact, if you go to http://www.un.org/en/peace/, you will see that the home page is entitled, "Peace and Security." In addition, Rus-

sian Foreign Minister Sergey Lavrov recently called for world efforts "to create the appropriate international atmosphere" to resume the peace process in the Middle East, with a common goal to achieve the concept of the two-state solution, which means an independent Palestinian state to live side by side in peace with a secure Israel. "Our common goal is to achieve the implementation of the concept of the two states, Palestine and Israel, living in peace and security," he said. "This point is reflected in the presidential statement that was adopted at the outcome of the discussion. The Security Council, in its statement, expressed its resolve to continue to provide necessary assistance to the parties to achieve this." (See http://news.xinhuanet.com/english/2009-05/12/content_11355977.htm, originally posted at www.chinaview.cn on May 12, 2009, accessed May 12, 2009.) Also, the UN Security Council "reiterated its call for renewed efforts by the parties and the international community to achieve a comprehensive and lasting peace in the Middle East . . . where Israel and Palestine would live side by side in peace within secure and recognized borders." (See http://www.reliefweb.int/rw/rwb.nsf/db900SID/ ASHU-7RY3XR?OpenDocument, posted May 11, 2009, accessed May 12, 2009.)

Moreover, there are numerous groups and Web sites working toward "peace and security," such as the Peace and Security Initiative, which exists "to influence U.S. policy to promote a more secure, peaceful and just world" (see http://www.peaceandsecurityinitiative.org/, accessed May 12, 2009); http://www2.spfo.unibo.it/spolfo/PEACE.htm which lists close to three hundred Web sites for the promotion of "peace and security" (the heading at the top of the page); the Council for Peace and Security, which "is a voluntary body with no party political affiliation, bringing together some thousand members . . . and which "considers Peace to be a necessary component of Israeli National Security" (http://www.peace-security-council.org/, updated May 12, 2009, accessed May 12, 2009); and Economists for Peace and Security, which "works to inform social scientists, citizens, journalists and policy-makers worldwide about the full costs of war and conflict, and to propose feasible alternative approaches to building international security" (http://www.epsusa.org/, accessed May 12, 2009). As the day of the Lord draws nearer, it would be expected that this phrase will be used more and more by international leaders.

23. As mentioned, it is likely that peace and security will be connected with an announcement of the treaty with Israel in which ten nations will guarantee the terms of the treaty. This will be the treaty (covenant) presented in Daniel 9:27.

24. *http://www.israelnationalnews.com/*, accessed May 2, 2009. Also see "Netanyahu's Peace Plan," by Caroline Glick, May 21, 2009 22:09 | Updated May 22, 2009 15:58, http://www.jpost.com/servlet/Satellite?cid=1 242212438938&pagename=JPost%2FJPArticle%2FShowFull, accessed June 19, 2009.

25. According to the king, Israel faces all-out war within eighteen months if it does not come to terms with the Arab world and allow the establishment of a new Palestinian state with its capital in Jerusalem (Ibid).

26. See: "Opportunity is knocking at Israel's door", *Jewish World Review* May 12, 2009 /18 Iyar 5769, by Caroline B. Glick, http://www.JewishWorldReview.com, accessed May 12, 2009. This is more in line with the treaty that kicks off the day of the Lord as presented in the book of Daniel. *http://www.israelnationalnews.com/*, accessed May 2, 2009; "Netanyahu's Peace Plan," by Caroline Glick, May 21, 2009 22:09 | Updated May 22, 2009 15:58, http://www.jpost.com/servlet/Satellite?cid=1242212438938 &pagename=JPost%2FJPArticle%2FShowFull accessed June 19, 2009; "US-MIDEAST: Regional Players Key to Salvaging Peace Process," December 4, 2008 by the editor, http://globalintel.net/wp/2008/12/04/ us-mideast-regional-players-key-to-salvaging-peace-process/, accessed June 29, 2009; "U.S. Envoy Talks Middle East Peace with Syria's Assad," Reuters, June 13, 2009, *http://www.silobreaker.com/mitchell-says-no-mideast-peace-at-lebanon-expense-16_2262382370436939801*, accessed June 29, 2009; "Clinton Promises New US Proposals for Mideast Peace," by David Gollust, The State Department, May 27, 2009, *http:// www.voanews.com/english/archive/2009-05/2009-05-27-voa50.cfm?CFI D=244606798&CFTOKEN=54798652&jsessionid=8830f5a2f41513f8 e5933230593996949685*, accessed June 29, 2009.

27. See "What Israel's Arab Neighbors Grasp that the Obama Administration Won't," by Caroline B. Glick at http://www.jewishworldreview. com/0409/glick042709.php3 , April 28, 2009, accessed April 28, 2009.

28. See "U.S. Trying to Push for Peace between Israel, Syria," June 12, 2009, http://english.people.com.cn/90001/90777/90854/6676972.html, accessed June 13, 2009.

29. Israeli prime minister Netanyahu has stated that there can be no peace in the Middle East as long as Iran is a threat to the region. See "Opportunity is knocking at Israel's door", *Jewish World Review* May 12, 2009 /18 Iyar 5769, by Caroline B. Glick, http://www.JewishWorldReview. com, accessed May 12, 2009.

30. See "Christians on the Run in Iraq," by Peter Wensierski and Bernhard Zand, http://www.spiegel.de/international/world/0,1518,587345,00. html, accessed October 31, 2008; "Iraqi Archbishop Decries Christian Slayings," by Yahya Barzanji, The Associated Press, *http://www.philly.*

com/philly/wires/ap/news/nation_world/20090427_ap_iraqiarchbishopdecri-eschristianslayings.html, Posted on Mon, Apr. 27, 2009, accessed April 28, 2009.

31. "Iraqi Parliament Betrayed the Persecuted Assyrian Christians," by Shamiram Daniali, *The Assyrian Times*, http://www.assyriatimes.com/engine/modules/news/article.php?storyid=3334, accessed October 29, 2008.

32. See "Christians on the Run in Iraq," op cit.

33. Op cit, "Iraqi Parliament Betrayed the Persecuted Assyrian Christians."

34. Op cit, "Christians on the Run in Iraq."

35. "Emerging Threats: Iraqi Christians Forming Ad Hoc Militias", http://www.upi.com/Emerging_Threats/2008/10/29/Iraqi_Christians_forming ad hoc militias/UPI-77471225314406/#top, published October 29, 2008, accessed October 31, 2008.

36. Interestingly, these militias have been formed in and around Mosul, which is near the ancient capital of Assyria, Nineveh.

37. Cf. Mark 16:15; also see Matthew 28:19–20.

38. For an indicator of the current state of the church, see the next point.

39. This can be seen by the vast majority of Christian publications and pre-sentations (including sermons, tracts, blogs, etc.) that add to, or com-pletely change, the biblical presentation of how one receives eternal life. While Jesus shows us in the gospel of John—the one Bible book written to show readers how to receive eternal life (see John 20:31 for the purpose statement)—eternal life is received only as a gift by simply believing in Jesus Christ for it. Any change of that, therefore, is a false gospel (cf. Galatians 1:6–9).

40. See 1 Timothy 2:3–6.

41. See Matthew 24:14; Revelation 14:1–6. As we have discussed, this will be accomplished by the 144,000 Jews who will go out from Israel.

42. By the church universal, we are referring to all who have believed in Christ for eternal life from the time of Pentecost until the rapture of the church.

43. Among those who take the approach that the seven churches are both literal first-century churches as well as representations of seven periods of the church age are: Theodore H. Epp, *Practical Studies in Revelation, Volumes I & II* (Lincoln, NE: Back to the Bible, 1969), pp. 67–70; Gary G. Cohen and Salem Kirban, *Revelation Visualized* (Chattanooga, TN: AMG Publishers, 1981), pp. 50–51; Tim LaHaye, *Revelation Unveiled* (Grand Rapids, MI: Zondervan Publishing House, 1999), pp. 43–95; G. H. Lang, *The Revelation of Jesus Christ* (Miami Springs, FL: Conley & Schoettle Publishing Co., Inc., 1985), p. 84; Charles Caldwell Ryrie, Revelation (Chicago: Moody Press, 1968), p. 21; J. B. Smith, *A Revelation of Jesus*

Christ (Scottdale, PA: Herald Press, 1961), p. 61; and John F. Walvoord, *The Revelation of Jesus Christ* (Chicago: Moody Press, 1966), pp. 52–53.

Clues that indicate that these churches are representative of periods of the church age include the order, the churches chosen, the number of churches, and the names of these churches. Regarding the order, one could argue that there is a geographical order beginning with Ephesus, the church closest to Patmos from where John wrote, and continuing around a clockwise formation. Yet, might the Lord have ordered these churches and the letters to them to reflect eras of the church age?

In addition, why were these specific churches chosen to receive these letters? After all, there were many more churches in existence at the time, some of which were most likely larger, dwelling in the midst of larger cities with greater potential of impact for the kingdom. The best answer is that these are representational churches.

Moreover, the number of these churches indicates that they reflect a representational purpose. After all, there are seven of them, which reflects the number of God—perfection or completion. Thus, these seven provide a complete representation of the seven epochs of church history.

Their names indicate that they are representational. Each church name has a significant meaning.

Ephesus means *desired one*, portraying its apostolic heritage. Smyrna means *myrrh* (http://eastonsbibledictionary.com/smyrna.htm, accessed March 6, 2009), a symbol of death, refers to a period of untold persecution and death in the Christian church.

Pergamos stems from two Greek words: *pergos*, meaning *city* or *high tower*, and *gamos*, meaning *married* or *united in marriage*; thus, the literal meaning is something like *married to the high tower*. The most famous high tower in Scripture is the tower of Babylon, a city which is linked throughout the Bible to the kingdom of Satan. This compromised church contained the throne of Satan (Rev. 2:13), who is always behind the compromise of Christianity.

Thyatira stems from two words meaning *sacrifice* and *continual*, marking the introduction of the denial of the finished work of Christ upon the cross and the false teaching that obtaining eternal life is a process. This corrupted doctrine provided the basis for many other false teachings that were also introduced during this time.

Sardis means *escaping ones* or *those who come*, signifying the reformation period. However, overall, the reformation churches became state churches and did not sufficiently change many of the false teachings that had developed up to this point, such as infant baptism, amillennialism, sacramentalism, and the muddling of the gospel.

END NOTES

Philadelphia means *brotherly love*. This pictures not only the love of one another Christians exhibited during this period, but also indicates the love believers had for reaching others with the gospel.

Laodicea is formed from two Greek words, meaning *people* and opinion or *a decree*. Thus, Laodicea indicates a focus on people's opinions or rule rather than a focus on the Lord's decree. This emphasis lends itself to lukewarmness among the church, and it certainly seems to mark the age in which we now find ourselves.

44. The first four of these church ages agree with church historian Philip Schaff's first four major periods of the Christian church. See http://www.ccel.org/s/schaff/history/About.htm, accessed March 5, 2009, based on Philip Schaff, *History of the Christian Church* (Peabody, MA: Hendrickson Publishers, 1858).

45. Certainly, this period was characterized by zeal, as we can see that in the lives of biblical characters in the New Testament, such as the apostle Paul, as well as the other apostles. However, Jesus also chastised the church of Ephesus for leaving its first love. Was that also true of the apostolic age? It is very possible that with the deaths of the apostles, the love of the church waned; however, there is scant information about the end of this age.

46. Philip Schaff indicated this was a period of protracted and cruel persecution. (See, for example, http://www.ccel.org/ccel/schaff/hcc2.v.iv.xv.html, accessed March 6, 2009.) Church historian Bruce Shelley suggested that though the church was persecuted, "prior to A.D. 200, Roman attempts to silence Christians were half-hearted at best"; then persecution began in earnest—Bruce Shelley, *Church History in Plain Language* (Waco, TX: Word Books, 1982). Tim LaHaye wrote of this period: "During the second and third centuries this persecution age saw hundreds of Christians brought into the amphitheater of Rome to be fed to hungry lions while thousands of spectators cheered. Many were crucified; others were covered with animal skins and tortured to death by wild dogs. They were covered with tar and set on fire to serve as torches. They were boiled in oil and burned at the stake, as was Polycarp in the city of Smyrna itself in A.D. 156. One church historian has estimated that during this period, five million Christians were martyred for the testimony of Jesus Christ" (op cit, p. 52).

47. At the beginning of this period, Constantine elevated Christianity as the religion of the state, which melded the church with Roman laws, institutions, and heathenism, among other problematic issues. In addition, a number of false doctrines were introduced during this period, including worship of saints, angels, and Mary; the doctrine of purgatory; postmillennialism; and replacement theology (the "casting off" of Israel and being replaced by the church).

48. This was the "Dark Ages" of the church, marking the beginning of the merging of paganism with Christianity.

49. The missionary movement began due to the revival of the teaching of premillennialism, which had been all but dead since the end of the third century.

50. We are currently in this period, characterized by greater apostasy and ecumenicalism. This period is also characterized by the birth and insurgence of the charismatic movement, leading to a focus on experience (including "whatever feels good, do it") and a movement away from biblical teaching, including the gospel of grace and the doctrines of premillennialism and the pretribulation rapture of the church.

51. "Economic Crisis Prompting Israeli Expats to Return Home," by Dina Kraft, April 27, 2009, http://jta.org/news/article/2009/04/27/1004696/economic-crisis-prompting-israelis-expats-to-return-home, accessed April 28, 2009. According to this article, there are as many as one million Israelis who live overseas. Last year, the number of returning Israelis rose to 11,000 from a recent annual average of 4,500, according to the Israel Absorption Ministry.

52. See Ezekiel 36:16–37:28.

53. "U.S. Backs Global Alternative to Dollar," Jerome Corsi, posted March 19, 2009, http://www.worldnetdaily.com/index.php?fa=PAGE.view&pageId=92207, accessed April 20, 2009.

54. Rebbe in English means master, teacher, or mentor: a Yiddish word derived from the identical Hebrew word rabbi. It mostly refers to the leader of a Hasidic Jewish movement.

55. Chabad-Lubavitch is one of the largest Hasidic movements in Orthodox Judaism. The name Chabad is an acronym for Chochmah, Binah, Da'at ("wisdom, understanding, and knowledge"), while Lubavitch is the only extant branch of a family of Hasidic groups once known collectively as the Chabad movement. (The names are now used interchangeably.) Hasidim refers to the pious or righteous ones.

About the Author

John Claeys has written and taught Bible courses at LeTourneau University for more than sixteen years and has been teaching the Bible in fulltime ministry for more than twenty-five years. He earned a B.A. from the University of Northern Iowa, a Th.M. from Dallas Theological Seminary and did doctoral work at Phoenix Seminary. John has written twenty adult Bible studies and more than fifteen Bible curriculum workbooks. In addition, he has spent more time than he could calculate (but that may be because he is not good at math) studying eschatology (which John says is a fifty-cent word for the study of future events predicted in the Bible), which has prepared him well for the writing of this book.